No Communication with the Sea

No Communication with the Sea

Searching for an Urban Future in the Great Basin

Tim Sullivan

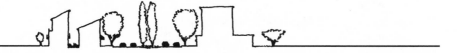

The University of Arizona Press   Tucson

The University of Arizona Press
© 2010 Tim Sullivan

www.uapress.arizona.edu

Library of Congress Cataloging-in-Publication Data
Sullivan, Tim, 1978–
    No communication with the sea : searching for an urban future in the
Great Basin / Tim Sullivan.
        p. cm.
    Includes bibliographical references and index.
    ISBN 978-0-8165-2895-0 (pbk. : alk. paper)
    1. Urbanization—Great Basin—Case studies. 2. Urbanization—West
(U.S.)—Case studies. 3. Cities and towns—Great Basin—Growth—Case
studies. 4. Cities and towns—West (U.S.)—Growth—Case studies. I. Title.
    HT123.5.G73S85 2010
    307.7609792'4—dc22

                                                    2010018849

Manufactured in the United States of America on acid-free, archival-quality
paper containing a minimum of 30% post-consumer waste and processed
chlorine free.

15   14   13   12   11   10   6   5   4   3   2   1

To Mom and Dad

for showing me how to be a Utahn and for everything else

The Great Basin: diameter 11 degrees of latitude, 10 degrees of longitude: elevation above the sea between 4 and 5000 feet: surrounded by mountains: contents almost unknown but believed to be filled by rivers and lakes that have no communication with the sea, deserts and oases which have never been explored, and savage tribes, which no traveller has seen or described.

—John C. Frémont

Velocity reveals
    How far
The faith of pioneers
    Will you fade at the frontiers?

—Chris Whitley

And the carpet at the Thunderbird has a burn for every cowboy that got fenced in.

—Craig Finn

Contents

Illustrations

All illustrations are by the author unless otherwise noted.

Figures

Photographs

Preface

The Great Basin, that vast, dry hole in America, is not often associated with great cities. It's understandable. The region is the most sparsely inhabited in the continental United States. The cities at its edges, chiefly the metropolitan regions surrounding Salt Lake City, Utah, and Reno, Nevada, are regarded as overgrown mining camps, Wild-West theme parks, zealous religious colonies, or—worst of all—bland American suburbia. The lore of the Great Basin, instead, is gleaned from its exoticism, from its differences from the rest of the country: the unbounded freedom, the space, the natural resources, and the scenery. The Basin has the loneliest road in America, bombing ranges and chemical incineration plants, and the legendary steep-and-deep skiing made possible by its strange hydrography.

But great cities are possible here. They'd better be. Ghost towns dot Nevada, and the old Mormon farm towns along the wagon road are emptying out or converting to bedroom country for the growing metro areas. The seemingly paradoxical urban life of this region, the core of the Intermountain West that lies between the West's two great mountain chains, the Sierra-Cascades and the Wasatch-Rockies, is the subject of this book. When you think about it, the Great Basin is a logical place to study the American city. In recent years, more people have moved to this region than to almost any other part of America. Some have begun to call the interior West the "New American Heartland" because of its growth, the attraction of its airy, recreational lifestyle, and its increasing economic importance and political sway.[1] And, almost everyone who lives in the Great Basin lives in an urbanized area. In fact, a higher percentage of Great Basin residents live in urbanized areas than in almost any other part of the United States. The cities of the Great Basin also face extreme degrees of the environmental problems that challenge much of urbanizing America. Here in one of the continent's driest deserts, we have a tough time matching our neighborhoods, downtowns, suburbs, and streets to the Great Basin's environmental reality of scarce resources and the inhuman scale of its vast, stark spaces. The cities of the Basin are some of the largest consumers of water, fuel, and land per capita in the nation. We are hard-pressed to temper our grand visions for the Basin's spaces and to read the real opportunities that lie in its patterns.

In late 2006, at the height of a long real estate development and employment boom, I set out to explore these changing cities. As one developer told me, ground was hard to find: It was being carved and scoured like a desert flood event, and the rapid changes taking place were telling in the manifestation of both bad ideas and good ones. Over a few years, I visited the cities' centers and their edges, encountering people who wanted to escape the city into the wide open of the Basin and people who were looking inward to rebuild the city. I encountered rural dreams and urban activism. I encountered connection to the natural environment and utter disconnection from it. Most important, I found people who were grappling with the fact of urbanization and struggling to make urban places in the Great Basin—places that might endure through the booms, busts, bounties, and scarcities of decades to come.

This book is about urbanism, the shaping of the city, the city not just as a collection of buildings and streets and parks but also the way people occupy them. Urbanism is different from urbanization. While *urbanization* is the movement of population to cities often brought on by large-scale economic forces, *urbanism* is a smaller-scale change within that reality—making the best of urbanization by making humane places. The conditions of urbanization created by economics are alleviated by the solutions of urbanism: designing densely packed houses or apartments to be livable homes, leveraging the economic activity of a city into proud public parks, bringing economies of scale down to a human scale, and making busy thoroughfares enjoyable streets. It's a kind of lemons into lemonade. If suburbanization was the great cop-out to America industrializing into cities, urbanism is the cop-to. Urbanization is a force that is manifested over regions by swaths of humanity and the whims of economies. Urbanism is a choice that can be manifested in as small an area as a street, a block or a building, by just a few people. The process of urbanity can lead to the result of functional, enjoyable urban places. Urban is trade-offs and balance. Urban is a diversity of land uses—residences, stores, offices, parks—put together compatibly in a small physical space. Urban is private buildings engaging with the public realm of the street through its entrances and windows. Perhaps most important today, urban is the predominance of a form of transportation other than the automobile. The automobile thwarts functional, comfortable, and enjoyable urban places in a number of ways: It takes transportation to the private realm, therefore diminishing the public realm; a motorist doesn't interact with the places he or she passes the way a pedestrian does; and the sheer amount of space to accommodate autos in streets and in parking lots distort the scale of the built environment to something inhuman. Most of the autos we drive today—and the way we drive them—pollute the air, demand nonrenewable fuel, and endanger the safety of people walking and bicycling. Urbanism doesn't have to look like New York City or Paris. What it looks like depends on what there is to work with. There is, for example, an urbanism to be pulled from the Great Basin Desert. I was out to find it.

And so this book is also about the land of the Great Basin, the famous Basin and Range, the salt playas, the hundreds of miles of seeming emptiness that has some of the most interesting ecology in the world. The Basin is lonely mountain peaks, it is crowded wetlands, it is gradients in between. It is adaptations of plants and animals to water, salt, and elevation. These adaptations are like urbanism: fitting into an environment, learning to live with one another in constrained space and with constrained resources. We can learn from their patterns. What is the marriage of urbanism to the Great Basin landscape? This is what I hoped to discover.

What is at stake here in the dry lands between the mountains is pertinent to all of America. In the Great Basin, we see the state of our nation's obsessions with growth, good jobs, quality of life, space, environmental transformation, and escape. The building of the Great Basin's cities shows us how people today are fitting themselves in by the thousand to one of the nation's most baffling regions. The Basin is at once inhospitable—in its high-desert climate, its lack of water and navigable waterways, and its isolation—and attractive—in its space, its affordability, its protection, and its promise for rebirth. The cities of the Great Basin, as throughout the West, are surrounded by some of America's most beautiful, unique landscapes. One of the best chances we have for preserving these landscapes is to build better cities that use resources efficiently and make urban living comfortable and enticing enough to reduce the urge of so many to flee to the unbuilt edge. While it may be an impulse of someone championing the land to cast a wary eye toward the region's urbanization, I focus my attention in between these coarse grains—to urbanism, the process of creating the great city.

A Note on Methods

This book is the product of a number of different methods of research, some of them that might count as scholarship, others as old-fashioned reporting. Generally, my process was to begin broadly and review census, employment, and business data, current literature, newspaper articles, government reports, photographs, dusty library books, blogs, and anything else I could find about the cities of the Intermountain West and their place in the Great Basin. From this information, as well as through road trips through the region, I picked specific places that would evoke the themes emerging from this mountain of data. As such, while my initial reconnaissance was comprehensive, the places I chose to tell the stories of the urban Great Basin are relatively few. Yet I hope these stories can serve a multitude of places, in the Great Basin and outside of it.

Acknowledgments

I give many thanks to my family, friends, and colleagues who supported me on this long journey. Michael Teitz, Michael Southworth, Mark Brilliant, and Vicki Elmer at UC Berkeley all read and commented on early versions of this project and offered needed encouragement. Paul Groth provided insight and a great reading list on modernity at a critical period in the book's development. I am forever grateful that the manuscript landed in the hands of Kristen Buckles at University of Arizona Press, who saw the potential for it and shepherded me through the process. Thanks also to all the other great people at the Press who had a hand in shaping the book. Many thanks to my friends and family who read late drafts of the manuscript and offered their comments. I thank my sources for lending their names and stories to this collage, and for their insights and cooperation. I thank my colleagues at Community Design + Architecture for teaching me about urbanism big and small every working day. I am deeply grateful to those people who have mentored me as a writer and reporter, most especially Barbara Ganley, Julia Alvarez, Chris Smart, Peg McEntee, and Gordon Oliver. Thanks to Two Creek Coffee House and Coffee Noir in Salt Lake, Caffe Strada in Berkeley, Cole Coffee, Nomad Café, and of course World Ground Café in Oakland—the places where I wrote these words and revised them over and over. . . . Thanks and love to Mom, Dad, Paddy, Erin, Juliet, and Bud.

No Communication with the Sea

Of Sin and Salvation

The Architect and the Gardener

> That coarseness and strength combined with acuteness and
> inquisitiveness; that practical, inventive turn of mind; quick to
> find expedients; that masterful grasp of material things, lacking in
> the artistic but powerful to effect great ends; that restless nervous
> energy; that dominant individualism, working for good and for
> evil, and with all that buoyancy and exuberance which comes
> with freedom.
> —Frederick Jackson Turner, on the American character, 1893[1]

No one told Gary K. Estes that the Wild West left Reno a long time ago.
Estes had just taken on a project in a downtown casino, the Comstock,
on the block of West Street just north of the Truckee River. Actually, the
sixteen-story building wasn't a casino anymore. The saloon-style doors
on the slanted entrance at the corner of Second Street were boarded shut,
and the wall of hotel rooms had since become a rent-by-the-week, single-
room occupancy for the down-and-out.

Estes was an architect. Earlier in his career, he had worked as a drafts-
man for the Federal Bureau of Prisons, but he now operated a design-
build firm in downtown Sparks and specialized in commercial projects
for the burgeoning city, such as the new 7-11 at the corner of Pyramid
and Victorian. Occasionally he worked in Las Vegas, but he preferred
the crisp mountain air of Reno to the Mojave swelter. He combed his hair
straight back, kept a silver mustache, and draped a leather jacket over his
bony frame. He wore a pair of snakeskin boots that he ordered online,
only to find that the man selling them lived down the street.

In 2004, the Comstock was for sale. Estes knew the building: The
Comstock had been built in the late 1970s as part of that decade's

downtown high-rise casino-hotel building boom, and its 310 rooms became popular with Canadian tourists. Estes visited to eat the casino's quality one-pound steaks. Then, when it became weekly rentals, he designed a commercial laundry for it. The casino was a tired mockery of the Old West, with scenes painted on the walls and dummies welcoming patrons on the ground floor. Its façades were a canvas for nightly display of blinking lights, which helped make the Reno skyline a colorful chaos each evening.

But the Comstock closed in the 1990s, having become a victim of long-term changes in Reno's economy. Las Vegas had long since taken the Nevada gaming capital title, Indian casinos took what remained of the national gaming business, and many of the successful local casinos in the Reno area sprouted at the city's edges and in the suburbs. The city, which had been increasingly trying to keep up with Las Vegas' tourism attractions in the second half of the twentieth century, hoped to reenergize its downtown by pushing through the opening of the Silver Legacy in 1995, which became the city's tallest building. The project took up two city blocks, one for the hotel tower, the other for a giant dome that encased a 120-foot-high mining rig. Reno officials and Silver Legacy developers openly sought to make the project a Las Vegas–style themed project, like New York–New York and the Venetian but with the Old West as its theme, complete with a background story of a young man heading out west to find his fortune in silver.[2]

The Comstock, meanwhile, having been converted into weekly rentals, became the real Wild West: not a place of romance and the country but of urban squalor. The parking garage turned into a scary trap. Rooms went for $99 a week. Cops went in and out all the time and fire alarms sounded through the night. "I saw more uniformed police officers in my first week here than I have in my entire life," said one former tenant whose stay at the Comstock was short.[3]

In fact, the Comstock fit in more with what downtown Reno had been for a long time: a sanctuary for transients or refugees from the laws of stricter jurisdictions. Downtown Reno was packed with weekly rental motels and hotels, labeled by the Reno Area Alliance for the Homeless not as affordable housing but, like the other weekly rentals, "emergency transitional family housing," a term that seemed to give the whole district an air of triage.

"It was old and sad and dark. It was all pimps and prostitutes," Estes remembers. "Boy, there were some real fruitcakes. There were more police calls down here in one week than in all of Reno. The mayor said he wanted it to burn down."[4]

But Estes saw potential. It still had a good steel frame. It had location. The architect thought about the factors that had drawn him and his family to Reno years earlier from California, a place toward which he still harbors harsh prejudices. "San Francisco is filthy. They tilted the earth and all the nuts ended up in San Francisco," Estes says. While Nevada has long been a place of sin to the rest of the United States and especially to California, to Estes, it was Shangri-la, a family-friendly escape in the pure mountain air.

He liked that the Comstock was a half block from the Truckee River and its Raymond I. Smith River Walk, built by the city in 1991 in response to the loss of its economy and identity to Las Vegas, and its need to take advantage of the natural attraction of the Truckee. For a while, it languished as an island of beautification, but within a few years, once Reno began repositioning its image and identity around recreation, the River Walk became a critical piece of its active downtown. It framed the new kayak park on the river, and the granite-banked island where people sunbathed, swam in the roiling eddies, and watched free outdoor movies. The River Walk saw the construction of a new movie theater, a microbrewery and an outdoor café, all at a pleasing pedestrian scale that contrasted with the awful experience of walking on the casino blocks. The City planned to extend the River Walk and build another whitewater park and an "eco-channel" that would excavate a deeper, meandering trough within the Truckee River to accommodate more fish, kayakers, and inner-tube riders.[5]

Reno no longer tried to project sin but salvation. It was now "America's Adventure Place." Skiers flew to Reno-Tahoe International and caught the shuttle to the Sierra. Kayakers surfed on the waves of the Truckee downtown. Mountain bikers rode from their houses up the mining roads in the bare hills. As historian Alicia Barber observes, the Silver Legacy was Reno's last gasp to try to become Las Vegas. The city began to project a new image and embody a new identity. That identity was changing along with the Comstock. As Gary K. Estes says, "We [visited California after moving to Reno] and came back and I said, 'How can people live there?' My wife said, 'They're not, they're moving here.'"

So Estes had a plan. He would undertake Reno's first major hotel-to-condominium conversion. He would strip the Comstock's interior down to its frame and turn the Comstock into the Residences at Riverwalk, a bastion of clean, upbeat urban living. In the weeks leading up to the closing of the Comstock, tenants were locked out of their rooms, escorted to them by security guards. "This room has been shut down courtesy of the Reno Police Downtown Enforcement Team!" read signs tacked to room doors. Still, Estes didn't take any chances when eviction day came. "Everybody was carrying a gun in plain view," he said at the time.[6] So, on the day that he took over the deed to the building, the architect walked into the building with one gun in his jacket and one gun at his hip. He went from door to door personally evicting the tenants. "The pimps and the prostitutes," he tells me, "all went back to Oakland."

Reno sits against the eastern face of the Sierra Nevada, a mountain rampart that forms the western wall of the Great Basin. To the east, casinos, McDonald's and industrial sprawl thin out into open country: 430 miles of sagebrush, shadscale, and salt desert in long valleys pace mountain ranges that finally end at the Basin's eastern wall, the Wasatch Mountains (see fig. 1.1). Anchored below the Wasatch's tawny foothills, in downtown Salt Lake City, is the headquarters of the Church of Jesus Christ of Latter-day Saints, also known as the LDS Church, or the Mormons. The church's campus looms large in the center of Salt Lake; like the gaming industry did in Reno, the church created the place and occupies approximately a quarter of the downtown.

At the center of the campus are two blocks: the famous Temple Square surrounding the Salt Lake Temple and, across Main Street, the church administration block, the Mormon motherboard. Even in winter, on days of white snow storms, newly sealed couples emerge from Temple Square across the Main Street Plaza to the series of pools and fountains that mark the middle of the block. They wait in line in long-sleeved white wedding gowns and tuxedos to get their picture snapped in front of the wall and gothic spires of the Salt Lake Temple. "When the fountain goes off, I want you to be standing there because then I can get you and the fountain and the Temple all in one picture," the photographers say.

The keeper of these grounds is a man named Eldon Cannon. He is the gardener of the quarters of the Lord. When he looks at the trees framing the entrance of the twenty-eight-story Church Office Building, still holding on as the tallest in the state of Utah, he sees younger pine trees that have sprouted to take the place of older ones that are succumbing to insects. The entrance to the office tower, a 1970s modernist lobby, is guarded by turnstiles and church officers wearing boxy black suits and bland ties.

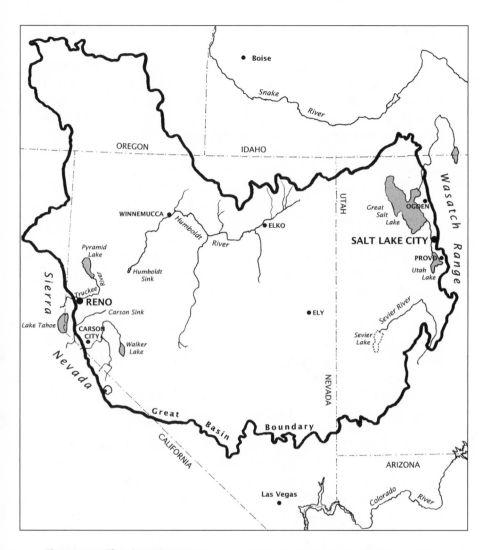

Figure 1.1. The Great Basin

Cannon, with a head of honest thick white hair, in contrast, favors a svelte wool overcoat and plaid scarf smartly whisked around his neck.[7]

The campus is changing, and Cannon is watching over the process. Kitty-corner to the Latter-day Saint administration block is a newer addition to the church's headquarters. This is the Saints' conference center, the church's millennial augmentation of the campus and successor to the

Tabernacle on Temple Square, the religion's primary meeting hall for more than 130 years.

The church constructed the new building with granite-like rock excavated near the mouth of Little Cottonwood Canyon in the Wasatch Mountains, to match the Temple's rock, quarried from the same area over a century earlier. The building holds some twenty-one thousand people and in some quarters is known as the "Supernacle." The conference center is massive and state of the art, in marked contrast to the Tabernacle, a stately and simple building. To some, the contrast of the conference center to the Tabernacle displays the church's transformation from a regional religion of the American West to a global player. The church, one of the fastest-growing religions in the world, claims thirteen million members and counting.

Now Cannon's job is to maintain the campus of a multinational organization in a manner consistent with its message. He renders the global and civic expressions of the church headquarters through the medium of landscape. Walking in front of the conference center, Cannon pointed out the elm trees along North Temple Street, on either side of an extension of City Creek flowing parallel to the street. The trees on the south side of the sidewalk sit in regular native topsoil. They have grown tall and have retained their leaves, though brown and crinkly, into December. The trees on the north side of the sidewalk, sitting on top of a parking garage, had to be planted in a lightweight soil called utelite. They are much shorter and have no leaves. Cannon believes the difference in growth is mostly due to the soil types, but it could also be attributed to the effect of the creek water, steaming in today's storm. Further complicating the picture is the fact that the fast-growing south-side elms are prone to retain snow, cracking branches in the winter. Which is better, which will be more effective in helping the church send its message? It's not yet clear.

As a midday December blizzard gains intensity, Cannon and I are standing on the conference center's roof, seventy-five feet above the Mormon campus. The church now owns a massive swath of downtown that is two blocks wide and five blocks long in places—and these are blocks that are ten acres each. We see the administration block, Temple Square, the Family History Library block, the Crossroads Mall block, the Zion's Cooperative Mercantile Institution (ZCMI) block, a whole block of surface parking, and the newly acquired Triad Center block. In all, a tidy nest of production, consumption, and government. But we can also see farther out west to the railroad depots which were the traditional neighborhoods

of minority laborers, and east to the Avenues, the city's densest and usually least-Mormon neighborhood. Salt Lake's center has always felt the
tension between Mormon and Gentile, and as Utah continues to become
a more heterogeneous place, the Mormons must find new ways to assert
their church locally.[8] One way the Saints' leadership is trumpeting the
church's nearly 180-year-old message in the changing city is behind us: In
the center of their headquarters, the Saints have built a green roof.

The roof of the conference center is accessed either by stairs that are
gated at the top, with a sign stating "Roof may only be accessed by tours
starting at Gate 15" that wards off the curious, or by an elevator taken
from the building lobby. At the top of the elevator is an airy room and a
church matron who asks if we have permission to be here. Naturally, the
gardener does. When we exit the room onto the roof we are presented
with stately rows of spruce, maple, and aspen trees dividing walkways,
which lead to a granite sculpture with four waterfalls pouring into a pool.
Behind it is a wall with a passage from the *Doctrine and Covenants*: "And
the gospel shall be preached unto every nation and kindred and tongue
and people."[9]

Terracing down from the roof on the north and east sides are giant
planting boxes with more spruce, maple, and aspen. And at the far end is
what Cannon calls "the meadow," a field planted with bunchgrasses. The
church has been selective here, reaching to the mountains for its floral
references instead of the valley, with its shrub communities of shadscale,
rabbitbrush, and greasewood. "We stayed away from the brush ecology
and went with the meadow ecology instead," Cannon explains. In the
spring, wildflowers will germinate from the ground, creating a scene
meant to resemble Albion Basin, which lies within the Alta ski resort at
the head of Little Cottonwood Canyon.

There are some discrepancies. In the summer, it gets hotter at four
thousand feet in downtown Salt Lake than at nine thousand feet in
Albion Basin. So, the church occasionally irrigates its meadow so the
forbs and columbine can compete. And, in a natural meadow, fire would
keep the land clear of larger vegetation. "As you could imagine, I don't
think anybody would want a fire on top of the conference center," Cannon says. So they mow it once a year, turning the organic matter back
into the soil, imitating the process of burning.

The green roof is just the beginning of the changes the church is
bringing to downtown Salt Lake. In October 2006, the church leadership unveiled plans for the City Creek Center, a two-and-a-half block

redevelopment of the Crossroads and ZCMI mall blocks just south of Temple Square and the Latter-day Saints administration block. The twin malls, both built in the 1980s, were failing and the church hired nationally recognized mall builders Taubman Centers, Inc., to start over. Taubman designed a new mall spanning both blocks, with the addition of housing and quasi-public open space. The new plan featured inner-block plazas and fountains that recalled Temple Square itself. "It literally vaults Salt Lake City into the future," proclaimed one downtown booster.[10]

The roof was meant to be a vault for Salt Lake's past. With all the changes happening around it, the roof was designed for the visitor to feel as if he or she was seeing what Brigham Young saw when he walked into Great Salt Lake Valley for the first time. Like the church campus, it's a controlled experience: Because of liability, one can only access the roof with a guide. And when it snows like this, no one is allowed up here. On cue, a large box-suited man emerges from the doors at the end of the roof terrace, walking over to Eldon Cannon, who is casually sauntering through the snow, his scarf unmoved. The gardener knows the message before it is delivered: We need to go inside.

Into the Hyper-West

This architect and this gardener demonstrate the opposite ends of the Great Basin's great divide: A 400-mile-wide desert has, for over a century, separated the gaming and divorce industries from the teetotaling Mormons, sin from salvation, one strange, isolated encampment from another. But in recent years at each end of this expanse, these city builders have made offerings of urbanism amid the tension of change in the power centers of the region—each with its pitfalls and prejudices but nevertheless emboldened with the adventurous élan that defined the settlement of the desert in the first place.

I set out to explore the Great Basin, though it was a different kind of route than most might choose. The Basin, with its meter of dry mountains and valleys, of outsized vistas, and its lack of very many people, has the comparative advantage in the American landscape as a place of emptiness large enough for any human soul to carve out its own piece. But I was after a different frontier—the one faced by the American West in the coming decades. The desert had been occupied with what Wallace Stegner called "Oasis Cities." Salt Lake City and Reno, exploding in population while their hinterlands die, bear testament to this term.

Cities of the Great Basin: Salt Lake City (above) and Reno (below)

While the Church of Jesus Christ of Latter-day Saints reinvents its downtown Salt Lake City headquarters with a green-roofed conference center and rising condominium towers (above), developers build a new Reno with the Truckee River Walk, casino-to-condo conversions, theaters, bars, and parks (below). Source: Top photo by Alan Sullivan

These two urban areas sit a day's drive apart on opposite ends of one of the nation's fiercest landscapes. One side of each city is pushed against a major mountain range that supplies it with water, spectacular views, and a growing tourist economy. But on the other side lurks the Great Basin Desert. The cities like to associate themselves with the high, wet mountains that rise above them, but they must exist in this strange, salty desert.

Can it continue? The city of the Basin is full of paradox—the most urbanized region in the United States has perhaps the least urban culture. People call Salt Lake and Reno cities but often with a disparaging edge, with none of the reverence that comes with calling New York or San Francisco "the City." Few seem as excited about them as cities as about what lies outside them. At the same time, this apparent abundance around the Wasatch Front and Truckee Meadows, of space to grow out into the desert and up sky-high mountains, isn't really abundance at all but severe limitations on basic resources such as water and fuel. The Great Basin, like the rest of the West, needs to face the reality of urbanization. Urbanism, that careful sorting of space, relationships, and resources in places that have a lot of people in them, is what is needed here. The Mormons' green roof and the condominiumania in downtown Reno are calls for urbanism in the Great Basin, but they are only the beginning of what can happen when an urban mentality is applied to the region's landscape.

As a native Salt Laker, I knew the city from growing up and working as a newspaper reporter, but I had never been to Reno. My father's family goes back five generations in Utah, mostly southern Utah Mormons who included ranchers, lawyers, grocers, and miners. But I knew nothing of Nevada. If a trip through the Wasatch Front became an unearthing of the familiar, a trip through the Truckee Meadows was blazing new personal territory. If I understand the landscape around my hometown through the city and all of its ties and roots, I would come to understand Reno through its landscape, a two-way cognition of land and city.

The city and the landscape around it—this is the modus operandi of the American West. And the Great Basin is the heart of the West. It possesses all of the mythical qualities of the interior West in extremes, both the fearsome and the alluring. It is the largest desert in North America, and with most of its land receiving less than ten inches of precipitation a year, is as dry as all other North American deserts except its neighbor to the south, the Mojave. Unlike the other American deserts, though, much of the Great Basin Desert's precipitation comes in the form of winter snow, compounding its harshness. And further preventing life are its soils, which are so salty in many places that nothing except saltbush or glasswort can grow. Salt Lake and Reno are the only American desert cities to exist in a climate at the same time four-season and temperate; you have to go to Tehran (Iran) or Kashgar (China) to find substantially sized cities in comparable four-season, temperate, mountainous, arid climates. According to one estimate, the Great Basin is home to more mountain ranges per square mile than anywhere except Afghanistan.[11] And in contrast to other North American deserts, the Great Basin sustains a high elevation even in its valleys, mostly staying over four thousand feet.

More of the Great Basin is public land than any region in the United States. Large portions of western states are too dry to be farmed and were retained by federal agencies. As of 1999, about nine-tenths of federally administered lands lay in the thirteen western states. Utah and Nevada are the extreme examples of this pattern: About four-fifths of Nevada and nearly two-thirds of Utah are managed by the federal government, ranking first and second in the contiguous forty-eight U.S. states.[12]

The Great Basin is the emptiest region of human habitation in the lower continental United States. Outside of its urbanized areas of Reno and Las Vegas, Nevada has the lowest population density of any western state of about three people per square mile, one whole percentage point below the nearest state, Wyoming. Utah, whose non-urban population lies primarily outside the Great Basin portion of the state, is nevertheless fourth, with about six people per square mile in its non-urbanized areas.[13]

But the corollary to this sparse population is another extreme of the American West—urbanization. Behind California, Nevada and Utah are the most urbanized states among the eleven western states, with 92 percent and 88 percent of their populations, respectively, classified by the census as "urban" in 2000. For comparison, the census classified 79 percent of the United States population as urban. Nevada and Utah also rank first and second among western states in percent of population in their largest two metropolitan areas, with 88 percent and 81 percent of residents living in Las Vegas/Reno and the Wasatch Front (the latter of which forms two census-designated metropolitan statistical areas). Looking at the Great Basin as a whole, one finds that 90 percent of its approximately 2.5 million residents in 2000 lived in a census-designated urban area, and 85 percent of residents lived either along the Wasatch Front or in the greater Reno metro area. Not only is the Great Basin's population highly urbanized, it is also concentrated in only a few large metropolitan areas. It is in—and along the edges of—these expanding urban centers where the region's growth is occurring. Elko, the only real population center in the middle of the Basin, failed to grow at all from 2000 to 2005.

Underneath the obvious differences, the Great Basin's cities are strikingly similar to each other—and distinct from others in the American landscape. And these cities are changing in similar ways, moving toward a shared path through the high desert. In Reno, the historic power of the gaming industry has waned, but the city's other attributes have lured growth over the past several decades: the jobs, the affordability, and the recreation of the nearby Sierra Nevada. The same attributes are helping to drive the population growth of the Salt Lake area, where the Latter-day Saints are adjusting to a more heterogeneous, urban city. Increasingly, the Wasatch Front and Truckee Meadows share a bond as a similar kind of place. Each is a new breed of city that is emerging in the Intermountain West: a safe haven between the mountains; a smaller, more accessible city where people can get involved more easily than in bigger cities; a landscape of recreation; a polyglot of new immigrants and refugees; a climate of crisp, mild weather; and a quality of life that is more affordable than that of the coasts. Here, many of the earth's major problems—overpopulation, deforestation, desertification, climate change, poverty, and a general paucity of resources—are, for now, to most people, hidden in the green between the mountains. Geographer Richard V. Francaviglia observes that "the Salt Lake Olympics subtly reinforced this belief that the Intermountain West is somehow buffered or sequestered from the terrors of the outside world. . . . Symbolically, the prospect of peace from a violent outside world is exactly what had brought Mormons to this stunning, mountain-protected location in the first place."[14] These Oasis Cities are increasingly connected to the rest of the world while, at the same time, remaining comfortably cutoff from it (see figs. 1.2 and 1.3).

And they have grown like mad. In the 1990s, Nevada and Utah were the first and fourth fastest-growing states in the nation (Arizona and Colorado being the second and the third), adding to their populations by 66 percent and 30 percent, respectively. In the next five years, Nevada remained the fastest-growing state while Utah leapt to third place. In the first half of the 2000s, Nevada and Utah grew by 19 percent and 9 percent, respectively.[15] Almost all of the growth in Utah has occurred along the Wasatch Front, and while much of the growth in Nevada can be attributed to Las Vegas, metro Reno has begun to catch up. From 1990 to 2000, the Las Vegas metro area more than doubled and was beat out only by St. George, Utah, as the fastest-growing metro area in the nation. But

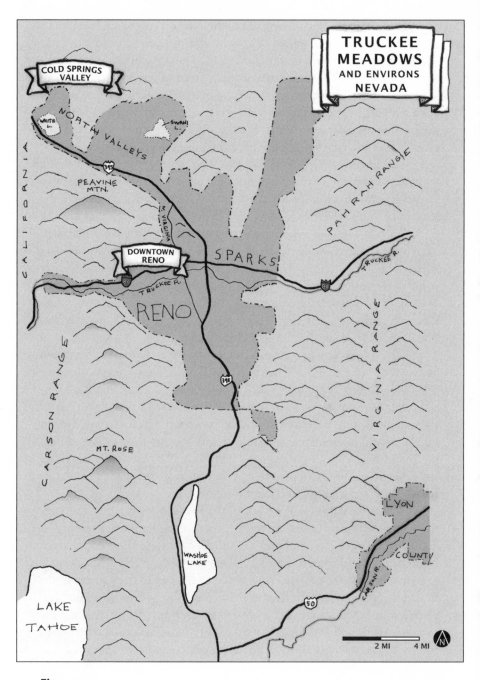

Figure 1.2.

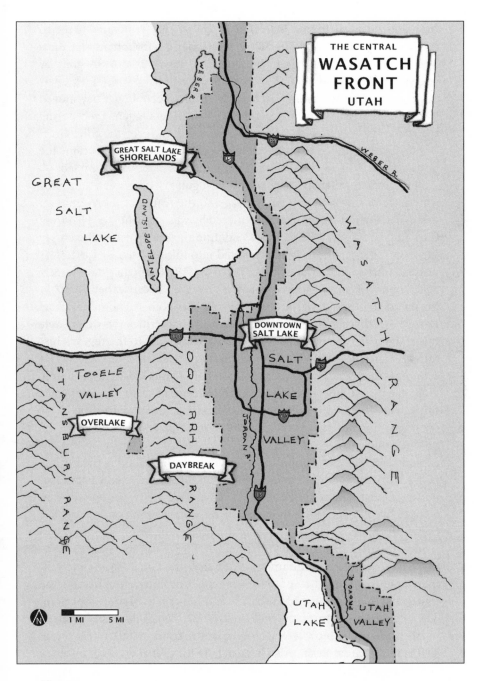

THE CENTRAL
**WASATCH
FRONT**
UTAH

GREAT SALT LAKE
SHORELANDS

GREAT

SALT

LAKE

ANTELOPE ISLAND

WEBER R.

WEBER R.

WASATCH RANGE

DOWNTOWN
SALT LAKE

SALT

LAKE

VALLEY

STANSBURY RANGE

TOOELE
VALLEY

OVERLAKE

OQUIRRH RANGE

DAYBREAK

JORDAN R.

PROVO R.

UTAH
LAKE

UTAH
VALLEY

1 MI   5 MI

Figure 1.3.

from 2000 to 2006, metro Reno grew by 17.5 percent, compared to metro Las Vegas' 13.7 percent.[16] The Salt Lake–Ogden Metropolitan Statistical Area (MSA) also grew 17 percent, and the Provo-Orem MSA grew by 20 percent. By comparison, the United States as a whole grew by 5.3 percent.[17] Between 2000 and 2005, an average of 30 people per day moved to the Reno area; 100 people per day to Salt Lake–Ogden. Even during the economic recession that began in late 2007, the growth of the Great Basin cities continued to outpace the rest of the nation; Utah became the fastest-growing state, and Nevada maintained its place in the top ten.

It is also here where perhaps the greatest gulf exists between the mythical image of the West as a rural place and the reality of the West as an urban place, a notion increasingly offered by western scholars. Historian Carl Abbott writes, "Americans . . . define the real West as the empty West. . . . Cities are not yet incorporated into this regional rhetoric."[18] As historian Alicia Barber adds more recently, "Western cities have largely been left out of conversations about the New West because they do not fit the picturesque image of the resort towns."[19] Economist Thomas Michael Power puts this slight in economic terms. He describes the way people think about the regional economy as "primarily tied to the region's historical economic experience," of natural resource extraction, "not present economic reality."[20] There is a spatial corollary to this idea: The economic ideas of a resource economy lead one to conceive of a vast, spacious place of individuality and freedom, when space is actually tied to the "New West" economy of urban services and, in some places, urban industry.

The consequence is that even as the cities of the Great Basin have exploded with jobs and population growth in the latest boom, their urban fabric has weakened. These cities of the Basin embody great paradoxes in that almost no one in the region lives outside a city, yet few seem to want to live in one. Those moving out to the developing periphery have their eyes trained on the openness and escape of the Basin, its valleys and mountains; they are loathe to love the city itself. So at a time when so many newcomers to the Intermountain West seek the Great Basin's increasingly unique combination of space, scenery, prosperity, and freedom, the imperative for a sustainable urbanity has never been more important. The interaction of large cities with such a raw, seemingly empty, strange, harsh landscape is nowhere as potent in the continental United States as it is in the Great Basin. Also pressing are the global crises of resource shortages and climate change—where the two driest states in the nation are its highest per-capita water consumers, and the bowl-shaped valleys perfect for collecting air pollution are host to some of the highest auto ownership rates in the nation.[21]

Still, I believe that the life of cities has much to offer this high-desert region. We know what we can celebrate about the "empty" Great Basin; what can we celebrate about the urban Great Basin? I hope to find some understanding of how, as Americans, we are adapting to life in one of the driest, coldest, emptiest, constrained—yet often booming—places in the nation, and the prospects for turning rampant urbanization into sustainable urbanism. Here, they are still seeking sin, and they are still seeking salvation. As the Great Basin city searches for a toehold in the desert, sometimes it's difficult to tell which is which.

Cities of Zion

The West's urbanization is not new but a long-established pattern. The commonly accepted notion of Frederick Jackson Turner that western American civilization evolved from trapper to farmer, then to "men of capital and enterprise," all while the edge of civilization swept west like a rake, is not accurate. As western frontier historian John Reps describes, the western city was the "instant city," a settlement built from scratch in one orchestrated act. Its site was usually selected by an individual, group, church, railroad, corporation, or government agency, and the founder would simply apply the gridiron pattern to streets and blocks, because its design was simple, easy to survey, appeared to be rational, and fit neatly into the mile grid established for the western United States.[22]

Early western cities were not the result of decades of agglomeration after settlement of the frontier but spearheads for it. The founders of mining camps and cattle towns laid down an urban template familiar to those coming from the east and sought to achieve coveted city status by filling it with urban institutions such as universities, banks, and seats of government. Urban settlements maximized efficiency of resources in the desert environment. Despite the myth of the Wild West, the development of western settlements was quite ordered.[23] At least that was the plan—for the instant city was also the boom town, its gridiron pulled by the ventures of not just the founder but anyone who appeared on the scene. In many cases, the boom town was just as soon the bust town.

Indeed, one reason the West was predominantly urban from the start was its relationship with unabashed capitalism on a monumental scale. Originally, in the late nineteenth century, the federal government worked in tandem with the railroads and other capitalist enterprise to turn its public lands, American Indian homelands, and Hispanic homesteads into private Anglo-owned land. Historian William Robbins has called the West's space an "investment arena for surplus capital, a source of raw materials for industrial sectors, and a seemingly vast vacant lot to enter and occupy."[24] The most efficient places to manage these investments were, of course, cities. The scale of the vision allowed these western cities to be born in an "instant."

The West has only become more urbanized. By 1890, urban residents and institutions dominated western culture and civilization, and after World War II, the West became a pacesetter for the nation. It became rarer for businessmen from points east to bring urban ideas to the western landscape than for the urban West to export new urban ideas like theme parks and retirement communities to the rest of the United States.[25] The West's urbanity was an optimistic version, embracing space and lack of past associations. The West became what historian Kevin Starr called a "testing ground for the national experience."[26] By 1967, Wallace Stegner, in *The American West*, urged contributors to be aware of the urban dimension: "The western American is, by the millions, a city dweller, even if he wears boots and a Stetson and grows whiskers for Frontier Days. Seven out of eight readers of this magazine are city dwellers," Stegner wrote. By 1980, 83 percent of westerners lived in urban areas, compared to 73 percent of the nation.[27]

The Mormons, as much as anyone in the West, were part of this pattern. Despite the agriculture and irrigation for which the Mormons are known, their Great Basin Kingdom began as a planned, urban settlement. Consequently, the tension between an urban system and planning on one hand and ruralness and the freedom of the Basin on the other was present in Salt Lake City from the beginning.

Followers of the Church of Jesus Christ of Latter-day Saints, founded by Joseph Smith in 1830, came to the Great Basin with the wish to be left alone and build the City of God while they awaited the millennial coming of Christ. They brought their city plans with them from Ohio, by way of Missouri and Illinois, where they had been drawn up under the direction of Smith as the "City of Zion." Smith was very much into cities. According to one account, inspired by the vistas of New York in 1832, Smith saw the city as the only work of man resembling God's creation.[28] Although the City of Zion was officially a divine revelation, Smith is thought to have drawn from plans for Philadelphia, Jerusalem, his boyhood New England towns, and the Jeffersonian grid. Smith was also interested in the city as economic efficiency: Property was stewardship, frugality, economic independence, cooperation, and equality.[29]

The City of Zion was platted as a settlement of one square mile. A grid of 132-foot-wide streets flanked by twenty-foot sidewalks created forty-nine ten-acre blocks. The plan accounted for public space: Three public squares were set aside for religious buildings, and there would be common stables south of the city, "so [there are] no barns or stables among the houses." The private lots were laid out alternately so that no lot fronted another. The lots were a half acre each, creating about one thousand half-acre lots. Yet because of the size of Mormon families, Smith estimated that each city would contain fifteen thousand to twenty thousand people, a population density that approaches that of New York City; that many people in a square mile unit could produce a vibrant urban neighborhood. Likewise, Smith saw the cities as building blocks: The plan ordered the development of more identical cities once the first was full.[30] The vision for such a city was startling in the 1830s, when the United States was still primarily agrarian. Smith's design predated by nearly seventy years influential, shockingly similar plans, like Ebenezer Howard's Garden City, which became an important template for progressive city planners throughout the twentieth century. The church tried to build the City of Zion multiple times during its early history: in Kirtland, Ohio; in Independence, Missouri; and in Nauvoo, Illinois; but were not completely successful.

After Smith's murder in 1844 in Illinois by political foes, the Latter-day Saints, under the new leadership of Brigham Young, left the Midwest after multiple threats from local communities and elected officials. Samuel Brannan, a Mormon leader, in 1846 brought a ship of Saints around Cape Horn to the Mexican town of Yerba Buena on the Pacific Ocean. He saw the potential of the bay and the beauty of the site, then went east to catch Brigham Young; meeting him at the Green River, Brannan made his pitch. But Young told Brannan that he was "looking for a country so poor, no one would want it, where his people would be left alone." As such, the Saints passed on the site of present-day San Francisco for the alkaline plains of the Great Basin.[31]

When Young led the Saints to the Great Basin in 1847, he inherited Smith's desire for a central urban settlement. Salt Lake City, founded at the mouth of City Creek, the northernmost of the streams emerging from the Wasatch Mountains into what is now called Salt Lake Valley, was the most pure expression of the City of Zion so far. In a valley of waist-high grass, nomadic Ute bands, and little Euro-American political occupation (the valley at the time was a far-flung part of the territory being contested by Mexico and the United States in the Mexican-American War), the Great Basin offered the Saints as close to a blank canvas as was possible on the industrializing continent. Young followed Smith's plans for the street widths, block sizes, lot sizes, and setbacks. The large-blocked, wide-streeted Salt Lake City grid was born, an expression of divine revelation in the desert.

In bringing the City of Zion plans across the plains, Young sought to build a permanent civilization. Young objected to mining as an economic enterprise, for example, because he saw it as transient and ephemeral. He deemed Salt Lake a "garden plot city," but it would be an urban type of agriculture, where church officials would mete out space in the city carefully and, as with the City of Zion's stables, would farm in the "Big Field" outside the city limits.

And while the Mormon city as designed by Joseph Smith was primarily a way station on the road to Heaven, when the faith's followers arrived in the Great Basin, they found a ready way to apply the message of redemption to the land itself. Once in the Great Basin, the Saints devised a system of irrigation canals to water their crops that capitalized on both their tightly organized social systems and the frequent streams flowing from the Wasatch Mountains. The Mormons had no experience in irrigation and, unlike settlers in the Rio Grande and Salt River Valleys in present-day New Mexico and Arizona, found no precedent on which to base their efforts. But the City of Zion plan gave them an advantage. What made the Mormon irrigation network innovative had little to do with the ditches themselves, which were quite ordinary, but how they fit within the Saints' systems of planning and resource management.[32]

Irrigation made Salt Lake City an urbane place. Ordinances required sidewalks to have grass, and trees spaced sixteen feet apart, all irrigated by open water ditches along the street. In its first years, the city's bountiful fruit and shade trees gave the impression of a garden.[33] In this isolated valley, city fathers were experimenting with landscaping techniques only beginning to be used with fanfare on the East Coast and the Midwest by landscape architects like A. J. Downing and Frederick Law Olmsted (though the Saints' version stressed orderliness rather than romantic whimsy). The overall effect was one that impressed visitors from all over the nation and afforded Salt Lake City cosmopolitan traits.

Salt Lake, from the beginning, embodied the tension that it would carry with it until the present: It was designed to be an urban center but, at the same time, an isolated escape. Yet it was never fully either. In 1849, travelers seeking gold in California began moving through Great Salt Lake City, tying the Saints' communal and subsistence economy to the national market economy. The completion of the transcontinental railroad in 1869 at Promontory Summit, on a peninsula extending into the northern portion of the Great Salt Lake, further integrated the Mormon economy into mainstream America. By the early twentieth century, the mansions lining South Temple street were built not by Mormon leaders but by mining magnates. Thus, since its beginnings, Salt Lake's utopia has doubled as a typical western urban center of resource extraction wealth that pulled at the Saints' utopia. "Incorporation took swift possession of the garden," as William Robbins writes.[34] This relationship strengthened once the Saints gave up their left-leaning socialist ways for flag-waving, right-wing business orientation in the early twentieth century. As a crossroads in a seemingly empty landscape, the idea of an escape on the Wasatch Front has dovetailed and been supported by strong ties to the national and global economies.

The continued dominance of the LDS Church has split the personality of the Wasatch Front. Like the Great Basin itself, it is middle America with some extreme jolts to the sides. Neighborhoods and social networks of Salt Lake City tend to be overwhelmingly Mormon or staunchly Gentile. In tough times for President George W. Bush, Utah as a whole remained his most loyal ally while the mayor of Salt Lake attended rallies to protest his administration's visits to the state. Utahns consume water and pollute their air more than almost any other state in the nation, yet Salt Lake City has emerged as a leader in environmental sustainability.

Reno has a much different story, but one that is no less entwined with the Great Basin landscape and geography, and serves as a contrasting western bracket of the desert to the Saints' eastern bracket. Reno's continued survival and growth, in contrast to Salt Lake's planning and theology, was due to scrappiness and luck. Reno was, like Salt Lake, a crossroads of north–south and east–west routes that became the target of an ambitious, half-cocked gridiron street plan. It grew around a crossing over the Truckee River. Originally, men and horses swam if the river was high, but a Mexican-American War veteran named Myron Lake arrived at the crossing, saw the traffic through the Truckee Meadows, and envisioned an urban future of an east–west railroad crossing. In 1861, he bought a log bridge, and then built a hotel and tavern for travelers, and Reno's haven for transients was born.[35]

The crossing's first taste of success was as a supply town for the nearby Comstock mine, located closer to Virginia City, in the mountains. But Lake believed his settlement's success hinged on luring the railroad and a depot, which he aggressively sought and received by giving land to the Central Pacific railroad. Thus, Reno was an instant city, though a different kind than Salt Lake City. Unlike the Mormon capital, which was platted fourteen years before its founding, Reno was not formally platted until 1868, a decade after its founding. Its name of Lake's Crossing was also changed to honor Civil War general Jesse Lee Reno. Its street pattern grew out of the intersection made by the river bridge at Virginia Street and the railroad tracks on Third Street.

Having grown from the influence of the Comstock mine, Reno—and all of Nevada—suffered when the Comstock ran out in the late 1870s. Nevada lost much of its population in the 1880s, and Congress discussed abolishing its statehood. At the turn of the century, gold and silver ore was discovered in nearby Tonopah. Reno again benefited, attracting downtown investment in the form of banks, hotels, and a mining school, and increasing its population from 4,500 in 1900 to almost 11,000 in 1910.

But by the turn of the century, Reno began to build itself around a group of industries whose common trait was that they were much more heavily regulated in other parts of the United States. As leftovers from Reno's frontier mining heyday, divorce, prizefighting, prostitution, and gambling all infused Reno's economy and identity in the early twentieth century as "Sin City." While the Saints saw the Great Basin Desert as a place for salvation, many of the boosters of Reno saw it as a place for sin.

Early on, divorce was the preeminent of these "sin" industries. Other states such as New York required proof of adultery to grant divorces. But Nevada's laws were suited to its population. The mining life was a transient one, where men seeking new fortunes met new women—Nevada allowed divorce on several vaguely defined grounds and required only six months to establish residence. Word of Reno's laws spread around the nation to the coasts, where California movie stars and New York millionaires made the move to Reno for six months, got in line at the Washoe County courthouse, and talked to a judge for ten minutes to obtain a divorce. Later in the century, Reno also innovated the quickie wedding now popular in Las Vegas. In contrast to the hallowed notion among Mormons of being sealed in the Salt Lake Temple, a wedding in Reno had the allure of anonymity.

Reno also took on boxing prizefights that were not allowed in other jurisdictions. In 1910, Progressive reformers in San Francisco convinced city officials to cancel a prizefight between former champion Jim Jeffries and current champion Jack Johnson. Johnson, who was black, had married a white woman, considered a scandalous indiscretion. Reno welcomed the fight, and many San Franciscans grew up thinking they could do almost anything in Reno.[36]

These industries coincided with the Progressive era, which, with its temperance movement and social conservatism, made Sin City stand out all the more starkly. But Reno and Nevada were not immune to the Progressives. Gambling, for example, was legalized in 1905, banned in 1909, then slowly crept back into the state until being legalized again in 1931. The residency requirement, the enabling mechanism of the divorce colony, was raised from six months to one year, then lowered to three months before being lowered again in 1931, in the same bill that legalized gambling. Indeed, eventually sin won out, and set the stage for the city's continued growth derived from gaming. E. E. Roberts, leading a successful campaign for mayor of Reno, proclaimed, "You cannot legislate morals into people. . . . You can't stop gambling, so let's put it out in the open. Divorce is the only solution when marriages are unhappy. And if I had my way in this prohibition year, I as mayor of Reno would place a barrel of whiskey on every corner."[37]

Keeping these activities legal was increasingly part of a conscious effort to support Reno's economy, of the city's intense desire to succeed dating back to Lake's Crossing. But in some cases, Reno's sin industries were tied to the land itself, to the city's desolation and isolation. Alicia Barber notes that gambling became "an established part of life in the Great Basin, capitalizing on the same psychological urges that had led so many to seek their fortunes in the state's mines decades earlier."[38] At the same time, the divorce colony, legal gambling, and prizefighting also brought cosmopolitanism to tiny Reno through the lifestyles of the coastal socialites who visited.

The change to Sin City also transformed Reno's economy from a natural resource economy of the traditional West to an urban, services-oriented one of the New West. While the Mormons predated planned communities with the City of Zion, Reno predated the service industry boom of the 1990s with its emphasis on gambling and divorce. These urban innovations were exported from some of the most remote outposts of the West.

Modern Reno was built on these ideas. Still a center for its hinterlands of gold and silver mines, the metro area itself was forged by services and entertainment. These constitute its second and first most important industries, respectively. Reno's downtown became the province of the whole-block casino embodied by the blank white-walled Harrah's, mixed in with tiny wedding chapels and souvenir shops, the alternately dim and blinding cityscape that some now consider "Old Reno." Into the 2000s, Reno was being called "the last remnant of the Wild West."[39] Nevertheless, times are changing: In 2004, for example, Churchill County passed an ordinance requiring a conditional use permit for those wishing to open a brothel.[40]

Remaking the Intermountain City

Reno and Salt Lake City were settled by refugee groups and fugitive industries and formed by both rural and urban ideas. The rural is found in the importance of isolation imposed by the vast open space and the mountain barriers to both cities, in the agriculture of the Saints' alfalfa and orchards, and the ingrained libertarianism of Nevada. Meanwhile, the urbanism of the Saints was the urbanism of efficiency, of a working system and allocation of space. The urbanism of Reno was transience and cosmopolitanism, of people of different backgrounds bumping into one another in "The Biggest Little City in the World." Even Ely, far into the Great Basin hinterlands of Reno near the Utah-Nevada border, had urban aspirations. The seven-story Hotel Nevada in Ely was, for a few years in the 1920s, the state's tallest building, and the hotel even built a walk of stars for movie actors such as Mickey Rooney and Ingrid Bergman.

One hundred years later, salvation, sin, urban, and rural, all mediated through the landscape, are still rubbing against one another. The urban forms of Greater Salt Lake and Greater Reno are in flux now because of their regions' growth. The Basin's internal urban growth—the majority of Utah's growth comes from residents having children—is colliding with outsiders' perspectives of these places as they move from more expensive or crowded places.

The most oft-cited engine of urban growth in the Great Basin is jobs. The Nevada state demographer believes it was new jobs that continued to bring migrants from other states to the Reno metro area during the booms of the 1990s and 2000s. Reno's economy, long dominated by the gaming industry and the tourism it brought, has diversified. In 2001, leisure and hospitality accounted for 25 percent of the Reno-Sparks Metropolitan Statistical Area's economy, but by 2005 it had dropped to 20 percent. Over that period, the sector lost some 3,300 jobs, most of them in casinos. The Reno economy grew in other areas, though. Professional and business services and trade and transportation added a combined 8,500 jobs from 2001 to 2005, meaning an overall growth rate of 8.8 percent, almost eight times the national rate. During a time period when the United States lost 13 percent of its manufacturing jobs, Reno's manufacturing sector grew by 2 percent.[41] In the mid-2000s, times were good throughout the United States, but in the Great Basin, they were really good. Along the Wasatch Front, in Provo, Ogden, and Salt Lake, unemployment rates in late 2006 were barely over 2 percent. Jobs were being created faster than people were moving into Utah to fill them. Even later in the decade, with the national economy in a tailspin, Utah's unemployment rate was half the national average.[42]

Affordability also clearly has been a factor for new residents: People have cashed out of California and Arizona for cities like Salt Lake, where they could get twice the house for half the money. The appreciation of Utah's housing market was third in the nation in 2006, despite its median housing price remaining at an affordable $186,250. They are also more affordable than the increasingly expensive mountain towns of the New West. And yet, with much of the same proximity to four-season recreation, the smaller intermountain cities have taken on some of the attraction of mountain towns while at the same time offering more affordable places to live and more good jobs to the educated young people who are often attracted to—and priced out of—mountain towns.[43]

Outdoor recreation is increasingly important in the urban Intermountain West. Reno had tried to market its outdoor amenities as early as the 1880s after the Comstock bust; a 1920s slogan promoted Reno as the "Recreation Capital of America." But the outdoors was always secondary to gaming tourism until the popularity of outdoor recreation in America caught up to Reno's amenities. Likewise, the outdoor industry is increasingly adding jobs along the Wasatch Front. As of 2007, the industry employed 36,000 people in Utah, which put $4.5 billion into the state's economy each year. The president of the Outdoor Retailer Trade Show, which has held its biannual show in Utah for years, remarked, "The best incentives are free in the state of Utah. If you want to own the mountain, you have to be on the mountain."[44]

The jobs, affordability, and recreation lifestyle have combined to lure migrants of all kinds from out of state, many buying houses with cash in hand. Californians, especially, began to dominate the Reno area. The state demographer estimated that one third of Reno's growth during the boom of the early and middle 2000s was due to the influx of Californians. Nevada and Utah, according to historian Carl Abbott, have long been part of "greater California,"[45] ensconced in the state's economic and cultural influence. Now, many Californians are using the state's hinterlands as a place for spiritual rehab. Feeling swamped by the size of California's cities, they feel that they can invest more easily in Salt Lake or Reno and can have a hand in making them their own. As one Californian who recently moved to Reno told me, "You have three degrees of separation with anybody here. In the Bay Area, you're lucky to have ten." William Robbins wrote that the West is "a region of metaphor and symbol, a place that provided rationale and definition for a larger sense of national purpose."[46] Robbins was writing about the frontier days of the late nineteenth century, but this idea is still alive. It's easy for people in other parts of the country to get the feeling that there are slices of American paradise still available in the Great Basin.

Yet it's not just newcomers. Especially in Salt Lake, development in high-growth areas has been fueled by native Utahns who want to continue to live in the Wasatch Front and enjoy what most people call its "quality of life." In 2005, for example, most fast-growing states saw 5 percent of residents having recently moved from out of state. In Utah, the number was 3.3 percent, yet Utah had one of the nation's top growth rates.[47] The State Office of Planning and Budgeting forecasts that two thirds of the state's growth will continue to come from reproducing Utahns.[48]

And while Intermountain Utah and Nevada are growing as fast or faster than the Sunbelt West of southern California, Arizona, and Las Vegas, Intermountain natives and newcomers alike are bent on distinguishing the urbanizing Great Basin from Sunbelt metro areas. Many Utah developers are wary of the speculation that fueled the growth in the residential housing markets of Phoenix and southern California. And they are wary of Las Vegas. Hal Rothman, in *Neon Metropolis*, emphasizes that in the new Las Vegas, so much of the landscape and culture is brand-new and imported.[49] Despite all the growth in their corner, northern Nevadans don't necessarily think of their cities like this. It is noteworthy that when deliberating the theme of the Silver Legacy casino, developers decided on a theme of something familiar, not fantastic, as is common in Las Vegas.[50] Many Reno boosters continually fought the Sin City image and promoted the "Real Reno" of the university and pleasant neighborhoods.

This contrast bears out in the Great Basin hinterlands. Ely, Nevada, the tiny, shrinking town of 4,000 people, which is roughly at the center of the triangle formed by Reno, Salt Lake, and Las Vegas, is one of the Great Basin's isolated communities, smack in the middle of the Basin and Range, and in the winter, one of the coldest places in the nation. Residents must rely on the cities, but they rely on them for different things. Residents usually go to the Las Vegas area to shop for the simple reason that it's closer and the road has fewer mountain passes, and in the winter for recreation and vacations, because it's warmer. But in culture, Ely is much more closely aligned with Reno. Its kids usually prefer University of Nevada in Reno over UN in Las Vegas. "Vegas is a rat race. Reno is more of a small city," an Ely city clerk told me when I visited. "Even though it's farther away, they have big summer picnics. The kids seem to hang out together. When I go to Vegas to visit my daughter, I have people waiting on me from Wal-Mart to restaurants, and all they have is dollar signs in their eyes. It's all about the money. In Reno, they ask, how are you doing today? Cold isn't it?"

In northern Nevada and northern Utah, there is a sense that the natives and the newcomers are jointly building the place. The recreation seekers, the refugees, the immigrants, and the 'fornians are all converging on places they think will give them another chance. Those already here feel that there is a quality of life worth defending like a castle. The result, for many, has been a vision of wholesomeness that dovetails with the four seasons, the tight enclosure of the mountains, and a feeling that there is enough room here for everybody. In an essay about moving from southern California to Reno, Eric Dieterle writes, "We had left that place, and California with it, in a small U-Haul, bringing with us all that we had salvaged from two separate lives . . . flowing north in a confluence of hope. . . . In Reno, we found good work and got well—spiritually, financially—and we began to dream again . . . images of a home, of a place that meant something to us."[51]

Despite the wealth and the boom and the hope, the origin of the attraction of these cold desert oases tucked between the mountains can still be defined in what they are not, by what they don't allow or what laws aren't on the books. In comparison to the coasts, they are not expensive. They appear not as violent. The spectacular natural amenities have little to do with the fabric of the cities themselves—to access them you leave the city, and the attraction is that the city doesn't get too much in the way of you leaving it. And to many, like the Mormon pioneers, the Great

Basin's space represents the geographical guise of new beginnings. The attraction of today's Intermountain West for much of America remains, despite its increasing urbanity, escape.

Gary K. Estes saw the escape, but he saw something else, too: Reno was the perfect place for a very livable type of urbanism. He had a plan to make Reno a city where people wanted to live, right in the center of it. To make it palatable, the Residences at Riverwalk would be just like a suburban subdivision, with a homeowners' association, a clubhouse, and security, and a river in walking distance. Thinking of the Truckee, he channeled San Antonio's original River Walk. He envisioned adding color to the city's skyline. While, for some time now, Reno's casino-hotel high-rises have projected plenty of color at night, the casino walls encountered by the pedestrian are drab beige and gray during the day. "I was on a cruise," he is telling me as we take the elevator to the third floor, relating a story about how he came to a decision on how to paint the Riverwalk, "and we went by St. Martinique and saw Diana Ross' house. It was light green and mauve. I said to my wife, 'get the camera.' She's from the Ukraine where all the high-rises are bright colors."

Estes opens the door to reveal the empty unit, the last one-bedroom left. It has wooly white carpet and a kitchen in the main room. The only window is the door that leads to a faux balcony. Frankly, the place seems to have retained some of its sadness and darkness, but Estes bounds through the condo, rapping on the counter, "Travertine. I got the granite from China. The glass," he points to the sliding door to the balcony, "will withstand 160 mile-per-hour winds. The steel frame allowed me to do 9-foot ceilings. Very well made. It was an architect's dream."

Later, Estes steps outside to West Street to light a cigar. "Two and a half years ago I was crazy," he says. "My friend said, 'You have balls the size of grapefruits.' I didn't see it as a gamble." He sold the units for prices that ranged from the mid-$200,000s to the mid-$500,000s. By October 2006, only thirteen units remained out of 130. By that time, national developers had descended upon the Truckee and taken Estes's innovation to the next level. Twenty-story steel-and-concrete frames began to hulk eerily above the sidewalks, like half-finished remnants of third-world oil booms. The colors of Reno were indeed changing: The outrageous sunburst hues of the 1970s were giving way to the calming wasabi and mauve of the 2000s. Names were flipping along with the property. The former Sundowner casino became the luxury condominium Belvedere by the grace of a Bay

Area developer. And kitty-corner to the Riverwalk, on Second Street, the Golden Phoenix casino has become the Montage due to the efforts of a Chicago builder. In this vision none of the sadness and darkness of the old Reno would remain. "Discover . . . your style," the Montage Web site urged in its intro, flashing a green color scheme and an image of a kayaker. The building was rebuilt much like a cruise ship: massive, with windows and balconies on its sides and a huge deck that holds a pool, a clubhouse, and a dog park. The marketers hoped to attract empty-nester seniors and single professionals.

Downtown Salt Lake City, too, is a giant construction site. The Great Basin Kingdom is adapting to Salt Lake's evolving urbanity. Like Reno, Salt Lake built its own 1990s downtown salvation project, the Gateway mall, constructed along the Union Pacific rail line at the west end of downtown, and squarely in the city's historic area of Gentiles, immigrant workers, Latinos, artists, punk rock clubs, and gay bars.

And the Gateway was several blocks from the Mormon campus. As downtown began to be recentered by this development, the church went on a construction spree of its own, which has included the conference center, a Main Street plaza, and the use of a parking lot as the 2002 Olympic Medals Plaza. And in October 2006, in the biggest development yet, the church released a bird's-eye rendering of what the Crossroads and ZCMI blocks will look like once the City Creek Center is finished in 2011, with a U-shaped open-air mall spanning the two blocks and four condo towers. "This can set the course for Downtown Salt Lake for generations to come," said LDS Church bishop David Burton at the unveiling of plans of the City Creek Center. "The church for the last 160 years has heavily invested in Salt Lake City. We need to do it right."[52]

There were vigorous objections to the church's plans, as there usually are to anything that involves both the center of Utah's largest city and its most powerful institution. Bitterness still remained from when, in 1999, Salt Lake City sold the block of Main Street between Temple Square and the church headquarters block to the church, creating a church super-block in the middle of downtown.

Had the church and the city sinned against urbanism again? Members of the public objected to the foot-traffic stealing skyway over Main Street and to the planned demolition of historic buildings at two of the blocks' corners. But no one could deny the benefit of housing to reinvigorate a downtown. Even the Utah Transportation Authority's Trax light-rail, which exceeded ridership expectations, had not revived downtown businesses. The City Creek Center plan offered 700 new residential units in four buildings. And the plan to break up Salt Lake's City of Zion blocks, now obscenely large for the pedestrian, was called by former Salt Lake City planning director Stephen Goldsmith "a quantum leap from where we've been."[53]

"We need to accept it," Goldsmith said. "The Vatican is the Vatican. Temple Square is Temple Square."

A new fake City Creek would run through the middle of the mall blocks, cascading through a streambed and waterfalls. City Creek Center would become a subtle echo of Temple Square and the administration block, extending the sense of the campus. As Burton said, "We're trying to pick up the same type of ambience we have on Temple Square on to 100 South." That means that there will now be three fake versions of City Creek flowing through downtown Salt Lake: the one going through the park at the mouth of the canyon near Brigham Young's grave; the one going in front of the conference center by the elm trees; and now the one going through the mall. Neither uses water from the "real" City Creek, which ends in a pool farther up its canyon. But the Latter-day Saints are maxing out the creek's cultural capital. Like the Truckee with Reno, City Creek was the original reason for the location of the Salt Lake settlement. And like the Truckee, with its new kayak park, City Creek has been engineered to fit the city's new image of itself.

The Saints like to phrase these changes in terms of a continuum that has multiple beginning points—the stories told in the Book of Mormon; the revelations of Joseph Smith; the founding of the city in 1847—and, according to the church's theology, an endpoint. Up on the roof of the conference center, Eldon Cannon is telling me that the garden on top of the building isn't simply the product of a trend like green roofs.

"Brigham Young said that there will come a day when we will plant on top of the buildings," Cannon says. That day has come, and according to Cannon, it has been evolving since the beginning. "If you turn and look at these blocks, there is very little that is not sitting on top of structure," he continues. Much of the administration block lies on top of five levels of parking; there are old underground tunnels leading between important buildings; dressing rooms sit beneath Temple Square, all of which is planted with trees and flower gardens. Thus, the view of the headquarters is rendered differently, as an urban continuum and cross-section of buildings rising over gardens and gardens on top of buildings on top of parking garages, sunk into the earth.

Like the buildings of the headquarters, the message of the Saints has been engineered in granite and foliage like so many public works projects. Now, as before, the message has taken on urban form. And yet it plays off the emptiness of the Great Basin. While the conference center roof is clearly adapting to Salt Lake's increasing urbanity, it does so by recalling the big open at the beginning of the story, by shielding the city with the trees to re-create the sense of the original emptiness presented as the opportunity to make a garden.

That is the message. "Christ is the creator with his father," Eldon Cannon tells me. "Father placed the first people in the garden and said dress and take care of this garden."

The city builders of the Great Basin are dressing their gardens—are they taking care of them? Outward from these centers of Reno and Salt Lake, to the edges where the city meets the desert, the garden is really growing. And the illusions of space, of emptiness, of new lives, are multiplying. The escapes, the utopias, the schemes, and the transgressions are accumulating like the snow, piling up, making this particular bottom of the Basin heavy.

Scaling the Basin

Peak to Playa

> We begin to think that there is something wrong with us if
> we cannot live under the conditions of desert life. Insofar as
> psychology tries to "help" us, it helps us to "adjust" to those
> conditions, taking away our only hope, namely that we, who are
> not of the desert though we live in it, are able to transform it into
> a human world. Psychology turns everything topsyturvy: precisely
> because we suffer under desert conditions we are still human and
> still intact; the danger lies in becoming true inhabitants of the
> desert and feeling at home in it.[1]
> —Hannah Arendt

Rising above Truckee Meadows, the broad basin that has become home
to Reno, Sparks, and the scattered settlements of unincorporated Washoe
County, are two major mountains visible from almost anywhere in the
region. The first is Mount Rose, the crest of the Carson Range, which separates Reno from Lake Tahoe and is the first Great Basin range heading
eastward. Naturalist Stephen Trimble describes how Mount Rose is par-
ticularly a Great Basin mountain, and not a Sierra peak, in its "instantly
recognizable tone—major, rather than minor, but not a heroic major like
the Sierra. A secondary, spare, less important key."[2]

The other peak is Peavine Mountain, north of the Truckee River divide.
It is more minor than Mount Rose, a few thousand feet lower and lacking
any alpine qualities, and thus has come under less scrutiny of public land
managers. Peavine is criss-crossed by a mine and jeep trails going straight
up its face. There is no trail to the top, so you have to walk on the jeep
roads. As one of the most popular recreation areas in the city, you might
assume a multitude of signs would lead the way to Peavine. But there isn't
even one sign, just an unmarked steep dirt road turnoff between houses.

This is my conundrum as I arrive in Reno for the first time late on a July night. Driving over Donner Pass from California, I listened on AM radio to J. T. The Brick interviewing Charles Barkley live from the Tahoe celebrity golf tournament—a century after the Johnson-Jeffries bout, Northern Nevada is still king of the getaway sports event but now with an America's-Adventure-Place twist. When I pull into downtown Reno just before midnight, I feel action crackling in the hot night. I stop at a Winner's Circle gas station/mini-casino and buy a street map from a rugged-looking guy with a mustache and a mullet ponytail. On Fourth Street, gangbanger-types are cruising in convertibles under the Casino skybridges, and a few blocks away, a local arts nonprofit is showing a movie to young families gathered at the outdoor amphitheater along the River Walk.

The city quickly becomes much quieter as I drive north on Virginia Street, seeking out a place to camp on Peavine Mountain. I buy some food at the new Smith's in Lemmon Valley, and then continue northwest to what I figure must be the apron of Peavine, where light industry, storage facilities, and mobile homes whiz by sporadically in the glare of my headlights. I squint, looking for a "Peavine Mountain turn left" sign, but I see none and have to take a chance on a steep, rutted dirt road heading uphill. It continues and soon enough, I find a turn-out that puts me on top of a small hill—likely a pile of mine tailings—and I look out into the night.

Peavine is a separate state of mind from the city, a place apart, where you can be away from Reno but look down on it. In early 2006, a group of students at the University of Nevada–Reno's journalism school documented how neighbors of Peavine Mountain interact with its landscape. The project superimposed the neighbors' voices over sequences of photographs. The photos show Peavine in the muted colors of winter, the glare of summer, the green of spring, the color transformations that make the Great Basin Desert a canvas of seasons. In each photo you can't help but notice how small the person looks, how small is the city in the distance, how overwhelming the folds of the mountain.[3] "We call our neighborhood the 'I'm On I'm Gone' neighborhood, the neighborhood around Peavine because we're real close to all the trails, there's probably a hundred, at least a hundred miles of roads up there," the mountain biker who was interviewed says. "You get a little bit of four-wheel people there, but it's not too bad." A geocacher[4] who lives below Peavine says that, "When I first moved here there were no houses, so I just crossed the street and started walking up the hill. If you're from back east you think, oh it's just a bare ugly mountain because it doesn't have any trees on it. If you're from Nevada it's what you're used to. People in the city see one side of it, and there's a whole other side." A four-wheeler states that, "When I have something wrong at home, just stressing, I'll go up there, look at this face, and be like oh dude, I gotta get up that thing, hopefully get out of it without rolling your car down the hill. It's self-reinforcement. I go up there and I don't have to worry about what's wrong. I can just be myself. It's a good escape, to get as far away from everything as I can. It's my serenity, it's my solitude. It's beauty everywhere you look."

A land of here and there, above and below. Places like Peavine surround the Wasatch Front and Truckee Meadows, where people move back and forth between city and raw backcountry. These are urban places because the activities undertaken here are necessary parts of urban life—and with urbanization creeping up the mountain, the line between mountain and city becomes more important. It's the condition, like the four-wheeler says, of living on the edge of two versions of oneself. I know because I grew up at a similar edge. Peavine, even at night, recalls the Wasatch foothills lining the north end of Salt Lake Valley. I grew up at the bottom of the slope and the foothills were the place for my friends and I to move between city and wilderness, between the shadows of the Gambel oak and the oval of city lights around the corner. I felt the effects described by those interviewed for the Peavine Mountain project: Of mountain biking out the back door whenever I wanted; of a hundred miles of jeep roads and trails; of a love for hot dryness in the summer; of the humility of living next to a mountain; of the feel of the grain of home. The nightshade of the hills where we spent our nights was holy, but so were the lights of the city. More than anything, I think this is what defines the life here, the moving between mountains and city, or between desert and city. How do we strike a balance between these vast landscapes and the concentrated activity of the city?

"The life of country and city is moving and present," Raymond Williams writes. "It is now and then: here and many places. When there are questions to put, I have to push back my chair, look down at my papers, and feel the change."[5] Having set up my camp chair at the tailgate of my truck and opened a Pabst, my dog sniffing around at the strewn junk and sagebrush, I look down on the lights of the city and wonder what Saturday morning holds for this city of the Basin.

My small collection of trips through the Great Basin can begin to give you a sense of this overwhelming landscape. The Great Basin isn't a tempting vacation attraction for most Salt Lakers, not with the Wasatch providing just about everything a mountain range should and the compelling Colorado Plateau quenching most thirsts for the desert. I never intended to see and explore the Great Basin, I just had to cross it on the routes to a variety of intentions. There were all the Thanksgiving family drives from our Salt Lake home to visit my grandparents in St. George, through the November juniper-studded bleakness of Central Utah along the last uncompleted stretches of the Interstate Highway System winding through too many distant mountain ranges to count. There was my fourth-grade field trip to Stansbury Island with our teacher who was a birding expert, and who taught us to look for the great blue heron on the smelly shores of the Great Salt Lake. There was the time my now-wife and I, interested in connecting Utah's dots, drove out to the Deep Creek Mountains near the Nevada border, following the trail of the Pony Express and finding surprising outposts of wildlife in the wet basin bottoms, and the time a friend and I spontaneously decided to explore the skiing in the Ruby Mountains' glacially carved U-shaped canyons and, after enduring one of Elko's $30 motel rooms, ended up snowmobiling up Lamoille Canyon with a group of backcountry ski fanatic gold miners in the nil visibility of a blizzard.

A few years later, when I was a reporter at the *Salt Lake Tribune*, I was lucky enough to have an editor who encouraged me to get on the road more. One of the trips I took was for a story about the Paiute Indian tribe's economic development. I spent several days visiting the disparate Paiute reservations, one for each band, scattered along the Great Basin's edge. The Paiutes claimed land from the Grand Canyon to Nephi and from Ely to Blanding but had been "terminated" from the United States' official list of Indian tribes in 1954 after several attempts by the government to remove them to other reservations. But after a decade of lobbying by a core group of Paiutes, they had been reinstated in 1980. I drove to Kanosh, to Koosharem, to the outskirts of Cedar City. I drove the long way from Cedar to St. George, around Pine Valley Mountain, past Mountain Meadows, where Mormons had dressed up as Paiutes while they ambushed and murdered a group of travelers from Arkansas in 1857. I drove to the Shivwits Paiute reservation in the lava fields below the red cliffs outside St. George. It was near the white brick house in the town of Santa Clara where my grandparents lived out much of their retirement. I met the band chairman, Glenn Rogers, there and he told me his story of growing up on the reservation, which the Paiutes call Sham City. Sham City was then a group of shacks without plumbing or electricity, and Rogers spent his youth partying and doing drugs and drinking and bouncing around from Enterprise to Cedar to other Indian reservations. When he returned to the Shivwits reservation, becoming a Mormon, he joined the tribal council and began bargaining for water rights with the City of St. George to replace the shacks with sturdier, plumbed buildings. I sat with Rogers in the band building as it got dark outside, thinking how far back both of our families went in these lava fields, maybe to the days of Jacob Hamblin, the Mormon ambassador called by Brigham Young to make friends and farm with the Paiutes, and he told me, "I want people to understand who we are. I want people to know we're just doing our best to survive."[6] The smallest band, the Indian Peaks Paiutes, had a reservation out on the western edge of Beaver County near the Nevada line. None of the members or anyone else lived or worked there, or within a hundred miles of it, but I wanted to see it anyway. From Sham City, I drove north across the Iron County desert. At the junction of the highway and a railroad line, I found a ghost town called Lund, my grandmother's maiden name. From there I had to maneuver my truck onto a graded dirt road, which quickly dissipated into a four-wheel track when it had to overcome a pass to reach the broad valley at the foot of the Indian Peaks. The reservation was a square of juniper-covered slope at the mountains' flanks. Not valuable real estate, though as recently as a generation earlier, members of the band had farmed turnips and wheat there before giving up and moving to Cedar City. Now they had thirty-eight members, who, the band chairwoman had told me, make the trip to the reservation once or twice a year. She had told me there was a cemetery here among the junipers and water-crevassed desert hills, but I couldn't find it.

Together, the Great Basin's characteristics separate it from every other part of North America and sum up to a perplexing place to explore, exploit, study, work, and live. The plants and animals, geology, and hydrography of different environs of the Interior West overlap to signify a distinct high mountain desert region. For example, Nevada and western Utah are the northern part of the sweeping Basin and Range Province that extends to southeast Oregon, California east of the Sierra, Arizona and Sonoran Mexico, and into New Mexico and Chihuahua. Here, mountain ranges alternate with desert valleys in a nearly one-to-one rhythm. Geologists note a Great Basin section of the Basin and Range Province, pinched off like a balloon, that encompasses the nearly parallel seventy-five ranges running between the Sierra and Wasatch: An east-to-west cross-section of these ranges from Reno to Salt Lake might include the Carsons, the Pine Nuts, the Stillwaters, the Desatoyas, the Shoshones, the Toquimas, the Monitors, the Hot Creeks, the Pancakes, the Rubies, the Goshutes, the Deep Creeks, the Stansburys, and the Oquirrhs. In the West, whose mountainous character is often assumed to be monolithic, the Basin and Range stands out as distinct. If you look at a topographic relief map of the entire United States, only a few large-scale landform patterns stand out: The school of fish of the Appalachians; the wispy clouds of the Great Plains' river basins; the dinosaur fossils of the Rockies; California's oval Central Valley—and the basins and ranges of the Great Basin. What is notable about this landform region is not only the number and isolation of its ranges but also the flatness of the basins between them. There is nowhere else in the United States that is as flat as the Great Salt Lake and Black Rock Deserts. This is a testament to the relative youth of these basins and ranges, which formed with a stretching and lifting that started only eight million years ago (compared to the 480-million-year-old Appalachians). As a geologist tells John McPhee in *Basin and Range*, "This Nevada topography is what you see during mountain building. There are no foothills. It is all too young. It is live country."[7]

Much of this Basin and Range section overlaps with the Great Basin Desert, North America's temperate desert in the rain shadow of the Pacific ranges, which has hot, dry summers, and cold, wet winters.[8] Under earlier definitions, the Great Basin Desert included much of the Four Corners–area Colorado Plateau, which came to be known as the Painted Desert, and then not a desert at all, by later biogeographers. The Great Basin Desert took its place with the continent's other, less temperate deserts, the Mojave, the Sonoran, and the Chihuahuan.[9]

The desert environment, like the Great Basin's mountains, is recent on a geologic time scale. Only twelve thousand years ago, during the height of the last ice age, the Basin was largely covered by two massive lakes, Lake Bonneville in the east and Lake Lahontan in the west, both of which were bigger than present-day Lake Superior. The land around the lakes was wet and cool and supported conifer forests.[10] The juniper trees now ubiquitous throughout the Basin came to the region as recently as the Late Pleistocene Epoch, when archaeologists believe the first people were spreading through North America. The landscape's demeanor has evolved with its humans.

The precise extent of the Great Basin Desert is really its relationships to other biogeographic zones in the West. The eastern and western boundaries are easy to agree on because the Wasatch and Sierra provide big mountain ecology distinct from the smaller, isolated ranges of the

Basin. But the northern and southern extents are trickier because similar landscapes extend north into Idaho and south to Las Vegas, California, and Arizona. Many biologists define the southern edge by the appearance of the creosote bush and the Joshua tree just north of metro Las Vegas. In the northeast, the Uinta Basin's sagebrush-dominated plant life mirrors the Basin's, but its animals do not, thus excluding southwest Wyoming.[11]

Idaho's Snake River Plain is not part of the Great Basin for another important reason. The Snake River Plain, as its name implies, was made by one of the West's largest rivers, which merges with the Columbia River before emptying into the Pacific Ocean. The most defining feature of the Great Basin is that its water does not reach the Pacific or any other ocean but instead drains internally, in salty bodies like the Great Salt Lake, seasonal lakebeds called playas, or big drainage basins called sinks. At the end of the Pleistocene, as the latest ice age was ending and the climate was drying, the levels of lakes Bonneville and Lahontan were falling. Because they had nowhere to drain, and the lake levels were plummeting as a result of the new climate's higher rate of evaporation than of recharge, the water left but the salts stayed in the remnant of Lake Bonneville, the body of water that came to be known as the Great Salt Lake. Thus, the Great Basin is a somewhat misleading name since the region is really made up of hundreds of tiny subbasins, some as small as a few square miles. This hydrographic definition would include not only the Great Basin Desert but also much of the Mojave Desert between the coast mountain ranges near Los Angeles and the Colorado River.

We overlap these three ideas of the region: the Basin and Range, the temperate desert, and the internal drainage. We emerge with a place defined by ruggedness, dryness, and isolation, characteristics that have vexed humans for centuries—explorers, capitalists, scientists, Caucasian settlers, and Native Americans. It is a region that is western Utah and northern Nevada, with a slight cut into the very eastern edge of California and hornlike extensions into southern Oregon and Idaho. The Sierra and the Wasatch are its west and east walls, the Snake River Basin its northern wall, with a leaky gradient of temperature and plant life at the south. It includes Reno and Lake Tahoe but excludes Las Vegas and Lake Mead. It includes Salt Lake City, Provo, and Ogden but excludes Boise, Logan, and Pocatello. It includes Cedar City but excludes St. George. Today, it is dotted with small, isolated ghost towns, boom towns, and bust towns: Winnemucca, Battle Mountain, Ely, Eureka, Austin, Caliente. And it is now rimmed with exploding cities.

A Hydrographic Mystery

The Spanish, the French, the British, and eventually the American explorers and conquerors became familiar with the temperate desert's winter fits and vast, confusing stretches of sagebrush. They came to endure its rhythm of basins and ranges. But they did not have a grasp of the Basin's internal drainage, and for centuries they attempted to solve the Interior West's riddle of emptiness and hydrology. In an era when navigable water meant access and connection, the Basin's vexing hydrography, its lack of human habitation, and its central location among the powers vying for expansion into North America led to the dominant notion of the region for several centuries. It was the inhospitable vastness that must be crossed—and must surely contain the means to create a new civilization. As much as the Basin's natural definitions, this perception helped create the region in the minds of Americans.

While European explorers were documenting and conquering other parts of western North America like the Rio Grande Valley and the California coast, the Great Basin was a blank area on maps. As Richard V. Francaviglia explains, "Overall, North America, like other continents, generally came to be understood in stages; first by her oceanic margins, next by her riverine ribbons of navigable water, and finally by overland expeditions into her landlocked heart."[12] The Great Basin was the extreme center of North America's landlocked heart. Consequently, for centuries, the Basin was defined by what wasn't there or by what people didn't know. It was terra incognita, a blank space on maps. On a Johnson and Browning map from the mid-1800s that hangs above my desk, the area of western Utah and eastern Nevada labeled "The Great Basin" is blank for hundreds of square miles except for a note explaining that "This vast Unexplored Region is supposed to be inhabited by tribes of Indians. Altitude nearly 5000 feet."

Other characteristics helped to deflect explorers and conquerors. The region had few native inhabitants compared to other parts of the West. High native population density had drawn the Spanish to areas from the Valley of Mexico to the Rio Grande Valley to present-day Peru and made conquest easier and more profitable. And massive obstacles stood in the way of expeditions, such as Coronado's 1540 *entrada,* which was stopped short of the Basin by the yawning crevice of the Grand Canyon. It would be another 200 years before anyone recorded setting foot in the Great Basin.[13]

The first inkling Europeans had of the hydrographic Great Basin was, in fact, the massive salty lake in the Interior West to which the rivers surrounding it all drained. But explorers found it hard to heed this clue. Fathers Escalante and Dominguez's search for an overland route from Santa Fe, New Mexico, to Monterey, California, in 1776, noted the lake's presence, as well as its connection to the freshwater Utah Lake. The group's cartographer, Bernardo de Miera y Pacheco, wanted to portray the present-day Wasatch Front as a good Spanish settlement site. In the map that he produced, Miera drew a river running from these lakes to the Pacific Ocean, making this valley in New Spain not only plentiful of water but also connected to the coast via a navigable river.[14] Miera's name of Rio de S. Buenaventura, meaning "River of Good Fortune," led generations of explorers to search fruitlessly for a navigable river connecting the Great Basin and the Pacific coast.

None of the Basin's rivers, then or now, resembles a great trade river like the Mississippi. The edge rivers that drain the mighty snowpacks of the Wasatch and Sierra—the Bear, the Weber, the Provo, and the Sevier on the east side and the Truckee and the Carson on the west side, are short, swift mountain streams that barely pierce the Basin before ending in terminal ponds like the Great Salt Lake, Sevier Lake, Pyramid Lake, and the Carson Sink. The Basin's only significant interior river, the Humboldt, meanders eastward across most of Nevada before giving up in the Humboldt sink outside Reno. It spawns no grand allées of cottonwoods or willows. While driving alongside the Humboldt, you barely realize it's there.

Peaks to Playas

Biologists have been equally baffled. They have spent careers studying how plants respond to the Basin's closed hydrologic systems, their ephemeral water, their stark differences in precipitation and the salts left behind by evaporating lakes. While European explorers tried to understand how the Basin's hydrology could support a human civilization, modern biologists struggle to understand how the region's waterways and water cycles—left alone to precipitate, melt, flood, settle, evaporate, and sink—support the life that already thrives.

The first concept of Great Basin ecology is the playa. Just as the bottom of the Basin is a sort of way station for the watershed, it is a baseline for life within it. It is the one place where water is stored and available to wildlife, the place that expresses the seasons of the Basin. When the newly formed lake is two inches deep, crustaceans, phytoplankton, and insects come to life through eggs and spores.[15] This temporary life zone drains throughout the summer, and the fun is over by the fall when the lake bed is dry again. Each year, the cycle repeats, the water saturating the cracked earth and creating a thin, silvery sheen, then drying up again.

Many Great Basin biotic communities orient around playas: Drainage defines not only the Great Basin's geographic parameters but also its ecological characteristics.[16] In the playas, plant life begins tenuously. Here, the most stringent limit on life is not water but salt. The salt is here because it has nowhere else to go. The minerals from the water end up in the playas, and there is not enough precipitation to wash them away. Here live the plucky plants adapted to life in alkaline soil, all with alchemical names: saltgrass, iodine bush, desert blite, greasewood, glasswort. All can reside in a playa through long-evolved adaptations to a high-salt content. Salt and aridity are linked not only through quickly evaporating water bodies but also at a smaller scale, through plants' relationships with soil. Salts in soil suck the water out of plant roots until the salt content on either side of the root membranes are equal, and the plant is facing drought. Plants that survive on the playa are able to take in and survive with salts in their tissues.

Heading outward and upward, the playa chain of plants gives way to the rolling valleys that are dominated by two primary plant communities, shadscale and sagebrush. Too dry for trees but not so salty that the strange playa vegetation is allowed to run amok, valleys are suited for these one- to three-foot shrubs. Like the playa plants, the shrubs have paid the price of their adaptation, living with smaller leaves, a slow growth rate, and a small stature.[17]

If the sagebrush and shadscale-dominated valley floors are the Great Basin's sea level—or ocean floor, as the more historically correct analogy may be—then its mountains are islands. They are cooler, moister places whose temperatures and precipitation spawn other sets of plants and animals. The mountains hold multiple life zones building up toward the peaks and saddles of the ranges: piñon-juniper woodlands; mountain mahogany and aspen; the subalpine forest of limber pine and five-thousand-year-old bristlecone pines, the earth's oldest inhabitants. While the craggy bristlecones and weathered mountain mahogany lend an air of eccentric dignity to the high ridges, aspen groves add lushness foreign to the dry basins below.

But animals living in the small conifer or brush forests face a sea of unlivable landscape around them. Like the Galápagos Islands, they are cut off from one another, leaving each range to evolve different species. Most plants here are likely remnants from the Pleistocene, when seeds were dispersed in a much wetter, cooler overall climate. Each range is left to evolve its own personality, and this process of biogeography still confounds the most noted experts. In fact, biologists have looked to the Great Basin—even as a landlocked desert—to study island biogeography. E. O. Wilson, the father of this field, wrote that island biogeography processes of "dispersal, invasion, competition, adaptation and extinction" are among the most difficult in biology to study and understand.

Hydrologists, meanwhile, must be comfortable with divining the Great Basin's mysteries of water with even less certainty. Water takes an interesting, complex journey in the Great Basin. The most important concept to grasp is that each of the Great Basin's individual hydrologic basins is a closed water system. It is a microcosm of the Great Basin as a whole. Underneath the watershed is a closed aquifer, so without human intervention, moisture can only enter through precipitation and can only leave through evaporation. If you graphed the valley's annual precipitation month by month, you would see a U shape, with the highest precipitation coming in the winter storms of December and January on each end of the year, dipping down to nearly nothing in June and July. Much of the winter precipitation falls in the form of snow, especially where there is more moisture in the high elevations, so it is stored until it melts. When it rains, or the snow melts, some of the water infiltrates into the porous, sandy soil while some runs off down the slopes, eventually coming to rest in the playa. Because of the clayey mud of the playa, little of the water infiltrates into the water table, instead evaporating and leaving its salts and other minerals behind.

Exactly how much moisture watersheds in the Basin receive has been vigorously debated by hydrologists for almost a century. The climate's high rates of evaporation, freezing, and strong winds can enervate the use of gauges. The evaporation can be thwarted with some oil, the ice with some antifreeze, but the wind remains an obstacle: A thirty-mile-per-hour wind can reduce a gauge's capture by about one third. "You could have a gauge network of one hundred gauges and your estimates might be off by 50 to 80 percent," one Reno hydrologist told me. So, scientists have resorted to making educated guesses and creating models. Even today, there is no surefire method to know the details of the system.

Here in the Great Basin, rocks and salt and water have created a place in the middle of North America full of desperate adaptations, but where humans have a hard time feeling at home. It walls us in and dries us out. The valleys have been maligned because they are too dry and their ground is not ripe for human paradise. The concentrated wetlands are disliked for the opposite reason, that they are too pungent. Its rivers go nowhere and its mountains always look far away and lonely.

Scaling the Basin

What challenges, then, await the urban designer in the Great Basin?

Northwest of downtown Reno, hugging the California border, is a long, sinuous watershed called Cold Springs Valley. It is one of the hundreds of closed, internally draining basins that make up the Great Basin. While much of northern Nevada civilization has clustered in the basins drained by perennial rivers such as the Humboldt, Carson, and perhaps most of all, the Truckee, more typical of the region is a basin like Cold Springs, which lacks constantly flowing water and whose center is a playa that changes with the seasons from dusty dirtscape to shallow lake to mudflat and back again.

You can see the Great Basin's difficult hydrology and gradient of biological communities most clearly in a microcosm such as Cold Springs Valley, where the eight-thousand-foot ridges of Peavine Mountain steeply descend, mellowing only shortly before flattening in the alkali flat that has been named White Lake—over three thousand feet below the peak but only a few miles away. It's a different world down here: Gone are the cool junipers and pines, which have given way to cracked mud and thin coats of standing water. "Crossed over a ridge to a valley which is perfectly level without any vegetation. . . . Soil is of a whitish color," were the words of traveler Alpheus Richardson upon entering the valley in 1852, according to a historical marker. Now, builders are moving in. Like the explorers, they are trying to figure out how to make this environment work for people, and like the biologists and hydrologists, they must know, guess, or override the Basin's patterns of life and water.

Yet designers of the built environment have their own additional challenge in the Great Basin—proportion. In almost every way, this region challenges the principles of proportion that underlay the greatness of classical architecture in providing an environment comfortable to humans. That cradle of urbanity was formed four thousand years ago by

The runoff of Cold Springs Valley creates White Lake playa's thin seasonal sheen of water (above), which eventually dries as Peavine Mountain looms (below).

Woodland Village's brand-new Reno (above) yields creative desert yards of grass and gravel (below).

thinkers such as Pythagoras and Plato, who were searching for a way to organize space in conjunction with a higher order, including the proportions of the human body. Renaissance designers adopted these principles, positing that man is the image of God and the proportions of his body are produced by divine will, so the proportions in architecture have to embrace and express the cosmic order. For these thinkers, spatial harmony also correlated directly with musical harmony, and they designed the proportions of their churches in step with consonant musical intervals, falling into an order they believed pervaded the cosmos.[18] These laws of proportion applied not only to buildings but also to the smaller and larger things of the world—including whole landscapes. Today, many of our most pleasant urban landscapes recall an inherent consonance to those of us walking through them. Many older residential streets in San Francisco, for example, whose houses and flats are half as tall as they are spaced apart by the street draw the pedestrian to them, in part because they have this resonant proportion and they conform to a human scale. In general, a human-scaled, man-made environment is more comfortable than one in which a person is drowned in a larger scale, such as the stark, sweeping plazas of modernist skyscrapers in downtown San Francisco. And walking down a forest glen where trees arch over a creek bed at a consonant interval probably puts the average person more at ease than walking through a stark desert canyon.

Take these ideas to the Great Basin, and watch out. Here, human proportion is thrown out into the dry desert air. The region's vast basins are, on average, a dozen or so miles wide; the ranges rise up to five thousand feet above the valley floors. Without much vegetation rising up to define smaller spaces, these are the spatial parameters of the Great Basin. Scholars of the region have realized this—and have come up with their own tonal analogies. William L. Fox, in *The Void, the Grid and the Sign*, calls the Great Basin the "American Frontier of cognitive dissonance." Cognitive dissonance, Fox says, is trying to hold two contradictory ideas or perceptions in mind at the same time. A human's preconception of looking at a landscape, for example, includes vertical objects defining a foreground, middle ground and background; sharp objects fading to blurry ones, a range of colors also defining the space. But the Great Basin's vertical interruptions are tens of miles apart, so it has no foreground or middle ground; its faded range of colors is narrow and its air is usually so clear and dry that objects in the far distance appear sharp as if they were a few miles away. "The Great Basin is a place where our eyes have trouble getting a grip," Fox writes. "The pattern of mountains and valleys is on a scale so large that we can't get our minds around it just by looking at it. . . . You have to travel through it to gauge for yourself what its size is in relation to your body."[19]

Designers, planners, architects, and gardeners of the Great Basin must reconcile its strange scale and aridity with human comfort. Just as generations have sought to understand the order of the cosmos, generations have sought to understand the order of the desert and humans' place within it. They seek the natural architecture of the desert, the "instructive patterns" in the land sought by Joan Woodward in *Waterstained Landscapes*, a book about a landscape architect who moves to Denver and begins to learn again how to design in a dry environment. Woodward is looking for more than drier versions of Andrew Jackson Downing landscapes. She notes disappointingly that even some xeriscaping simply copies the patterns of wetter environments but with desert-hardy plants.[20]

John Tillman Lyle attempts to define these instructive patterns in desert "archetypes." Lyle distills arid landscapes into archetypes: "The Wash" is a channel that collects and conveys water to a basin or sink and allows the water a place to pause and infiltrate the ground and recharge the groundwater table. "Plant adaptations" means that desert plants all must deal with lack of water, strong winds, and solar radiation. In response, they tend to grow low, spread wide, sprout small leaves and are often spiky and point upward, thus presenting a low profile to the wind and a small surface for losing water through evapotranspiration. "Occasional concentration" means that desert plants tend also to concentrate in small groups around patches of water. "Dryland rivers" have supported some of the world's first cities, "ever-changing ever-moving patterns of braiding, interlacing movement," Lyle writes. "Typically, we encase them in concrete to prevent flooding, thus killing the ribbon of life." Finally, "The Oasis," the subject of fables and legends, is a well-watered island in the desert created by wells or natural springs. "In modern times, oases are more often cities where water has been brought . . . by artificial means," Lyle writes. "Once it is there, urban dwellers usually ignore the natural aridity of the environment and use water in prodigious quantities."[21]

Can the designer employ these principles at different scales, like the proportioning ideas of the ancient Greeks? Lyle's examples range from his own small garden at the base of the San Gabriel Mountains in southern California to the Nile watershed. But he warns that these landscapes are experiments, that all of the great dryland civilizations have eventually declined, and that the long-sustained desert societies are "mostly nomadic and poor." Marc Reisner, in *Cadillac Desert*, notes the absence of any long-term desert civilizations on the earth, save Egypt, where the unique Nile, "the world's most reliable river, would engorge itself in a spring flood and cover most of Egypt's agricultural land," a process that deposited silt and carried away the harmful salt.[22]

Still, some past desert civilizations have used ideas similar to desert archetypes to design places that not only respond to humans' needs for water but also for a comfortable scale. The traditional Persian garden, for example, walls a limited space where water flows—often supplied by a *qanat*, a type of irrigation ditch that brings water from mountains. The scarce resource of water can be put toward concentrated plant and animal life while walls create a human-scaled courtyard.[23] Or, take Yemen, on the Arabian Peninsula across the Red Sea from East Africa, whose geography bears a striking resemblance to that of the urban areas of the Great Basin: A desert region nourished by the moisture of a large, 10,000-foot-high mountain range that has historically held up to four fifths of the Arabian Peninsula's population. Irrigation made possible urban settlements in this highland region as early as the second millennium BC. In the city of San'a, Yemenis built houses six, seven, or even eight stories high, out of mud, fourteen thousand of them all crowded into a walled city. The houses lined narrow streets and behind them were large gardens planted with fruit and vegetables. The buildings provided spectacular views to the gardens and the arid landscape, especially from the highest room, the *mafraj*, where relatives and friends smoked hookahs while speaking to each other in elegant formal language or even poetry and gazing out the windows.[24] They may be antiquated, but these designs embody the floods of the desert wash and the concentration of moisture and green. Efficient use of water and density has led to the creation of urban environments that scale space and use resources in ways that made urban life here livable, and even brought out enjoyable aspects of the harsh high-desert environment.

Modern Americans have reacted differently to their dry landscapes. We've concentrated not on what is in the desert environment but what is not in it. While we have tried to reproduce Eastern America in our towns and cities, we have also made use of our deserts' open spaces. We've treated our most arid and inhospitable deserts—the Great Basin and the Mojave—as sinks for things that won't fit or are undesired elsewhere. The Basin has become a forum of hidden American violence in the Department of Energy's 525-square-mile weapons testing range at Tonopah; the combat training grounds in western Utah; and even a fake German city built in Utah's west desert during World War II. It has become a landscape of frictionless extremes in the salt flats that hold land-speed records at Bonneville and the Black Rock Desert. It has become the home for the great Bay Area escape of the Burning Man festival. It has become the largest of canvases in massive works of "earthwork" art such as Robert Smithson's *Spiral Jetty* at Promontory Point and Mike Heizer's *City* in Railroad Valley. It has become the receptacle for pollution in the Skull Valley Goshute tribe's desire to import spent nuclear fuel rods to its tiny reservation. And, of course, it has been a promised land for the salvation of the Saints and the industries of sin.

Amid these layers, though, the Great Basin Desert has become not an empty landscape but one whose starkness simply makes the accumulations more visible and potent, including the presence of a single person. It is these qualities that make the most dissonant of landscapes resonate with many of its inhabitants. Terry Tempest Williams writes, "If the desert is holy, it is because it is a forgotten place that allows us to remember the sacred. Perhaps that is why every pilgrimage to the desert is a pilgrimage to the self. There is no place to hide, and so we are found."[25] Thus, emptiness is not the ends of the desert but the means. Emptiness simply lays the foundations for desert life: Emptiness makes the per-capita impact greater, leading to the somewhat paradoxical axiom that that which is lacking makes a larger footprint, whether it be water or humans. Reactions to the lack of water inform the form taken on by desert life.

Reno: Urbanity in Motion

Our most significant mark on the Great Basin landscape is and will continue to be the large Oasis Cities at its edges. They are, as Marc Reisner writes, "beachheads" of civilization.[26] They are the saccharine frosting on the long-leavened dough of the world. They are strange versions of Miera's fantasy. When I wake up above Reno in the back of my truck on the slope of Peavine Mountain, I find the morning as quiet as the night, but a thick heat has descended upon it, and after some pancakes on the double-burner, my dog and I are off up the road to the summit to get a better look at the city.

You can reach the top of Peavine Mountain via an old dirt road that almost naively rides the mountain's south ridge, disappearing in some parts to a game trail clinging to the slope. The summit has been flattened to accommodate several giant radio towers. The best seat is the edge of the dusty parking lot for the service trucks. Here I am four thousand feet above the Truckee River and downtown Reno, which rises up like an atomic cloud in the green-on-brown of the valley below. From my position at the top of Peavine Mountain, the visibility of the casino-hotels and the vastness of the vista are hard to reconcile, and I decide that, if Pythagoras were here, he would hear a deep drone thumping into his gut from faraway.

The view from Peavine, as from the Wasatch foothills, presents the unique urban form of the Great Basin city. That is, the urban American West in the extreme. Nowhere in the United States, for example, are cities so close to mountains—real mountains. Bigger western cities like Seattle or Denver are indeed close to serious mountains—one could argue more serious than the Wasatch or Carson Range—but it takes dozens of miles in freeway traffic to move from the prairie or Puget Sound through the foothills to the crest of the Rockies or Cascades. The mountains are visible from downtown, but they feel secondary to the cities' impressive skylines. In Reno or Salt Lake, there is no mistaking it: The mountains are in charge, and neither city could ever build a skyline that could dominate the mountains. The mountains are in your face. The peaks above Salt Lake are even closer to the city, so when you are on top of Mount Olympus, you look down the sheer northwestern face and feel like you're on a diving board over the city. When Utah homebuilders market their products in renderings, they always add mountains to the background. Otherwise, the drawings would not look right.

And nowhere in the country are cities so close to such vast public lands. In both metro areas, public land directly borders densely populated places, such as the Avenues neighborhood of Salt Lake and downtown Provo.[27] Most of it is managed by the Forest Service or the Bureau of Land Management (BLM), federal agencies with millions of acres under their purview, compared to the local districts that manage the prized public parks around the Bay Area. The implications are found in places like Peavine Mountain, where you're on and you're gone: The public lands offer a place where urbanites can interact with vast, raw, rugged open space every day, without even getting in a car.

The crowding of the city by the mountains and the public lands lead to another telling trait of the West, and hence the Great Basin city: density. It's a secret that western metropolitan areas often have denser populations than those in the East. The reasons are many, but geographic constraints like steep slopes, water bodies, and federally managed land are major

factors to containing urban growth. The classic example is that the Los
Angeles (L.A.) metropolitan area has been measured to be denser than
the New York metropolitan area. But intermountain cities are up there,
too. A 2003 Brookings Institution study ranked Salt Lake City the densest
metro area in the nation by one measure.[28] Reno, according to another
Brookings study, is the fourth-densest metro area in the nation, behind
L.A., New York, and Honolulu.[29] The combination of natural and political constraints to development and the western instant city's explosion
onto the land led to fewer households spreading out into the rural fringe.

Yet within this containment, the urbanization spreads out to an even
distribution. The density of the western city is often called "dysfunction
density," because it is evenly distributed, disregarding concentrations of
resources and amenities like water, transit, and jobs. Unlike a city such as
Philadelphia, which grew around a central city and rail corridors, western
cities were built around autos that had access to anyplace anytime and did
not need to cluster. Figure 2.1 shows how, within its urbanized boundary
(outside of which is primarily public land), the Wasatch Front displays
relatively even density, and that residential growth in Salt Lake Valley
has actually avoided the central north–south transportation corridor.
Reno is similar, although recent annexation has captured more sparsely
populated areas at its metropolitan fringe.

And because of the lack of a need to agglomerate around any central point, development in western cities is predominantly horizontal.
The auto has allowed them to become a new kind of city, the realization
of an "expansive, relatively unrestrained and innovative capitalism," as
William Robbins writes.[30] The Great Basin Kingdom incorporated its
own horizontality—the City of Zion plan fit strangely well in the wide
valleys of the Great Basin, where the 132-foot width of the streets locked
in step with the scale of the landscape, opening up broad views to the surrounding desert and mountains. The wide streets are not complemented
by grand apartment buildings but by single-family homes. Horizontality also means that the land uses common to a city—residences, stores,
offices—do not mix on top of one another, and are instead segregated into
groups that make it necessary for a person to drive among their home,
the store, the workplace. The result of the dysfunction density and the
horizontality, as has been noticed by those studying this phenomenon,
is that western cities endure the worst parts of density and urbanization,
such as traffic congestion, without reaping many of its benefits, such as
walkable, exciting urban places.

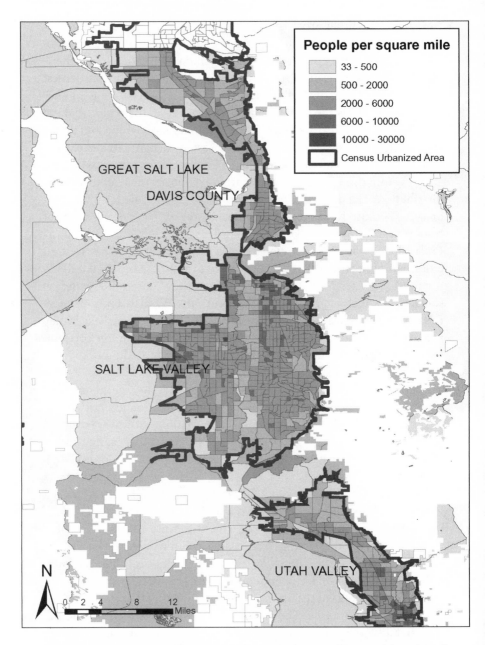

People per square mile
- 33 - 500
- 500 - 2000
- 2000 - 6000
- 6000 - 10000
- 10000 - 30000
- Census Urbanized Area

GREAT SALT LAKE

DAVIS COUNTY

SALT LAKE VALLEY

N

0 2 4   8   12
Miles

UTAH VALLEY

Figure 2.1. Population densities of the central Wasatch Front (above) and the Truckee Meadows (opposite) show the typical medium, evenly spread metropolitan densities for western cities surrounded by mountains and public lands. (Source: U.S. Census Bureau, "Census of Population and Housing," 2000)

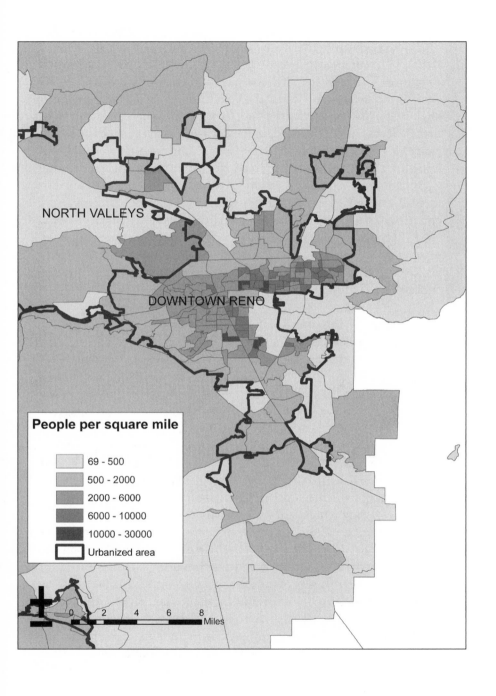

People per square mile

	69 - 500
	500 - 2000
	2000 - 6000
	6000 - 10000
	10000 - 30000
	Urbanized area

NORTH VALLEYS

DOWNTOWN RENO

0   2   4   6   8
Miles

From Peavine Mountain, you can understand this shape of the Great Basin city in one sweeping vista—you can get what urbanist Kevin Lynch called the "image of the city," the mental picture of a city held by its citizens. For many great cities, the image of the city is landmarks such as the Eiffel Tower, but in the Great Basin, the image is the shape of the whole city itself. The edges of the city—of the man-made oasis—are clear. This in itself is unique to the Great Basin. Even if you could find a way to climb four or five thousand feet above Indianapolis or Kansas City without an airplane, it would be almost impossible to distinguish their limits, and so the collective image of these places remains fuzzy and pixilated into smaller views and experiences. It's another paradox: Here, in the Great Basin, whose landscape creates a natural cognitive dissonance for humans, cities are more clearly defined than anywhere else in the country. Here, we get a sense of the identity of the city through the starkness and ruggedness of its land.

An image of the city of Reno, if you look around at its mobile homes, recreational vehicles (RVs), apartment buildings, motels, and casinos, is largely one of that age-old hallmark of the old West, transience. Statistics bear this out. The 2000 Census found that 40 percent of the city's residents rented their homes, compared to 33 percent nationwide. They were less likely to live in a detached single-family home, only 53 percent as compared to 60 percent nationwide. It is heavy on multifamily: One in twelve lived in a building with more than fifty units, 94 percent of them renters (see fig. 2.2). Overall, it's more transient than the United States in general, with 63 percent of its residents having moved between 1995 and 2000, seventeen points above the national average. With RV parks and weekly rentals still common in downtown Reno and Sparks, the city's modern urban form has stayed true to its roots: As one of the only American cities of its size to have started as a mining camp, it has remained a place of opportunists moving through.

Reno is a bigger version of the towns throughout Nevada in that it was created by mining and built casinos for entertainment and stray tourists. Now, like the smaller Nevada towns, Reno is looking to outdoor recreational tourism. Passing through Battle Mountain, Winnemucca, Austin, and Eureka, it's easy to notice their pluck. But because of their extreme isolation and wicked climate—as well as the fluctuations of the mining industries that have supported them—interior Basin towns have not snowballed into anything more. Their populations stayed relatively steady in the booms of the 1990s. Many of their residents are short-term, their housing is defined by mobile homes. More than half of the housing units in Battle Mountain—and one fifth of Fernley, Winnemucca, and Elko—are mobile homes. Nearly one in three residents of Winnemucca, a jurisdiction that is not growing, lived in a different county before 1995, 12 percentage points higher than the national average. And Reno doesn't have as many older houses as even the Wasatch Front: While nearly 10 percent of Wasatch Front houses were built before World War II (a small enough percentage as it is), only 3 percent of Truckee Meadows houses were built in that time period.

That percentage is declining more and more. In the North Valleys, where some of the city's most explosive growth has occurred, these modest subdivisions are like pods colonizing the string of mini-basins, moving outward and hopping over one another. In these neighborhoods, urban form is in motion: Nearly one in ten households lives in a mobile home (see fig. 2.2). Reno homeowners are four times as likely as other Americans to live in an RV. Along Virginia Street and U.S. 395 north of downtown, mobile homes and RV trailers infuse built form. The older houses are mobile homes; the newer houses have RVs in the back yards. And the link between northern Nevada's mining past and recreational future is the RV. At Nevada's largest dealer of RVs, on North Virginia Street, they sell to both sets. "We just sold some to a group of miners," the owner had told me when I visited. "I sell them to construction guys all the time, who are home on the weekends and can go from job site to site." It's cost-effective for someone on the move. You can buy an RV for $40,000–50,000 and pay as little as $300 a month for a space, depending on the utilities. By comparison, she said, any weekly is $150 a week.

But what their business is really about these days is a platform for the recreation lifestyle. Life for many Renoites seems to be like a set of nesting Russian dolls. Houses store RVs, and RVs store four-wheel recreational vehicles. In Reno, it's all about going out to the desert with your toys, transported in trailers to far-flung playgrounds. And, here in the North Valleys, RVs dovetail with the housing market. Many buy houses here for lower prices and so they can have RVs to enjoy. It's one way of living in the immense space of the Great Basin, to spread one's life over the miles of public land.

The choices range from the Jayfly, made by Jayco, a travel trailer made of sturdy wood and aluminum, for $30,000, to the Grand Junction, the most popular "fifth wheel," a trailer designed for recreational living.

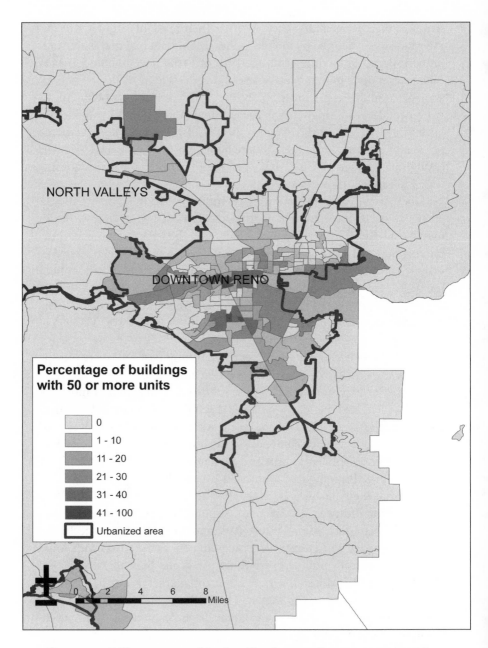

Figure 2.2. Different areas of Truckee Meadows are home to concentrations of large apartment buildings (above) and mobile homes (opposite), which help define its urban form. (Source: U.S. Census Bureau, "Census of Population and Housing," 2000)

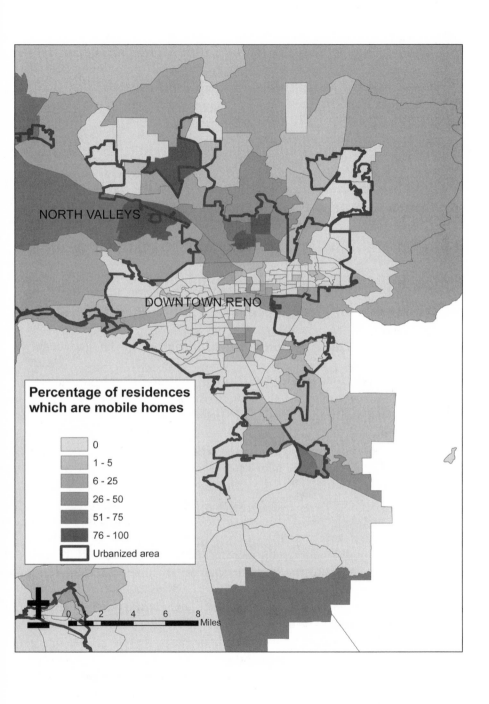

NORTH VALLEYS

DOWNTOWN RENO

**Percentage of residences
which are mobile homes**

- 0
- 1 - 5
- 6 - 25
- 26 - 50
- 51 - 75
- 76 - 100
- Urbanized area

0 2 4 6 8
Miles

Outside on the lot, a salesman showed me a souped-up Grand Junction. This one was going to a retired banker, the listed $70,000 negotiated down to $57,000. It came with a wine rack, microwave, oven, washer-dryer hookup, and a fake fireplace. "You got everything, guy, you really do," he said.

He said it used to be just snowbirds that bought the Grand Junction, but that's changing. Now it's people of all ages who want to live the mobile recreational life in Reno and explore the Nevada backcountry in style. I asked the salesman if any of his customers planned to take their Grand Junctions up to Peavine Mountain to set up for a few weeks.

"I wouldn't try it, guy," he said. "If you want to go up on Peavine, get a Jayfly."

Growth Just Goes: In Cold Springs

One arrives in Cold Springs Valley via a freeway from the center of the city that runs through the various valleys—Stead, Golden, Lemmon.[31] The road curls along the broad toe of Peavine Mountain, providing a sturdy compass for these places. Sixteen minutes after leaving downtown—when there is no traffic—you crest a little rise and pop into Cold Springs Valley.

Cold Springs embodies all of the tensions of the Great Basin city, between the desert and the need for green, between the natural closed basin hydrology and urban infrastructure, between rural and urban, between center and edge, between destruction and renewal, between isolation and connection, and between adaptation and illusion. When you exit the freeway and dip into the valley, the first thing you see—besides the collection of makeshift signs advertising the Cold Springs Church now meeting at the new Cold Springs Middle School, and a number to call for housecleaning service—is the blue-white playa of White Lake, stretching in a disk between the freeway and the neighborhoods. When I arrive on another trip to Reno, in October, I am surprised to see a thin film of water remaining over the playa, which has usually dried to cracked mud by now. An old barbed-wire fence marks where it edges out from thick grasses below the freeway, and looking out into the sunny glare of the morning, it's hard to tell exactly where the water starts.

The nature of the playa is like others in the Great Basin, a constantly changing stage; the playa's and the valley's visual emptiness becomes a mirror for past experiences and the imagination: "The valley's aspect changes with the light, the weather, and the season, offering a new perspective at each viewing," writes Eric Dieterle about White Lake. "Each drive home brings anticipation of how the valley will appear. The playa is a deep alpine lake, or a desolate stretch of Sahara sand, or a mirage of waves shimmering."[32]

The playa, though, is clearly part of Reno, having developed with the familiar pattern of the neighborhood casino and gas station. Next to the lake bed is Chuck's Market, and Discount Cigarettes and Liqueur, and across the street, a sign: "Congested area. Livestock at large prohibited. Discharge of Firearms prohibited. Dogs at large prohibited." Up the hill is the Bordertown Casino and its adjoining gift shop–convenience store, restaurant and RV park. The casino restaurant is the only one for a several-mile radius. Most of its employees aren't old enough to go into the casino portion of the building, even though most of them are working second jobs. The place must make a killing serving take-out to weary parents migrating back to Cold Springs from a day at their Reno workplace.

The human layers of the North Valleys have been accumulating slowly. The Western Pacific railroad made its way along the skirt of Peavine Mountain, as if afraid to dip into the valley floors, spawning small foothill settlements. Large herds of wild horses once roamed the area, caught by wranglers and turned into glue. Hollywood filmed blockbusters with Clark Gable and Marilyn Monroe, Rocketdyne tested the engines of the Saturn V rocket mission, and the U.S. military built the Stead Air Force Base.[33]

For the buyers of Woodland Village, though, Cold Springs is brand-spanking-new, produced and polished for the new Reno. The promotional signs to this new subdivision begin at the freeway exit and tell me to head east. The signs keep coming, encouraging turns through the neighborhoods on the edge of the playa, past the new fire station, and down the newly paved parkway running along the base of the hills.

In his book *Edge City: Life on the New Frontier*, journalist Joel Garreau notes that suburbs aren't "sub" to anything anymore.[34] It's all just urbanization, units of human civilization moving out into unbuilt squares of land. Such development isn't just residential; it's industrial, commercial, even civic. Lifestyle Homes is bringing this approach to Cold Springs Valley, where Woodland Village is just the beginning. The company was founded in 1989 when it took over the building of a golf course subdivision in Stead Valley that had sat dormant for two years. Lifestyle completed the houses, and was off and running. In 1999, it moved to Cold Springs Valley, where it purchased a larger chunk of the Great Basin. Woodland

Village is the first phase of Lifestyle's plan for the valley. At completion, it will contain some 2,000 houses, a large park, and a commercial center. Then, Lifestyle plans to begin work on its next phase, 750 ranch-style homes on one-acre lots in a valley beyond Woodland Village. Across the playa and freeway, the company plans to build an industrial complex at the foot of Peavine Mountain. The completed result: a sparkling pod of living and working plunked down onto the Great Basin.

Lifestyle operates out of two of its model homes on Georgetown Drive, the first Woodland Village street that hooks off the Woodland Village Parkway. They've set up shop in the high-ceilinged, thickly carpeted living rooms of the houses, breeding a homey atmosphere. Lifestyle's marketing manager, whose office is a corner of the living room, is telling me, "The North Valleys were just a place that was ready to be developed at an affordable rate." Lifestyle Homes has built and closed on a little over half of the houses planned for Woodland Village. It's in the process of building fifty more and has fifty more subdivision lots approved by the county. "Growth just goes," the marketing manager says. "You have to expand outward."

To offer houses at the entry level, Lifestyle created an efficient design-build setup. Lots lie mostly at the small end of the company's 6,500- to 16,000-square-foot range. The houses range from 1,040 to 2,660 square feet. The engineers designed the street pattern for maximum efficiency, with only a few collector streets. Mail is delivered to a "clusterbox" instead of directly to houses.

The company's skeleton crew designs its own house plans with basic software on an old computer set up like a shrine in the living room. The computer spits out the plans on tidy eight-and-a-half by eleven sheets. They are designs whose basic layout hasn't changed since 1989. The two- or three-car garage is the largest room in the house and is usually in the front left, the entrance at its side off a small covered front porch, opening into a vaulted living room. The bedrooms and kitchen are arrayed around this central axis in an arc, and that's your house.

We head out "in the field" for a ride around Woodland Village. We drive past the main park, where there have been public safety problems. A few kids who live in a house across the street had pulled a knife on a Woodland Village facilities employee. The Woodland Village Homeowner Association, whose home base is in another of the Georgetown Court model homes, runs a twenty-four-hour security patrol. It's one of the perks cited by new Woodland Village homeowners on why they moved here.

Another perk for this desert subdivision is that the residents have water available to them. Strangely, even with all of its development, Cold Springs Valley has not shown a lowering in its water table but a raising of it. This is because Cold Springs' modern shapers have been manipulating the closed basin. They have been taking water from Long Valley, the next basin over, in California. The water sucked up from these wells is used in Cold Springs households and then piped to the valley's own sewage treatment plant, where it is cleaned and left in small basins to infiltrate—into the Cold Springs aquifer. Not only has the water been taken for one-time use by Cold Springs households, but it will also cycle through the system over and over. They have also been trying to keep water away from White Lake. While much of the Cold Springs watershed is underlain by porous, large-grained sandy soils, the playa is mud and clay. So, when water finally does reach it, it is almost sure to evaporate rather than infiltrate back into the aquifer—lost, as Nevadans say, to "beneficial use." Hydrologists everywhere in Nevada are tasked with increasing this recharge, to keep water from ending up in the death of the playa.

The water treatment basins accomplish this. And in Woodland Village, Lifestyle Homes has built several large drainage basins to handle peak floodwaters and to drain the water back into the system. In fact, it's one of the things you notice about the subdivision: The drainage network, mimicking a new and improved Great Basin hydrologic channel and sink system, has become a centerpiece of the neighborhood. At the center of the project is a large, rectangular park bordered directly by houses and the stubs of culs-de-sac. So while the culs-de-sac cut off vehicle access, they allow for walking and bicycling connection through the park. Next to the park is a football field–sized drainage basin that, for the most part, sits empty of water. It's crossed by streaks of vegetation where water has collected and bicycle tracks: another kind of informal park space in addition to the park. The basin is the center of a drainage system that has a hand in organizing the whole subdivision. From the central park, dry channels radiate outward that double as walking and bicycling corridors that connect the culs-de-sac.[35] Around them are other, smaller drainage basins that also act as common open spaces between houses.

The other thing I notice is the gravel. Woodland Village's entrance parkway is organized by gravel in a two-tone pattern that is spawning tiny shrubs. Pedestrian paths are paved with crushed rock. Grass is used sparingly in the subdivision's common spaces. The only grass parking strips are along the collector streets, where it's as if the turf, along with oaks and plane trees, mark the importance of these thoroughfares.

In Woodland Village's front yards, Lifestyle plants one tree for each house, usually a compact fruit tree in a little round concrete-lined well. There is the driveway on the left, and the rest is a palette for the home-owner. Here, homeowners have mixed together at least half a dozen types of medium-grained rock. Rock has become infamous to Truckee Meadows residents as a sign of growth and sacrifice. "I like my little patch of green grass. Don't make me put rocks in my yard," a resident of nearby Stead told the *Reno Journal-Gazette*.[36] Lifestyle Homes regulates its gravel. The Woodland Village landscaping agreement states that a yard may have no more than 60 percent gravel and 50 percent grass, thus carefully arbitrating desert nature and people's desire for green. The rules are specific about which rock is OK. "Rock mulch or gravel shall be selected from the approved list and can be no smaller than one half inch in size," the manual reads. Pea gravel, decomposed granite, and sand are not allowed because of "their dirt-like appearance" and their tendency to spill onto driveways and streets. The design guidelines recommend aesthetically pleasing gravel: "A variety of ground plane treatments such as four-inch-minus river rock, one-half-inch crushed rock, bark mulch, live groundcover, and turf provides visual interest, whereas a sea of one ground plane type, such as gravel, etc., is monotonous and uninteresting," the landscape manual states.[37]

In many cases, it's as if the rules have spawned innovation. Some home-owners have swirled together white gravel and gray gravel, some gray gravel and black gravel, some put islands of grass in their gravel. There is sharp gravel like pieces of broken up slate and shale and weathered gravel like loose scree on top of a mountain. Some go for the salt-and-pepper look. The rocks create a mini-topography of people's yards. Gravel seems to have inspired the placing of sculpture. Amid these mini-landscapes, plants make more of a visual impact, and their makers have seemed to place plantings like yucca and dwarf pines selectively. Such use of the small yards seems to be a uniquely Reno-style urbanism at work of bal-ancing priorities in small spaces short on resources.

The ubiquitous gravel not only substitutes for grass but also becomes a medium for drainage. Within their front yards, some residents have used rocks to construct small swales with check dams so water can infil-trate into the ground, taking the stormwater off the street and into their small yards, or else keeping the water away from their foundations. Some residents have taken this concept further and created little wetlands in their rock swales. Here, the little Woodland Village yards express the limits and function of Great Basin ecology in one hundred square feet.

Lifestyle Homes built Woodland Village's houses with other forces in mind. It gets windy here, blowing up to 120-mile-per-hour gusts onto the houses. We arrive at what will become the new model village once Lifestyle packs up from Georgetown Drive and sells its existing models, farther along the Woodland Village parkway, farther out into the expanse of basin. Here, the Lifestyle construction process is visible: An engineered wood shear-panel exterior board works as both structure and siding. Then the builders caulk it and paint it, and hope it can defend against the wind and snow, which can come in three-foot dumps at a time.

But despite designing a neighborhood somewhat adapted to its Great Basin valley and climate, Lifestyle Homes markets Woodland Village as what it is not. These are not, for example, luxury houses, but Lifestyle is trying to create "a more solid, heavy look" in its new façades with fake rock and fake brick. They offer granite-option countertops, raised countertops in master bathrooms, and rounded corners. They've added arches inside. Woodland Village is only sixteen minutes from downtown Reno, but that's all behind the mountain. In many ways, the attraction of Woodland Village is its un-Reno-ness. There's a nice family feeling out here, the Woodland Village people tell me. You don't see high-rise casinos. Many out-of-state buyers, including California refugees who pay cash for Lifestyle Homes, don't find downtown Reno attractive. "Creepy, nasty downtown Reno," is how one Las Vegas émigré put it. Woodland Village is "new and clean and the view's gorgeous." And for those who are from Reno, it's an escape. One resident used to live in an apartment complex near downtown where he witnessed two people being thrown out of an upper-story window. "We plan on living here a long time, unless we can move further out," he told me.

And there are no woodlands. Looking around at all the brownness, I ask the burning question: Why did Lifestyle name this place Woodland Village? "Nice tree-lined community," the marketing person muses, cruising down the Woodland Village Parkway, which is lined by trees. "Old-fashioned street lighting. A different type of community. Makes it pleasant to the eye." He means a different type of community in the scorched earth of Reno. "I've been amazed that the trees have changed color this year," he remarks.

The crux of Woodland Village is that it has adapted to the Great Basin landscape on one level and has pretended to be Anytown USA on another. It has tried to create the illusion of escaping from Reno while becoming another urban pod through its affordability and highway access. Residents can just as easily see the subdivision for their reflection in the glare of White Lake playa as for the landscape and the playa's actual ecological function.

The problem for closed basins like Cold Springs Valley, though, may be the other side of the watershed's advantage—not what's happening outward but inward. Sucking water from outside the watershed and preventing it from taking its course to the playa allows basin aquifers to recharge, even so much as raising water tables as homebuilding explodes in these valleys. And this, the ability to hoard water, the internal drainage basin's greatest asset, could be its downfall. As Americans, we rely on importing cheap labor for our goods, and once we are done with them, we export our waste. Largely, it's the same with water: We take water from rivers and reservoirs that comes and goes through our watershed, and then expunge it once we're done with it, outside the watershed. The Great Basin has no such luxury. The water that its residents use usually stays in its tiny individual watersheds. While treatment plants clean out much of the harmful substances, plenty could remain in the water: nitrogen and phosphorous, dissolved solids like salts, and even pharmaceuticals such as birth controls and penicillin. And for the most part, surface storm-water runoff, carrying oil and particulates from autos, is not treated before it filters into the sandy soil. There is a chance the waste from meth-amphetamine labs likewise ends up in the stormwater. Hydrologists say they don't know exactly what is going on, but as is the tradition in Nevada hydrology, they can guess. "Each time it goes through the system, it picks up a little more," one hydrologist told me. "Sodium chloride, magnesium, potassium, arsenic, it's probably what's going to kill the human race." The image of the big wide open is at odds with its reality of the closed hydrology and possibility of a slow pollution boomerang lurking underneath.

When we return to the model village, the sun is low in the horizon, hanging above Peavine Mountain. Between it and us is White Lake. Like its layers of human history, Cold Springs' natural history is locked away in hard-to-see places. In Cold Springs and other terminal basins, the mudflats of a playa hold not only organisms but a record of past precipitation, the lifeblood of the watershed. "We actually own that lake, and we don't have any feasible idea of anything to put in it," the Woodland Village marketing manager says when I ask about the playa. "We would probably develop it for commercial means if we could."

And so the eggs and spores of phytoplankton hang in the balance. Lifestyle allows the public to use the playa as a marginal recreational resource. In the winter, the valley's snowmelt drains into it and creates an eighteen-inch-deep lake frequented by kiteboarders. By this time of the year it's usually dry and caked over and is mostly a public nuisance.

"It gets very dusty," he says. "When that lake bed is dry and the wind hits it, it just blows. You can see the cloud coming."

Between Mountain and Marsh

Out through the expanses of other North Valleys, Woodland Village coexists with products of more well-known national builders. In adjacent Stead Valley, the giant Lennar is building Horizons at Stonefield, a higher-end subdivision whose houses have three and four bedrooms but with none of Woodland Village's eye toward parks, stores, and gravel microcosm. Stonefield's expanding construction edge disintegrates outward into the void of the old Stead Air Force Base, where clear evening air pierces through three thousand acres of range after range.

In Stead, the industrial development, like the houses, has hungrily consumed the valley's space. Tilt-up concrete distribution centers of several hundred thousand square feet crowd along Stead Boulevard, elbowing next to the Lennar projects in the coarse built grain of the valley. These monoliths cover up an even better treasure than White Lake. Out beyond the horizon of Horizons, and the space slated for the new Wal-Mart in Lemmon Valley, is Swan Lake, Stead Valley's seasonal playa. Unlike White Lake, Swan Lake has its own freshwater-recharged wetlands that support habitat for birds. The giant box warehouses point their ass-ends toward Swan Lake and a little dirt road that leads to a small parking lot at the edge of the lake and wetlands. The only sign of humanity here is a guy asleep in his car.

This source of life is directly connected to Peavine Mountain. Springs at the edge of the playa feed Peavine water into its silty clay. Swan Lake also receives almost five hundred acre feet of treated wastewater from the City of Reno each year—valuable water, remember, that could be put to another, more "beneficial" use.[38] As I walk down the path, the noises concentrated in the marsh become louder, the buzzing and thwacking of bulrushes. There is so much life here in the amphibians and reptiles alone: Pacific Tree Frogs, Bullfrogs, Western Toad, California Toad, Great Basin Spadefoot, Great Basin Whiptail, Great Basin Rattlesnake, Long-nosed Leopard Lizard, Western Racer, Northern Desert Horned Lizard, Northern Sagebrush Lizard, Great Basin Fence Lizard, Side-blotched Lizard, Ground Snake, and Night Snake. Like the water, the playa and wetlands are the meeting place for dozens of avian species. Five hundred Black-necked Stilts and American Avocets once congregated here. There are eighteen species of waterbirds, including Coots, Buffleheads, and Shovelers. The regal herons stand among all of them.

Unlike the top of Peavine Mountain, the playa and its marsh are more difficult for me to relate to. Where the heights of the peak offered views of Reno and the clarity of the Great Basin city, the bottom of the basin brings confusion and vulnerability. While the serene tops of the mountains are celebrated, the bottom of the basins are pushed away and often forgotten in their ever-shifting pungency.

But like a guide, Robert Frost's poem "Directive" surfaces in my mind as I walk through the thicket of reeds, rushes, grasses, and horsetails at dusk. "Your destination and your destiny's / A brook that was the water of the house," Frost wrote. "Cold as a spring as yet so near its source / Too lofty and original to rage." John Elder, in *Reading the Mountains of Home*, interprets the "water of the house" to be "not the runoff from a single season's snowmelt but the circulation of groundwater pulsing throughout the year."[39] This hydrologic system so bound any life to its natural cycles that it calmly created both "destination and destiny." Frost and Elder were both reflecting on the Green Mountains of Vermont, where water is everywhere at all times, but in the Great Basin Desert these words have a more concentrated, powerful meaning in the rush of Swan Lake. I have found the destination of the developments surrounding the playa, but what is their destiny in the gravity of the sink?

The noise of the birds overwhelms anything else occurring outside the playa. I emerge from the thicket to open water, where startled ducks make for the sky, peeling off the water in a ripple of flight. The lump of Peavine Mountain rises above the pool, which reflects its silhouette; lights flickering on in houses, warehouses, and the Stead Airport surround it. In the words of Frost, these are your waters and your watering place. Drink and be whole again beyond confusion.

Shorelands

Life at the Edge

At latitude 41 degrees north, the Great Basin crashes into the Wasatch Mountains at a ten-foot rise in the earth known locally as "the Bluff." It's where Gentile Street pushes out from Davis County's Main Street spine north of Salt Lake City, brushing past old downtown Layton and plodding past lines of Lombardy poplars and beige stucco-walled castles in culs-de-sac to where it can't go much farther, treading into the beginning of the Great Salt Lake's murky gradient of influence. A straight, brave road named after the first white non-Mormon families to inhabit the area, even Gentile Street withers when presented with the lakeshore: a marshy, mucky territory where one never knows if he or she is walking on water or solid ground. These mud morasses and salt marshes, wrote historian Dale Morgan, have preserved the Great Salt Lake's "atmosphere of desolate strangeness."[1]

The Bluff slashes in a diagonal across these lands, providing a terrace of solid ground and a slight but significant vantage over the shore. As such, the Bluff has had a road almost as long as the Mormons have been in the Great Basin. It was part of the historic emigrant trail to points north, and on it are some of the richest alluvial soils found by the pioneers, who farmed it in a patchwork of fields integrated with their city grids. To obtain water, the settlers had to go beyond the Bluff to the springs bubbling up from the wetlands.

Out in the shorelands, you can get the impression that you're below the earth looking up at it. The tops of cattails and reeds snake up from an undecipherable ground plane, washing into the horizon in unending swaths. Away from the Bluff, the next relief westward is the supple rise of Antelope Island a dozen miles away, and the next person westward may be in California or Japan. Even with a look back to what is now a thin, almost unnoticeable strip of civilization—Ogden, Roy, Layton, Centerville, Farmington, Clearfield, Bountiful, a sliver of Salt Lake, and the rush of Interstate 15—between the flattest country on earth and the steep mountain walls, time seems to evaporate in the desert air. The land seems to be ready for anything to happen in it, like an empty stage.[2] The openness and surreality of no appropriately scaled reference points breed possibilities of a groan of any magnitude.

Scholars of the Great Basin have found this sense of timelessness and surreality in other parts of the region. "The gray-green sage and greasewood seem withdrawn and unfriendly, the darkly green blotches of juniper immensely unrelated to human existence," wrote Dale Morgan about more distant shores of the Great Salt Lake. "You know that this is how it always was, back to the time when the first immigrant company to California went this way."[3] In more extreme playas like the Black Rock Desert, the seasonal lake bed that is the flattest of the flattest places on earth, American culture and physical possibilities stretch: the world's fastest land-speed records, the Burning Man festival. "Elemental time and space play 'round every perception of the Black Rock Desert," writes Stephen Trimble. "Nowhere else is the Great Basin Desert reduced to such simple elements. . . . Empty landscapes like the Black Rock Playa seem somehow to pay attention to the entrance of a human. Each of us makes a difference; we make the land more alive."[4]

But the Great Salt Lake is the Great Basin's ultimate sink, a vast year-round puddle sustained by the raging streams that drain the snowpacks of the surrounding mountain ranges each spring. In the lake's shorelands, a person's impulses can be deceiving: What seems like peripheral emptiness to Utahns treading out to the edge of their desert civilization is actually the center of this basin's hydrology and ecology. A walk around the perimeter of the Great Salt Lake, were it possible, would necessitate the crossings of the Jordan, Weber, and Bear rivers (the former of which nearly killed Jedediah Smith when he tried to cross its mouth in 1827). One would also find smaller drainages such as Kays Creek, whose short course from the steep canyons of the Wasatch through Layton and over the Bluff, where its water is lost to the salty death of the lake, is typical of the streams along the Basin's wet edges. As is the proliferation of life at this last checkpoint for freshwater: It originates in streams and from underground aquifers and creates natural wetlands before coming to rest in the terminal basin of the lake, where water from the prehistoric freshwater Lake Bonneville settled and evaporated faster than it could be recharged once the last ice age was over, creating a "dead lake" that can only support brine shrimp and brine flies, the robust links at the end of a very long food chain.

This chain extends around the Western Hemisphere. The combination of concentrated freshwater oasis and ecological dead zone beyond the Bluff creates some of the most important migratory bird habitat in the world. Birds come from as far north as Canada to places as far south as South America to eat brine flies and brine shrimp. In May, over 250 bird species descend on the Great Salt Lake shore; eight hundred thousand Wilson's Phalaropes, the second largest population in the world; twenty thousand White Pelicans; over one thousand wintering Bald Eagles; the world's largest populations of California Gulls and Cinnamon Teals; sixty thousand Tundra Swans; over one million Eared Grebes; and the entire Intermountain West population of White-faced Ibis.[5] Many species use the feeding they do along the lake to charge their bodies to pull off the thousand-plus-mile flight remaining in their migratory journeys.

If there is a caretaker for this strange Great Basin Garden of Eden it is Chris Brown. Beyond the Bluff is Brown's realm. He is the manager of the Nature Conservancy's Great Salt Lake Shorelands Preserve, four thousand acres of private marsh purchased to protect this particular stop along what ecologists sometimes call the international flyway. He has a staff of one: himself. I first met Brown at a truck stop on Interstate 215 south of the Shorelands, a node of interstate commerce of its own. The northwest part of Salt Lake County, pushed up against the southern stretches of the Great Salt Lake, is a land of warehouses and truck stops that frames the meeting of Interstates 15 and 80, one of the great crossroads of the West. It seems to be a regular stop for Brown, who despite his affinity for the preserve, has to scurry between meetings with local and state officials at the Wasatch Front's various power centers and seems to know the geography of its truck stops.

Now, it's winter and Brown and I are driving out through the preserve.[6] None of the regular storm systems that move across Nevada, pick up moisture from the lake, and pummel the Wasatch has arrived in over a week, and a nasty inversion has set upon the valley. In an inversion, the warm air rises and the cold air sinks, trapping pollution particles in the valley. Where, in September, I could see not only across the lake to the Oquirrh Mountains and its island continuation of Antelope Island but also across the entire lake to the Stansbury Range and its island, today the western horizon is just gray fuzz beyond a tower Brown tells me is used for nesting Peregrine Falcons.

Brown grew up a few miles from here, in Farmington, now a piece of the linear city that the Wasatch Front has become. It used to be a separate town when Brown was young, with a strong connection to the lake shorelands. He hunted ducks with his brother; other than birding, duck hunting is one of the only activities attracting people to the lake. Duck hunters were one of the first groups to attempt to preserve the lake's shorelands, when, in 1901, the New State Duck Club and others began buying up land.[7] As a kid, Brown climbed through fences on the farmland between town and the lake, with his shotgun and an increasing knowledge of the thirty ducks that flap along the lake as its permanent residents. By the time he was fourteen, he recognized every duck from three hundred feet away. He also knew he wanted to protect wetlands when he grew up. He went to college, then graduate school with the express purpose of returning to Davis County to work with the wetlands. He got hired at Farmington Bay, another nearby preserve, then won the job at the Nature Conservancy in 2002.

Brown, like nearly any person who crosses the gradient of the Bluff between the civilization hugging the Wasatch Mountains and the openness of the Great Basin, sees the shorelands as an escape, a place where he can get some time and space to himself. "I can leave my subdivision and drive five minutes to work, down a dirt road, and it's quiet, except for an occasional F-16 from Hill Air Force Base," he says. "I don't hear the bustle. I can see the birds. I can see the way things should be."

The way things should be is what Brown spends his time restoring, and sometimes, creating. His office is his white truck that bumps around the ag roads and dirt tracks of the preserve, with a row of feathers carefully arranged in the groove above his drivers' side window: Chucker Partridges, Pintail Ducks, and Mallard Ducks. He rolls with a box of Winchester bullets in the shelf below the dashboard and a jumbo Mountain Dew in the drink holder. He uses the proprietary "I" when discussing the preserve's projects, as in "The people from that subdivision over there messed with my fence last week." And why not? On any given day, Brown is the only human roving these lands, save for the duck hunters. On drives around the preserve, he'll run into camoed hunters he knew in high school who will ask him for a lift. They are the harvesters, he is the farmer. "I'm a bird farmer," he says.

With only himself to plow the fields, bird farming takes a while. To sow his bird habitat, Brown has grafted numerous man-made wetlands onto the preserve by himself. He's used an excavator to pile the dirt into

dikes that contain water and marsh plant life. He equips the dike enclo-
sures with release valves made up of boards preventing mountain creek
water from going down a pipe that leads to a larger, natural wetland. The
construction of each of these wetlands takes Brown about two months.
In the spring, he pulls the boards, draining his little wetland into God's
bigger wetland. Draining, he explains, reoxygenates the soil by exposing
it to the air, allowing more growth that will help along the migratory
birds. Brown opened the floodgates on his newest wetlands last summer
to the arrival of one hundred pairs of nesting Avocets.

Brown is thirty-six years old. He's tall, with round glasses and scruffy
blond hair, and when he gets out of the white truck to show me an example of his work, he unfolds his lanky six-foot-six-inch height. In high
school he had to give up skiing for basketball. And duck hunting. When
we walk around the back of his truck, I count six bright mallard carcasses
piled together in a corner opposite a bucket of crushed aluminum cans,
their metallic green shimmering even in the dull overcast light. Leftovers
from the family's weekend hunt. "There should be seven," he says. "Seven
is the limit allowed by the state, per day. Most people don't get seven."

We walk over to one of the dikes. This time of year, the water is frozen
over, the vegetation mostly a pale, dormant tan. But there is still work to
do. He points out where muskrats have dug a large hole into the dike,
which he'll have to fill soon. Such maintenance makes up most of Brown's
work. In the winter, it's mainly time to catch up with his war against
invasive weeds in the wetlands. Brown's primary enemy is a plant called
phragmites, the common reed. It looks deceivingly like the cattail, the
bulrush, and the other tall, slender natives of Great Basin wetlands, but
it is a cheaper version, with wispy strands at its top instead of the solid
cylinder of the cattail. And it crowds these natives out, eliminating the
quality habitat they provide to the birds.

It isn't just the wetlands that are Brown's province. The Nature Conservancy has also purchased several acres of farmland that Brown refers
to as "uplands." The purpose of the uplands is not only to provide a
buffer between the marsh and the Wasatch Front neighborhoods next
to it but also to complete the ecological system of the Great Salt Lake
bird habitat. There are some birds that nest by the lake and feed in the
uplands; some vice versa. White-faced Ibis, for example, nest near the
lake, but they feed in uplands, pulling worms out of irrigated fields.
Brown, as a consequence, uses old Mormon irrigation ditches and the
same board dams to flood the fields, longtime cow pastures. Along one

of the ditches, the last gasps of Homes Creek, which, like Kays Creek, shoots a short, steep course down from the Wasatch into the lake, is a row of new houses.

The shorelands of today are not the shorelands of Brown's youth. They are not even the shorelands of twenty, or even five, years ago. In 1983, when the Nature Conservancy began buying land along the Great Salt Lake, the purchase price was $500 an acre. The Conservancy recently closed on a piece of property for $22,000 an acre—and much of it isn't even buildable land. The shorelands of today, despite their surreality, are squarely an urban place.

"They just look like little boxes on the land, don't they?" Brown says as we approach the beige wall from the space of the preserve. Along the ditch of Homes Creek is a fence that Brown put up to mark the Nature Conservancy's property line. They don't like it when he floods the fields because the ditches back up, creating a potentially dangerous child trap. One of the homeowners cut out a section to put up a large white vinyl fence, slackening the rest of the barbed wire. He had to go to the home-owners' association for that one. Some of the residents throw bales of garbage or compost over the fence into the preserve. One pushed all the rocks from his yard out into the seemingly empty field. Once a year, Brown says, he walks along the fence, looks at what the residents have thrown over, scoops it up, and throws it back over.

Chris Brown also finds himself beyond the wetlands, past the meander line of the lake in the white playa, where the linear city is even thinner and quieter. Sometimes, past where the dirt roads turn to two ruts in the grass, and then, out onto the seasonal lake bed, to nothing at all, to the nesting territory of Snowy Plovers, Brown will just stop. "I'm out spraying phragmites for ten hours a day, and I just drive and get out there and I don't realize what I'm doing. I just stop, kick back, and eat my lunch. I just decompress. On 9-11, back when I was working at Farmington Bay, I noticed no planes were taking off from the airport. I got back to the office, and everyone's like, 'Haven't you heard?' I was like 'No, what happened?'"

Mormon Country Redux

"Wherever you go in Mormon Country . . . you see the characteristic marks of Mormon settlement," wrote Wallace Stegner in 1942's *Mormon Country*. "The typical intensively cultivated fields of alfalfa and sugar beets, the orchards of cherry and apple and peach and apricot, the irrigation ditches, the solid houses, the wide-streeted, sleepy green towns." Most of all, Stegner wrote, one sees the "Mormon Trees," Lombardy poplars. "Wherever they went the Mormons planted them. They grew boldly and fast, without much tending, and they make the landscape of the long valleys of the Mormon Country something special and distinctive . . . there is no place where the peculiar combination of desert valley and dark lines of trees exists as it does in this country."[8]

The Mormons have created a shore on the edge of the Great Basin. While the settlements throughout most of the Basin relate to Reno in many of their physical and social characteristics, the towns strung along its eastern edge relate to Salt Lake City. Unlike the mining towns of the Basin, whose semblance to Reno came about through economic means, as well as the acceptance of gambling throughout the state of Nevada, the relationship between Salt Lake City and Utah towns was carefully orchestrated. Brigham Young ordered that the Saints settle towns one day's wagon drive apart, which was roughly every fifty miles, the end goal being a Mormon "Corridor," stretching as far south as Las Vegas and San Bernardino, California, both originally Mormon settlements.[9] While the map of Nevada ghost towns is thick with dots representing vanished settlements, over 80 percent of the 537 towns founded by Mormons survive today as working communities.[10]

Thus, even today, the built environment of the Wasatch Front contrasts with that of Truckee Meadows: strong homeownership, lots of single-family houses, lots of vehicle ownership. The 2000 Census found that, in the Salt Lake-Ogden Metropolitan Statistical Area, 67 percent of housing was single-family detached, 7 percent more than the national average; 71 percent of households owned their homes, 5 percent more than the national average. In the Provo-Orem MSA, 3.7 percent of households owned five or more cars, three times the national average.[11] It is a different interpretation of more or less the same natural environment.

And Zion has become a super-America. Cars, capitalism, flags, parking lots, privacy, and bigness are all here in spades. In the late nineteenth century, the Church of Jesus Christ of Latter-day Saints that brought the City of Zion plan and socialistic utopia to the world made a U-turn. Humiliated by the federal government, which made it give up polygamy in order to become a state (Utah was granted statehood nearly a half century after Nevada) and confiscated all of the church's property in the 1880s, the church decided to become as American as possible—or, at least, on the outside.

In the early days of the city, church leaders were largely farmers and disapproved of the involvement of members in professions like law. But church leaders soon saw the advantage of sending its members to study law and of getting involved in business.[12] Ironically, as the United States entered the Progressive era of planning and social activism in the early twentieth century, the church abandoned its earlier programs of social planning, economic equality, and public ownership, instead aligning itself with business. As some of the more socialist ideas upon which the Wasatch Front was founded gained acceptance in mainstream America, the LDS Church went the other way, publicly renouncing its old values in exchange for those it perceived as essential to survival in the United States. "The church entered the twentieth century in anxious pursuit of respectability," wrote historian Davis Bitton. "The Mormons were becoming middle class with a vengeance."[13]

And they would do it on the narrow strip of shore on the edge of the Great Basin Desert. You can taste the last 150 years where Great Salt Lake meets the Wasatch. The land has been layered by generations who wanted to be here and wanted to stay here. Every time you look around, the strangeness of the lake and the robustness of the mountains make this place feel like an arrival. Or an easy chair with a tall, sturdy back, mountains to lean on and breathe in the alluvial soils. The rhythms of the poplars, the stout Victorian houses, and the spreading squares seem such a natural scale for the narrow human-friendly places in between the rugged Wasatch wall and the lake.

When the Saints first came to Davis County, named after settler Daniel C. Davis, they described "deep, crooked gullies" from the mountains to the lake. The numerous creeks had worn deep grooves into the land sloping down to the marsh. These were minor streams, not the rivers that feed the lake, small in potable water value but long in erosion on the landscape. The settlers disapproved of these watercourses. "The water running unchecked would run to the lake in the early spring, making it difficult to even get a drink after the middle of June," wrote the Daughters of the Utah Pioneers in *East of Antelope Island*. If five or six families settled on one of the creeks, that was thought to be the limit.[14]

The Mormons made the desert a moral place. They ingrained in their culture the settlement of the Great American Desert as an obligation. And so they approached it differently. Some historians note that the Mormons, as early pioneers of irrigation in the West, were among the exceptions to the early settlers who failed to come to terms with desert conditions, but few followed their example.[15] This is why their role as either "environmentalists" or "anti-environmentalists," or why their preaching "sustainability" while acting unsustainably has been misunderstood. As Stegner pointed out in *Mormon Country*, the faith lends itself to a certain stewardship of the land. And as Stegner also later pointed out, the faith lends itself to a rampant sense of entitlement to the human use of the earth's resources.[16] But their relationship with the land was their relationship with God. The desert distilled this relationship to an offering, a challenge. It's not that the Mormon land ethic has advocated a careless overpopulation and overuse of the land, it's that the Saints are on a different time and cosmological scale than many of us. The faith's view of the world extends beyond earthly matters to a detailed concept of an afterlife and second coming. The earth is in much worse shape than in 1847, but the Mormons keep working over the desert, chugging along with an eye toward the celestial kingdom.

In the nineteenth century, the land between the rugged mountains and the dead lake seemed like a gift. The beginning of the city of Syracuse was five families clustered around what was known as Miller's Spring, one of the oases of freshwater along the lake shorelands. They drilled wells a hundred feet deep, and the water tasted the slightest bit salty. The springs gave them drinking water, and the streams gave them irrigation. Joseph Hill was the first to settle on Kays Creek. He built an adobe cabin at its mouth in 1851. Within a few years, Kays Creek was irrigating pumpkins, potatoes, alfalfa, and sugar beets.

The Saints were efficient in their agriculture. Christopher Layton, who dry-farmed fifteen bushels of wheat per acre, described threshing and hauling forty acres worth of grain to a mill in Kaysville, grinding it into flour, and then milling it and making the flour into biscuits in one day. They turned wheat into flour, hops and molasses into yeast, wood ashes to lye and lye to soap.[17] The Bluff was Davis County's interstate highway. Travelers heading to Oregon or California passed along it before splitting ways near City of Rocks, just over the modern-day Idaho border. It was good grass for their cattle and easy to walk through the sand along the Bluff.

In such an inhospitable region, the Saints were particular about their land. Among the springs and the creeks, life was good, but conditions changed quickly in any direction. Between Hooper Spring and Kays Creek was a "desert waste." Eastward, above the Bluff, was for the Gentiles. Gentile Street, opened in 1882, connected the fertile Mormon agricultural communities with the only two families on the east end of the survey, who happened not to be Latter-day Saints. Here, the soil was sandy, and not until the early 1900s did Syracuse get water up on the Bluff. And, as it had been since the time of the Spanish explorers, what lay out west was a disturbing puzzle. In Syracuse, residents harvested salt from evaporation ponds, which would crystallize over a couple of years, but otherwise there was little use for the lake.

Strange things happened out there. Utah's most unredeemable landscapes were places for the territory's most unredeemable humans. In 1862, Salt Lake City authorities raided the Avenues house of a French-born gravedigger named Jean Baptiste. According to the story, they found clothing and jewelry from bodies Baptiste had buried. Brigham Young's innovative punishment after Baptiste was convicted of grave robbery was to tattoo "Branded for Robbing the Dead" on Baptiste's head and banish him to Antelope Island. Some versions of the story have Young ordering Baptiste to be shackled and his ears split like an animal. But Baptiste might have escaped. One legend has him lashing a raft together and sailing along the chain of lake islands north to Promontory Point. In 1893, duck hunters at the mouth of the Jordan River found a leg bone with an iron shackle around it.[18]

The edge between the fertility of the land and the perceived void of the lake remains. Near the intersection of Gentile Street and 3200 West, just before the Bluff Road, Grace Stevenson lives at this edge. The Stevenson place—she and her husband Mike, whose great-grandfather came to the shorelands with the Kays and the Laytons, have lived here for thirty years—is a brick house built in the 1960s on alfalfa fields. Mike Stevenson grew up in a white frame house next door, his grandma's family on the next farm over. Now, near retirement age, the couple runs a wholesale perennial business on their remaining two acres. Their property lies at the edge of the Nature Conservancy's preserve. They're one of the closest to the lake and yet, from here, it's nearly impossible to know the lake well. In the mid-1980s, when the lake level rose to a historic high of 4,212 feet,[19] the water only got within a half mile of here. They do get the creek water, though. Practically all yearround, it rushes through a ditch along their driveway, part of the water used and discarded by the farmers flooding their fields. Grace Stevenson is only happy to use it again before it goes to waste out in the salty void.

She likes lots of trees around her. The Stevensons have some of the last-remaining poplars along the shorelands, which surround the house and yard like a royal guard. "They're going down so fast," Grace Stevenson says, but then again, she admits, they're not a great tree in the first place. They get sick and die easily, and branches break off in storms. They send up awkward new shoots. Inside the line of poplars are oaks, and within those, in the semicircle driveway from which the house is finally visible, are the rosebushes and fruit trees, the heavy limbs of cherries and peaches.

Inside the garden of the Stevenson place, the birds of the shorelands give and take away. Robins get the cherries every year, stripping the tree of its bounty. Owls keep the mice down but regurgitate pellets on the grass. But the birds also drop seeds that sprout asparagus and plenty of other things that Grace Stevenson never planted. She hosts dozens of sparrows who return each year and build nests outside the house, as well as generations of swallows who bring their families. They come in spring, clean out their nests, lay three or four eggs, and leave again. "You became anti-social because you love the peace and quiet," she says. "We've made our own piece of heaven. We'll die here. I want to figure out a way to be buried here."

The Stevensons, like shorelands property owners before them, scoff at the ground that became the county's spine of the Wasatch Front. "Dad could've bought that sandy land up east for $50 an acre," Grace Stevenson says of her husband's grandpa. But you had to be careful not to go too far west. One of the Stevensons' neighbors drained some property that had been grazing land below the Bluff so he could sell it as farmland. He ploughed it and watered it, and it yielded a crop of grain. The next year, it went back to weeds and wild lettuce.

That's why the good land was hard to come by. Twenty years ago, you couldn't buy an acre, says Grace Stevenson. "The farmers wouldn't consider it." She reconsiders. "Even six years ago, they wouldn't sell." In the rare case that a piece of land did go up for sale, another nearby farmer usually bought it. "Ground was sacred," Grace Stevenson says. Farming is a good profession, she explains, because it's your own business and you're independent. Now, the kids in the neighborhood would give anything to farm, but land is too expensive. You can only do it if you inherit. Besides, the canning and processing plants are closing. The real farmers are starting to flee north to Tremonton, at the northern tip of the Wasatch Front.

She remembers the first sale. It was a cattle rancher in his nineties who had promised he'd never sell. He was the guy who had bought a piece of the original Stevenson property. The developer bought another piece and combined the two to create the Wildhorse Meadows subdivision.

That was it, says Grace Stevenson. Growth had begun in the west in the pioneer days, but it had moved eastward and had stayed there. Now, it was coming back.

Road Rage or Traffic Jam

When the city planner Rodger Worthen first met City of Syracuse government leaders in the late 1990s, he told them, "You couldn't afford me." They could. The tiny town along the shore of the Great Salt Lake was engulfed in a surge of building on its western flank, and having the comfort of someone to blame for all the chaos was apparently a good use of the newfound tax money generated from the development that was plowing the ground westward. Since the town was founded in the nineteenth century, its population had slowly climbed from one thousand to about four thousand and had stayed pat for decades. Even though the Syracuse City Hall is only about four miles from Interstate 15, the city considered itself a world away from the urbanity of the Wasatch Front. "You could say we were isolated in that we didn't consider ourselves part of the Wasatch Front," says Worthen, who is from Brigham City, just up I-15. "One day, it was like, 'Crud, we're on the map.'"

That was sometime in 1997, when Wasatch Front builders and house consumers began turning their appetites toward the shorelands' pastures. Originally, Syracuse was popular because its land was cheap and it was close to the interstate, perfect for Utah starter houses. By granting an average of five hundred building permits a year since 1997, the city has seen its population grow at an annual 12- to 15-percent clip, each year adding more houses to keep up with that rate. It's been exponential. From 1990 to 2000, the population doubled, from 4,658 to 9,398. Then, from 2000 to 2005, it nearly doubled again to 17,938.[20] Even the aerial photo on Worthen's wall is a nostalgic picture of the old town.

Syracuse also lies between two major transportation improvements that will likely alter the form of Davis County: West of I-15 is the Utah Transportation Authority's FrontRunner commuter rail between downtown Salt Lake and Ogden, with seven stations in Weber and Davis counties. Layton Station lies along Main Street about a block from Gentile Street; much of the new development along the shorelands in Layton and Syracuse is only a few miles from the rail station. And along the western fringe of the city, roughly following the Bluff, is the planned route of the Legacy Highway, designed to take pressure off I-15.

Like many people along the Wasatch Front, Rodger Worthen views growth and the way that it occurs in Utah as inherent, natural. "It's just a natural process of going where the land and ground is," he says. And like others in the region, when he thinks of growth, he thinks of those who grew up along the Wasatch Front, and want to stay here, like himself. Nothing wrong with that. "Most people moving here are young families," he says. He's right. Syracuse's median age is almost ten years below the nation's, and the average household size is almost four. Forty percent of the population is below age 18.[21] Worthen says that 80 percent of the new people who have come in are Utah natives and are looking for somewhere to continue the quality of life they knew growing up. The 10 percent that come from California are looking for a new quality of life.

He is aware that Davis County has the smallest land area of any Utah county because most of it is taken up by the Great Salt Lake, leaving only 36 percent for building.[22] "I think people think it's a big dead lake," he says. "People look at it as a wasted area. People view it as a big void." Being from the Great Salt Lake shorelands himself, Worthen has occasionally driven out to Antelope Island. "You get to the top of [the island] and you look out and there's just nothing there," he says. "You have to look back to the Wasatch Front to get back to reality."

The city's response to the growth has been rather slow, especially when you consider that it had some idea of what was coming. In 1993, it prepared a report that concluded, in the words of Worthen, "Crud, we're going to get hit here." The city was still mulling over its agricultural infrastructure, which hadn't been dramatically changed since families gathered around Miller's Spring. The streets were on the familiar Mormon grid, a numbering of four-digit streets radiating from old downtown Layton. Eventually, the city narrowed its tractor-grade 14-foot lanes on its streets, widened the roadways and added sidewalks, curbs, and gutters in 2001. "When I moved here 19 years ago we had more tractors go by than cars," Syracuse's mayor told the *Davis County Clipper*. "Now there's a yellow stripe down my street."[23]

The city has lured a Starbucks, a Wal-Mart Supercenter, and a new high school. "In living here all my life, I never dreamed as a child I would hear of a Starbucks coming to Syracuse," said one resident whose family has been in Syracuse for several generations. To much controversy, the Davis County School District located its eighth high school in Syracuse, prompting a flurry of suggestions for the school name—Island View High, West View High, Sandridge High, Legacy High; and for its mascot—Brine

Shrimp, Seagulls, Crickets and Salt Monsters. None satisfied a *Salt Lake Tribune* columnist, who wrote, "If I'm personally going to name the mascot what the area reminds me of, then how about Road Rage or Traffic Jam? I usually encounter a traffic jam when I'm traveling through Davis County on I-15, then have to suppress my feelings of road rage."[24]

Developers charged into Syracuse satisfied that the pastures they were bulldozing were developable because they weren't under a dead lake, they didn't need the U.S. Army Corps of Engineers' permission to build, they weren't on steep slopes, and they weren't on public land. Those were constraints enough. But what makes decent pasture and what makes good land for building foundations are different. Nationally prominent developers began to clear fifty acres at a time and encountered a rock-solid hardpan beneath the topsoil that ranged from three inches thick to three feet thick. The farmers knew the hardpan was there and wouldn't drain very well and used the land above it for grazing, especially because they could run the water across the top of it and it would wash off as tailwater, bound over the Bluff for the Great Salt Lake wetlands. But builders had to blast out the hardpan with explosives.

Once the houses are built, however, many of the realities of living in the Great Basin are practically invisible to the average busy Wasatch Front homebuyer. The city has tried to drain the land better here by building land drains, a pipe with a service lateral to the homes. The vast majority of the water discharges into a storm drain; the city reclaims some of the water, directing it into a pressurized irrigation system. This source, says Rodger Worthen, makes up most of the water that irrigates Syracuse's new lawns. "It's incredibly cheap water," the planner says. For $13 a month you can water as much as you want. And people do water as much as they want. They water like crazy. They water almost every day. "It's almost a nuisance," Worthen says. He finds sumps in new yards that have become swamps. "They just overdo it. Apparently people don't understand that the roots of a grass plant only go down two or three inches." This overuse is not unique to Syracuse: The U.S. Geological Survey found that in 2000 each Utahn used an average of 293 gallons of water per day for municipal and industrial purposes, which ranked second in the United States—behind Nevada's 336 gallons per day. This number had increased by twenty-four gallons from 1995 to 2000, one of the five largest increases in the nation.[25] Even in the desert, Utahns love their lawns. Utah homeowners are famous not only for watering but also for mowing. Salt Lake City's water conservation coordinator, an out-of-stater, said on a radio program that when she arrived in Utah, she'd never seen men cut their hair so short or mow their lawns so close to the ground.

But limits aren't popular in Syracuse. "Most people that come out here don't want to compromise," Worthen says. "They have to have sod, trees, the whole deal." Then again, he adds, as the Mormon land-use ethic surfaces in the planner, "Weber Basin sends down the water. If we don't use it, it goes into the lake."

Syracuse gave itself a checkup during a revision of its general plan in 2006. The key issue was the future of the shorelands, where declining agriculture, ecological need, a booming housing market, and imminent transportation projects were weighing down on one another. The city considered adding new areas for planned residential developments (PRDs) and office use, as well as how to designate the acres of agriculturally zoned land at its edge along the lake. The city's idea was to keep an agricultural "buffer" beyond the Bluff, an idea popular with planners throughout the Wasatch Front. But three old-guard Syracuse families, the Jensens, the Gardners, and the Cooks, pled with the city to allow their agricultural (A-1 zone) land along the Bluff to be built with houses. They warned the city that the large fields would simply become large, unmaintained weed patches. And, unlike the Stevensons, members of the Jensen and Cook families wanted out of agriculture and in on the real estate bonanza.

"We need a payoff," Leo Cook, who was told his land was too swampy for development, said to planning commissioners. "Ground people often refer to as swamp and marsh land, we've been farming the whole time." Cook said he had worked this ground with the idea the Syracuse master plan would keep changing agriculture to residential. "This is the reason for planning," he said, "so areas can be changed as time necessitates." He said he remembered when a sign welcomed people to Syracuse and announced the population as 590.[26] "Our machinery is worn out and we are getting old," Cook said. "Farming is a thing of the past, but we are told to keep farming." He concluded by telling the city to buy their own buffer—to purchase the properties from his family for what they've been offered.

At the same time, the new residents were uneasy about being crowded in by more subdivisions. A faction of the city's population launched a crusade against the PRDs, whose flexibility would allow higher densities and more amenities such as commercial enterprises and parks. They cited reasons such as "safety of children," "loss of the community feel," "storm-water problems," "residents do not want commercial or professional offices in their neighborhood," "PRDs could become transient communities," "commercial development devaluing homes," and "our area is an entrance to the city and should be aesthetically pleasing as people enter the city."

At least the old farmers had a context for the change. For those who knew Syracuse by "Road Rage," and "Traffic Jam," it was simply a clearing in the urban jungle. "With the old timers, you used to see the sense of history, but now two-thirds of people on the streets of Syracuse don't have any idea about the history," Rodger Worthen tells me. "They just think it's new ground."

Mountain Castles, Basin Bonanza

The subdivisions pushing the edges of the Wasatch Front are more fanciful than what we saw in the North Valleys of Reno. There is more grass, more automobiles, more space to store them. Gone is the modest gravel and the inexpensive, efficient siding. If the new Reno North Valleys house is an efficient hovel anchored to brave the elements, the new Wasatch house is more of a castle.

The largest residential builder in Utah is a company called Ivory Homes. It has been responsible for the construction of some ten thousand houses along the Wasatch Front, in St. George, and even out in Elko, Nevada. The company has a legend about it, a lore that circulates around today's corporate staff. It's a story in which the current company is only the most recent incarnation. The family is Utah's version of the urban entrepreneur gone boom and bust and boom again. The entrepreneur who never relents, like Charles Yerkes, the notorious developer of the elevated railway of Chicago in the 1890s, who was run out of the city, only to find rebirth as a major developer of the London Underground.[27]

Like most powerful Utah people and institutions, Ivory Homes traces its ancestry to the pioneer days of dugout cabins and poplar windbreaks. Its very own Moses was Matthew Ivory, a stern-eyed, thin-lipped, buttoned-up Pennsylvania homesteader who came to the Great Basin alongside Brigham. "Except for sagebrush and jackrabbits, when Matthew Ivory first entered the Salt Lake Valley in 1847 it was empty," begins the book penned by the company to tell its history, called "The Ivory Legacy."[28]

Matthew Ivory's grandson, Clark Ivory, saw potential in the post–World War II construction boom the United States was experiencing and moved from rural Utah to Salt Lake. The family built a house but had to live in its basement because Clark Ivory's construction and real estate ventures alternated between success and failure, and he could not

The sweeping view westward from the Great Salt Lake shorelands (above) may require glancing back at the strip of Wasatch Front civilization to get your bearings in time and space (below).

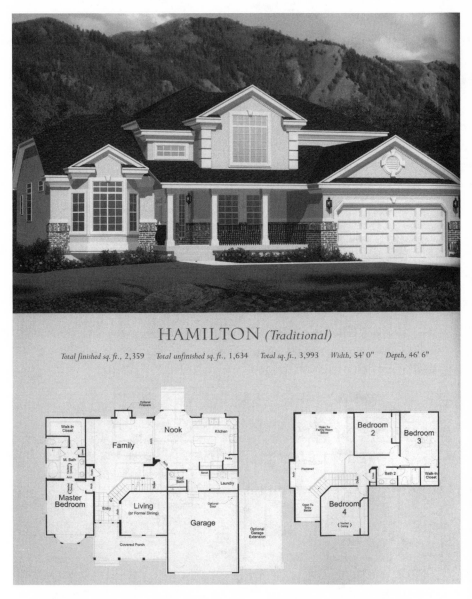

HAMILTON *(Traditional)*

Total finished sq. ft., 2,359   *Total unfinished sq. ft.*, 1,634   *Total sq. ft.*, 3,993   *Width*, 54' 0"   *Depth*, 46' 6"

Ivory Homes' best-selling Hamilton (above) would look out of place in the Ivory Homes Catalog without the Wasatch rising behind; the Savono Rustic (opposite) is the new Utah old-world mountain-lodge style that has taken over fast-growing places like the Great Salt Lake shorelands. (Both images courtesy of Ivory Homes)

afford to complete the house. Clark Ivory's youngest son, Ellis, was born in 1940 in the dark-brick bungalow that Clark had built. From his early teens onward, Ellis Ivory worked in a variety of construction-related jobs: hauling sand and gravel, driving trucks, carrying hod for his bricklayer uncle. When Ellis became the first in the Ivory family to attend college, he obtained his real estate license.

The family then fell into real estate development by happening upon a piece of property in St. George, in the southwest corner of the state. Beginning in the 1960s, the Ivorys developed the property into a resort subdivision they called Bloomington after a failed pioneer settlement, and the project helped transform St. George into a retirement Mecca. Ellis Ivory quickly worked his way into a seat among Utah's powerful real estate developers. Ivory's brother-in-law was Roger Boyer, the future patriarch of the Boyer Company, a big-time Utah commercial developer. The two men, still in their twenties, formed Ivory and Boyer Company, and after Bloomington's success, merged with another landholding company to become Terracor. Terracor became a giant. It ran wild all over the

As Wasatch Front growth spreads out to the shorelands, it trades the historic poplar windbreaks (above) for Utah-style urbanization (below).

With the arrival of the FrontRunner to the cities along the Great Salt Lake shorelands (above), can downtown station areas like that in Layton (below) capitalize with successful transit-oriented development?

West as executives flew in their three private jets to offices in Los Angeles, Denver, Kansas City, and Chicago. Ivory moved into an office in one of the mansions built by the mining magnates along South Temple Street in Salt Lake, a den of wood paneling, leather sofas, ornamental metalwork, and stained glass.

But uncomfortable with Terracor's insatiable appetite for growth, even as it overextended its capital, Ellis Ivory quit the company. He was thirty years old. He told his relatives he wanted to learn how to ski, and while doing just that in Vail, Colorado, happened upon the front edge of the West's luxury condominium boom. He returned to Salt Lake and created Ivory and Company in time for the inflation to lead to rampant property value appreciation. By 1975, Ivory and Company had created eighty residential subdivisions along the old pioneer trail from Brigham City in the north to Cedar City in the south. Ivory became nearly as dominant as Terracor: In 1975, it was responsible for one in eight Utah lots sold.

As the 1970s ended, so did that wave of Ivory's fortune. In 1979, the LDS Church called Ellis Ivory and his family to serve a mission in England for three years. When he returned, the economy had turned into a recession and all the pieces of land that were previously assets became liabilities. In his absence, the company could not unload them fast enough. Ivory found himself deep in debt: In the early 1980s, his company operated at a $2 million deficit.

The current phoenix of the Ivory family rose out of this seemingly devastating hit. With so much property in a dismal market, Ellis Ivory realized that the only way to get rid of the land would be to build inexpensive houses on it for first-time buyers. Throughout the mid-1980s, the company struggled to build thirty houses a year. Then, as in Bloomington, fortune smiled upon the Ivorys. The company received a contract to build four hundred houses for gold miners in Elko, Nevada. Ellis Ivory, onetime tycoon jet-setter, drove almost every day from Salt Lake past Tooele Valley, Skull Valley, the Bonneville Salt Flats, and over Silverzone Pass past the Ruby Mountains to Elko and back to manage the project. For the times when Ivory didn't feel like driving back, the company bought the Esquire Motel in Elko.

Once again, success in a far-flung part of Zion took Ivory to success on the Wasatch Front. By 1988, Ivory Homes had become the state's most prolific residential builder, a title it has held since, surpassing aggressive national companies such as Pulte and Lennar. When Utah experienced the population boom of the 1990s, the Ivory family was once again in the right industry in the right place at the right time. This time, their company would take a dominant role in defining the urban form of the growing metropolis along the Wasatch Mountains.

In 2006, Ivory Homes celebrated the construction of its ten thousandth home, meaning that roughly 2 percent of all the housing units in the Wasatch Front were Ivory Homes. Ellis Ivory had since handed the reins to his son Clark. "I figure it's going to take somewhere between seven and eight years to build the next 10,000," Clark Ivory said at the celebration. In 2006, the company built 1,202 houses on 52 Wasatch Front sites. It planned 1,300 for 2007. The Utah governor, Jon Huntsman Jr., attended the ceremony and proclaimed that "when we're gone I think the only thing we're bequeathing to the next generation is the land and the air that we breathe, and a sense of humanity. . . . That humanity starts in the home."[29]

Ivory Homes' headquarters is a two-building campus tucked away in the middle of the Salt Lake Valley. One of the buildings is the Customer Care Center, where future Ivory homeowners browse around the "color room," a room of house finishes, and then sit down with a company salesperson and finalize their house package. Upstairs is the office of Ivory Homes' head architect, Brian Apsley. Apsley is the other, newer kind of Utahn, the kind from California. He grew up in Sacramento and in 1994 moved to Utah and received his certificate from the Ivory Institute, the annual training camp that teaches employees about the Ivory lore.

Over the past decade, Apsley has presided over the evolution of Ivory Homes design, which in many ways has paralleled the population and economic boom of the Wasatch Front. In the mid-1990s, the company was still based on the concept of starter houses. It was still struggling to emerge from Ellis Ivory's debt. Design was price: Ivory chose floorplans and materials that wouldn't pass on too much expense to their customers. And so for much of the company's early existence, the most popular house style was what was known as a multilevel, or tri-level. From the entrance, a half flight of stairs led to the main floor and a half flight led to a half-sunk basement. The garage and other parts of the house were at ground level. As Apsley notes, multilevels were efficient to build, especially with the aluminum siding and slight brick accents the company used almost exclusively. In 1994, Ivory's runaway biggest seller was the "Heritage," which was one thousand finished square feet. Today, multilevels define much of the interior Salt Lake Valley, and in doing so they show one other trait of the early Ivory Homes: They were close to or within existing development. Ellis Ivory's near financial ruin had led him to seek properties that were already surrounded by neighborhoods and infrastructure, rather than speculative edge areas. For much of its early life, Ivory Homes built in this "infill" manner, helping to create the even density of the Salt Lake Valley.

But in the middle and late 1990s, changes in Utah changed the way Ivory designed their houses and neighborhoods, and thus, the urban form of the Wasatch Front. First came the population boom, a large part of which was made up of Californians and people from other parts of the country. Ivory saw its largest percentage of California buyers in 1996 and 1997, and with them came what Apsley calls "an increase in sophistication in the marketplace." And as the same aspects of Utah that were attracting people to the state also attracted jobs, homebuyers also experienced an increase in wealth. From 1990 to 2000, the median family income in the Salt Lake City–Ogden MSA increased from $30,882 to $48,594, almost one-and-a-half times the increase nationally.[30]

The Wasatch Front had imported California building trends before. The bungalows of the 1920s and 1930s came from California, as did, more recently, the light-colored stucco of the late 1980s and early 1990s that became known as the "stuccosaurus." But this time the stucco came darker and with heavy timber and copper, high pitched roofs, and four-car garages. The nudging toward this style of building came from more money and the influence of outsiders, but for better or worse, Utahns were forging a new style of their own, unveiling the identity of not necessarily who they are as a people but of who they want to be. As it turned out, they were creating a monster.

The new Utah house starts in the great room, a large combination of a family room and living room hitched onto the kitchen, a ground zero for a large family. It adds multiple bedrooms, usually at least three for even a starter house. And a basement is essential to add space. Many builders will offer additional square footage in the form of an unfinished basement for a lower cost. And there is lots of, as one Utah developer called it, "pizzazz." As much pizzazz as one can afford, in fact: Jacuzzi tubs, embellished entrances, massive garages, and large master suites.

On the outside, Ivory Homes take the surreal form of a mountain lodge blended with an old-world Italian cottage. On the cover of the 2007 Ivory Homes Catalog is a model called the Savono Rustic, a high-end house with timber and masonry (see the photo section in this chapter). In the renderings of most Ivory Homes, images of the Wasatch Mountains rise behind, as if the craggy peaks were part of the architecture without which the house façade would be incomplete. "It's sort of a mountain style," describes Apsley. "A lot of the elements come from Park City and Deer Valley. It's a style that's uniquely Utahn, a rustic mountain lodge. Or, as much as it can be while being built for mass production."

The European style emerged around the turn of the twenty-first century with the Tuscany, which presented buyers with a textured stucco façade rising above brick. It had a romantic iron balcony and majestic moldings over the balcony doors and windows. The Tuscany sold well, so the company continued in the vein of Italian cities. Apsley says he believes buyers want to feel like their house is old and has been here a long time. The current rave is a mishmash of the two styles that pits timber, copper, and rock against brick and preweathered stucco. You could argue that there's a little overlap between the styles, in the villas of the northern Italian Alps and hill country. Apsley says it's native Utahns who are embracing this style. "People coming from out of state are more likely to shy away from that style and go more toward brick," he says.

"They want to think of themselves as being in a treed, mountain setting," is the explanation of Ted Knowlton, a planner for regional coalition Envision Utah, who grew up in Davis County. Knowlton calls the style an "odd bastard hybrid" of California stucco and Park City–influenced mountain architecture. "The vernacular I'm seeing more and more is exposed wooden elements and darker color paletting. Look at Park City. What happens in Park City usually happens in the valley a few years later. People want to think of themselves as living in a setting like Park City. I don't know, maybe it was the Olympics' strange branding that did it."

For whatever reason and in whatever style, one thing is for sure: Houses have become bigger. As the state's increases in wealth and per-capita water usage suggest, households are living larger, even outpacing the nation as a whole. Ivory's houses begin at 1,754 square feet in the Nordic and run up to 6,350 square feet in the Tuscany, a far cry from the puny Heritage of the mid-1990s. Most have at least three bedrooms and massive unfinished basements. As figure 3.1 demonstrates, the central Wasatch Front's development has swept southwest and northwest from Salt Lake City, and the houses' sizes have increased with their newness. As I talk to Apsley, I get the feeling that the design of Ivory's homes is something that has happened to him, a force of nature, or consumerism, that has taken hold of the company, and he, as head architect, is simply obliging it. Despite the conservative ethic of its Mormon founders, Ivory Homes is only happy to indulge in Utahns' fantasies about where they live and under what conditions.

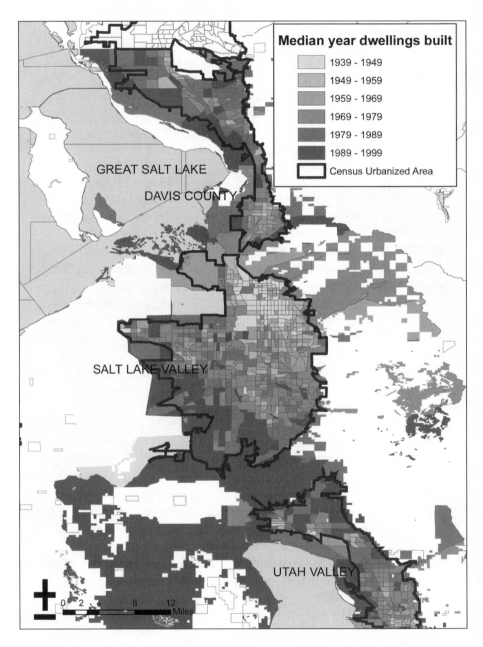

Figure 3.1. As urban growth has spread westward from the Wasatch Front's historic centers and into the Great Basin (above), houses have become much larger (opposite). (Source: U.S. Census Bureau, "Census of Population and Housing," 2000)

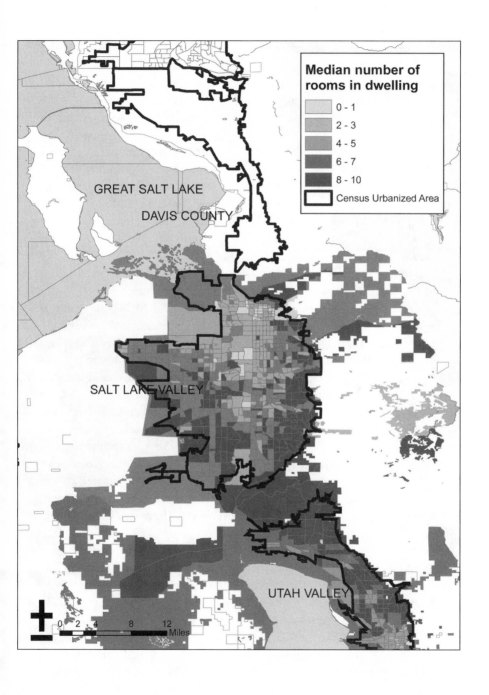

Median number of
rooms in dwelling

0 - 1
2 - 3
4 - 5
6 - 7
8 - 10
☐ Census Urbanized Area

GREAT SALT LAKE

DAVIS COUNTY

SALT LAKE VALLEY

UTAH VALLEY

0 2 4   8   12
                  Miles

Currently, Ivory Homes has ten subdivisions in the cities along the Great Salt Lake shorelands in Davis County, including three in Syracuse. Despite the company's ideal to stay close to town, all of its north Davis County projects are pushing toward the wetlands, including one below the Bluff, Fairmont Estates. The same thing that has happened to Ivory Homes has happened to the City of Syracuse. When you drive out Antelope Drive, you pass house after house of vinyl or aluminum siding painted a dull gray. Those aren't really being built anymore. Recently, the majority of the houses going up in the affordable housing market formerly known as Syracuse have conformed to the mountain lodge–old world castle style.

"They want a bigger home, more features, and more toys to play with," Rodger Worthen says. Part of it is a continuation of the population growth pressure of the Wasatch Front. Land has become more valuable and more expensive, pushing up to $80,000 an acre. The assessed values of some houses in Syracuse have approached $1 million.

But there is another element to this style trend, which is the desire of Syracuse to become a higher-end place. For 150 years, the city was happy to be a laid-back rural backwater. It was only when it perceived that it had been enveloped by the urban matrix, at the bottom of its totem pole no less, designated as a dumping ground for cheap houses, that it decided it would rather be snobby. Here, another reason for the current style becomes clear: status. The mountain lodge–old world castle style embellishes itself with expensive materials on its façades: rock, brick, timber, and copper. Cities like Syracuse have legislated this architecture, requiring a majority of the house to be covered in rock, brick, and stucco. In an effort to dilute Syracuse's vinyl siding, the city council mandated that at least 40 percent of each house has to be brick, rock, or man-made stone.

Brian Apsley is aware of this requirement. "They've made the determination that that is a better look," Apsley says, shrugging. "Places where homes have been lower-priced, the city officials have almost a fear of developers coming in and building a cheap housing product with aluminum siding. It's a fear of the past. It's debatable how much a city should be able to influence something like that." Or, as one homeowner tells me, "People in Utah are stuck up. Syracuse, they're sending a message. People in Syracuse don't like that transient nature."

Indeed, Utah seems to have invented this family-scale urbanization, and along the Great Salt Lake, developers and builders have worked double-time to produce it. One of the most prominent local Davis County developers is the Adams Company, owned by two brothers, Stuart and

David. Stuart Adams, who is a former member of the Utah Legislature, shares the belief that housing is an obstacle that Utahns need to overcome to continue to live in the state. "Too much money chasing too little product," Adams says of the boom times. "The drop in interest rates has allowed people to buy bigger, nicer homes. We went to siding when interest rates were at 18 percent. Now you see garages on the side, to fit four cars. People like the brick and stucco, but we blend the stucco and siding."

Land became hard to come by in the boom for the Adams Company. The high prices started to free up more ground, but it's still difficult to find. What's also difficult for Adams is finding cities that will allow him to develop at reasonable densities. Of course, the higher the density, the more money he makes, and the more efficient the infrastructure. But he doesn't understand the old farmers who fight for low density and the cities who mandate it. West Layton, for example, wanted one-third-acre lots for a recent project, but Adams was able to persuade the city council to approve some ten thousand square-foot lots. Once they're on the market, though, Adams plays up the spaciousness. "Modern Living in a rural setting," the Adams Company advertises in Syracuse.

"It's a struggle. Most of the farmers are demanding half-acre lots, to maintain a rural effect. Half-acre lots are really challenging to do to most developers. I don't think they understand it." Adams says. "How many people moved into Davis County last year? Divide that by ten dwelling units per acre, then divide it by one unit per acre. How much land does each of those take up? If you're really a farmer, you probably should prefer a higher density."

Grace Stevenson is not a fan of Adams' houses. She perceives them as high-density starter homes, bound to attract transient residents. "We didn't want starter homes so it wouldn't become a bad area," she says. "Two or three sellovers and you really get it run down. We fought for larger lots so people would stay.

"Syracuse has done wonderful things," Grace Stevenson says. "We've been really pleased."

Nothing Here, Nothing There

It all comes together down the road from the Stevensons, out to the intersection of Gentile Street with Bluff Road, where a small subdivision curls into the shorelands. Behind the last row of houses is the slope of the Bluff, beyond that a few privately owned acres, and beyond that, the Nature

Conservancy's shorelands preserve. Beyond that, no one, all the way to Japan. The houses are of the mountain lodge–stuccosaurus variety, boats and four-wheelers in their driveways, and their rooflines steeply gabled to punctuate their mark on the earth. The roads end in culs-de-sac where one's voice reverberates in the starkness of the concrete and asphalt. No trees. Along this contour, walking by the houses, you can see clear to Antelope Island, like the lake is not even there, transporting the viewer—when the smog isn't too bad—into the alien world of buffalo and marooned convicts with their ears clipped like livestock. This, at the edge of the Great Basin, is the edge of the Wasatch Front, and it will be the edge for a long time to come. Chris Brown is eyeing the privately held ag land next to the houses; the Nature Conservancy's purchase of it would seal up the interface between the bird farms and the city. This city isn't the ever-expanding radial American city of the eastern woodlands or prairie but the Great Basin city constrained by more extreme nature. What happens here will define the difference between the city and the country, or in the Basin, the city and the sink. Just like the users of Peavine Mountain who spoke of moving between the two worlds, the outward of the mountains and the inward of the city. Or vice versa.

The new homeowners here don't really see it that way. "We jumped on this one," says one homeowner about the lot he and his wife bought across the street from the model home. "Our last house was a cookie-cutter in Kaysville. You walk into your neighborhood and you feel like it's the same as all the others." This one's custom, or close. They selected the builder's open floorplan for a thirty-four hundred square-foot house. "This gives you the country feel," he says. "If I had my way, it would stay exactly the same."

A teacher living down the street bought his house while on the Parade of Homes, a Utah tradition of real estate marketing. He and his wife were living in a sixteen hundred square-foot starter house. They wanted a bigger place, but his wife wanted to stay in Davis County. The builder threw in some of the upgrades, such as two-tone paint, one-piece countertops, garden tubs, and it was a done deal. "We just sit here in our little corner, nice and quiet," he says.

These are Utahns who love the back of beyond of the public lands surrounding the city, and like the RV-bound Renoites, love their toys. One homeowner says he has been a hunter all his life and loves the noises of pheasants over his backyard. Another uses the pasture next door being cleared for another subdivision as his private driving range. But living at the edge also means owl droppings and mosquitoes. There is tailwater that comes off the pastures over the fence, so the homeowners build drains. Most mornings they wake up to the cows.

Beyond the pheasants and the cows, few really care about what lies out there. "I know there's nothing out there," says the owner of a seven-bedroom house. "I was a flight instructor for fifteen years, I flew over it a lot. Nothing there."

As we have seen, there is plenty out there but nothing here. There is a lot of house here, a lot of yard, a lot of LDS ward house and LDS ward house parking lot but not much else. If several vocal citizens who are trying to shoot down neighborhood commercial areas have their way, the planned commercial center for Gentile and Bluff won't happen. Any development that is built will likely be inhospitable to walkers.

Syracuse city planning has corralled Wal-Mart into designing its supercenter in the same mountain lodge–stucco style as the houses. It wasn't a problem—Wal-Mart was thrilled to come to such virgin retail territory. One city official knows the stigma about Wal-Mart's labor practices and commercial hegemony but figures, "You always hear Wal-Mart will destroy jobs in the community. Well, Syracuse wasn't like that. We have no jobs to destroy."

The city planning department is fighting a losing battle with the city council and developers in commercial parking requirements. "Recommend deleting 10 parking stalls to . . . improve pedestrian scalability, reduce overall storm water collection, reduce solar heat creation, and provide a more aesthetic development through additional landscaping," read one planning staff report. But the covenants, conditions, and restrictions (CC&Rs) put forth by chains like Wal-Mart often require high parking minimums so that shoppers don't have to worry about congestion and can "linger" in the stores without a hassle.

Not that many residents are planning on sticking around very long. "We'll probably sell in a year or two, build a house that *we* want," says one man. "It's always been so open here, and it's closing in." His neighbor's voice reverberates across the new hardscape of the cul-de-sac: "In twenty years, hopefully, we'll be gone."

This Is It

"I think we could've done some things better," says Rodger Worthen, leaning back in his office chair. The city's open distaste of multifamily housing, for example, bothers him a little bit. There have been a handful of condo and apartment developments among the large-lot, single-family developments, but when your highest density zone allows a maximum of five-and-a-half dwelling units per acre—that's about eight thousand-square-foot lots, "large" lots for many cities—multifamily is just the beginning of what you can't do. Such a density, combined with the city's façade requirements, excludes everything but the rock-stucco lodge-castles. And Worthen feels the land is being sold and annexed a little too quickly. The process of turning sacred farm ground into throwaway bedroom-community ground, formerly a closely scrutinized phenomenon, has become taken for granted. Such a lack of annexation procedure leads to an expectation from landowners. "There has been no formal procedure for annexing into the city," one landowner noted at a planning commission meeting. And so it becomes a game of political favors. The landowner added that, "Our families are owed something since we have given so much to the community."[31]

"The City of Syracuse is struggling to keep up with what we've got," Worthen says. "It's no longer a planning issue; it becomes politics. Planning is thrown out the door. There are 1,200 kids in the rec program, and no room. There will be 22 soccer fields in a new park and it will be booked every night. How are you going to address your stormwater, your drains, your sanitary systems? How are you going to address services, and you want to add 80 acres more? We're just consuming land at huge volumes." Worthen blames the city council and the planning commission for succumbing to the politics and not understanding the city as a system. But he also blames the consumer. "There's just a unique mentality," he says, "that I need my brick and rock as big as I want on green grass and close out the rest of the world."

Worthen's views aren't the consensus at Syracuse's City Hall. "There're a lot of people here who think Rodger Worthen's a fruitcake," Worthen says. At the Davis County Shorelands Regional Plan hearing, Worthen stood up and said, "Don't we have a right as a community to stand up and say, 'This is it.' It's not going to keep expanding like a donut that keeps growing."

Chris Brown is also angry. He's mad at the people who live in the crackerbox houses along his fence, the few starter homes that sneaked through, because they don't understand bird farming. The new neighbors flip him off on his tractor because he's blocking the freeway, and they bitch when the dust comes up.

We're now driving in Brown's white truck on the other side of his property line, on the new asphalt of the subdivision, looking out at the preserve. Out of curiosity, I am asking Brown if non-Mormons have a tough time fitting in in these new subdivisions like his and this one. Brown is a lapsed Mormon, having grown up in the faith and since stopped going to church and started drinking coffee. "Nah," he says. "I know people who aren't LDS and they seem so bitter about it. I'm like, do they bug you? They say no, and I say, what's the problem?"

Having explored the shorelands on either side of the edge that separates the urbanizing Wasatch Front from the wetlands, I see that the Great Salt Lake wetlands are an engineered place. It's part of a system that needs constant balancing and human maintenance. Chris Brown, unlike many of his neighbors, is comfortable with this reality. "People used to have a distorted view of the marsh," Brown says. "The Nature Conservancy used to sell it as the only natural wetland left along the Great Salt Lake. But that marsh is affected by humans in so many ways." But he's less comfortable with the same idea on the other side of his fence. Near the FrontRunner commuter rail station in Farmington there are plans for a large mixed-use project with multifamily housing, retail, and restaurants. It will be practically in Chris Brown's backyard, and he doesn't like it.

"In Farmington, we just barely got our first stoplight," he says, exaggerating. "Retail, restaurants, if I wanted to live next to that stuff, I'd move to West Valley City or South Jordan." For Brown, regarding any kind of development, less is better than more. "In a lot of ways, we're still a young city. And this is all new," he says. "We've grown so fast. Older cities knew what they had and preserved it. My generation, everyone wants it now." He pauses and looks out toward the lake. "I used to get really angry and really bitter about things."

So it is in the islands of life along the edge of the Great Basin. Like Cold Springs and Reno, Peavine Mountain and White Lake, the Great Salt Lake city lives and dies in the short watercourses between the steep slopes and the flat playa. This place that seems so open is actually very crowded, with birds and freeways, people on the make and people on the take and people on the move, space and water, reflections and realities. One landscape's edge is another's center. One landscape's natural history is another's blank canvas. A place that is all about pushing out has fewer and fewer chances to do so. What seem like endless possibilities at a glance are really very narrow choices that must be made in the same shrewdness as God's when he placed saltbush at the edge of the playa.

Even so, in flux, the new city's identity is trapped, between the long associations of the farmers and the blank-slate associations and fantasies of the new residents. The relationship between the new city and the Basin, between the human ecology and natural ecology, along the edge of the Bluff, is what must be found here. It's an urban relationship. In downtown Layton, the shorelands landscape of mountain walls and infinite lake views layer with the past of the historic human-scale commercial buildings and the future of rail transit to create the kernel of appealing, perhaps sustainable, urbanism. How can these urban layers grow out along the corridor of Gentile Street toward the Bluff? As one longtime Syracuse resident said, "The farming community is gone. Now it is a city." Syracuse is struggling to think like one. Indeed, it is a matter of adaptation. Like the natural landscape, which has evolved over geologic time, the human landscape must evolve, but much more quickly.

In the Great Basin city, edges such as the shorelands present the opportunity for vital urban places but must balance the orbits of both people and nature to achieve this goal. This dynamic edge, where the nature of the Great Basin meets its culture, should be a vibrant urban place, carefully calibrated to balance people and birds, waterways, and streets with a vanguard of public space, all the while considering that the region's central axis is only three miles away. Front it with the best we've got rather than turn our back onto it. This edge should be a dialogue between people and nature, not a random and unfortunate meeting of property lines and interests.

The forces at work have caused Grace Stevenson, at least, to turn inward. She'll never sell. She is frustrated with what, to her, seems like beastly traffic ("You just don't go uptown after 3 p.m.," she warns), but what really irritates her is the Nature Conservancy, which bought out most of the property near her family's land. How it's getting in the way of putting the Legacy Highway farther below the Bluff, so it can be farther away from her and her husband and their history. "The wildlife adjusts," she says. "Otherwise, they'll be tearing down homes." When the time comes, Grace Stevenson says, they'll just put another row of poplars around their garden.

Urban Realities of Rural Places
The Illusion of Space

> There are people who like things as they are. I can't hold out any
> hope to them. They have to keep moving further away. This is
> a great, big state, and there are other states. Let them go to the
> Rockies.
> —Robert Moses[1]

It's almost like going back in time: Take Interstate 80 west from Salt Lake
City, squeeze through the thin strip of land where the Oquirrh Mountains
meet the south shore of Great Salt Lake and then watch the landscape
open back up into another expanse. This is Tooele Valley, the next in the
series of basins running out into the Great Salt Lake Desert. Here, you
see the other side of the Oquirrhs. Whereas in Salt Lake Valley, they are
the dry range of a minor key opposing the grand wet Wasatch, they gain
new character here as the conifer-covered sentinels that loom above the
small town of Tooele, looking bigger and more assuring. The Stansbury
Mountains become the dissonant range *out there*, hemming in the valley
from the impossibly vast Great Basin. The resemblance of Tooele Valley
to its neighbor to the east is striking. The shoreline of old Lake Bonneville
cuts along the foothills, whose grassy slopes ease down to the valley. The
valley floor spreads out to a size resembling that of Salt Lake Valley, but
there is no orderly grid of ten-acre blocks, no thick cover of maples and
sycamores, no loops and lollipops at the edges. Only the town of Tooele
and a few outlying hamlets, farms, and a lot of shrubs. Here, in comparison to the LDS Church's conference center roof, you get a more authentic
sense of what Salt Lake Valley may have looked like to John C. Frémont,
Jim Bridger, or Brigham Young. Through gathering storm clouds coming
in over the Stansburys, the light hits it like an empty room.

From 2000 to 2003, Tooele County was Utah's fastest growing. Its population increased from about forty thousand to about forty-seven thousand. By 2008, it had reached nearly sixty thousand. A consulting firm hired by the county in 2002 projected its population to reach one hundred thousand by 2020.[2] The picture emerges of an intermountain civilization cloning itself westward in basin after basin.

When Drew Hall drove into Tooele Valley for the first time, he noticed that the Bonneville Lake line continued around the northern edge of the Oquirrhs, just like in Salt Lake Valley. He noticed the emptiness. And he noticed how long it had taken him to drive out here from Salt Lake City: thirty minutes.

Hall was a Seattle accountant who had evolved into a real estate developer, helping to put together projects in Washington, Canada, and Eastern Europe. In the early 1990s, Hall's brother alerted him to the Wasatch Front. Salt Lake stuck out as a market that had a strong upside potential in its affordability, Hall noticed. He began to research Salt Lake fervently, taking interest in its geographic peculiarities. He saw a lot of similarities between Salt Lake and Seattle, with respect to natural growth limits. The growth tended to be elongated because of all the barriers to growth such as the lake and the mountains.

Hall was visiting Salt Lake in 1994 when someone told him that he should go and check out Tooele Valley. So he drove out around the point of the mountain and into the next valley over, whose population at that time consisted mainly of the approximately fourteen thousand people who lived in the town of Tooele, which, like most other interior Great Basin towns, was tucked up against the mountains on one end of the valley. The higher he went in the valley, which, unlike Salt Lake Valley, slopes up slightly to the south, the more noticeable was the view down to the Great Salt Lake. In contrast to Salt Lake Valley, where, in most places, the view of the lake is almost pushed into a corner, Tooele Valley's view is more striking, with the valley floor hovering above the lake's silvery landscape.

That day, on the outskirts of the town of Tooele, he saw what he recognized as the bottom half of a withered "For Sale" billboard. It had advertised twenty-seven hundred acres just south of the railroad tracks on the south end of town. When he called to inquire, he found that the land was owned by an aviation buff and oil entrepreneur who had just died. The son was looking to unload the land from his new empire of holdings. So Hall and his brother negotiated a deal for the property and became one of the largest landowners in Tooele Valley.

When Hall made his land purchase in Tooele, he realized that the Oquirrh Mountains separated Tooele Valley from Salt Lake Valley, pushing it out of most of the populace's consciousness as a part of the metropolitan area and as a viable place for those employed in Salt Lake Valley to live. It was also on the west side of the metro area, which seemed like the opposite of everything residents wanted to associate themselves with. The skiing was on the east side, with prestigious resorts like Park City, and the wealthy traditionally lived on the East Bench. But Hall also knew it only took a half hour to get to Tooele on uncrowded roads. By most Utahns' conceptions of geography, Tooele Valley was a world away from Salt Lake. Considered in time, it was as close or closer than Utah County, parts of Davis County, and Park City. "I said, people don't realize Tooele's so close," Hall says. "What's close to us is what's within our frame of reference. When you say, let's go out to Tooele, people say, 'I have to pack a lunch.' The perception is that Tooele's "hell and gone" from Salt Lake City, but the commuting time to Salt Lake City is less than from residential areas that people deem close. I knew that Salt Lake City would have to make that transition to thinking of distance in time."[3]

At the time, Tooele, a picture of pastoral quaintness to a first-time viewer, was actually going through serious changes. In 1993 the Tooele Army Depot was ordered to close through a Base Realignment and Closure. Since World War II, it had maintained topographic equipment, troop support items, construction equipment, power generators, and vehicles, providing almost a thousand civilian jobs to those in Tooele.[4] Another Great Basin boom town had gone bust; as throughout the Basin, many believed Tooele would become another empty desert valley littered with persisting ruins. Not Hall.

"I'm a contrarian by nature," Drew Hall says today. "The smart money was saying Tooele was going to become a ghost town. I looked at it as, if you're willing to be patient, there are chances here."

Urbanization, Urbanism, and the Intermountain West

The United States has been urbanizing for a long time, and never faster than today. At the turn of the millennium, about four fifths of Americans lived in urbanized areas. Between 1982 and 1997, the total amount of urbanized land in the United States increased from around fifty-one million acres to about seventy-six million acres, an increase of some 47 percent.[5] And most people live not just in cities but large ones. The

2000 Census found that 58 percent of Americans lived in urban areas of more than two hundred thousand people.

The concentration of population in larger and larger metropolitan areas is accelerating. Urban geographers Robert E. Lang and Arthur C. Nelson point out the trend of the "megapolitans," supersized cities that combine two or more existing metro areas. We are already familiar with Dallas–Fort Worth and Washington-Baltimore, but Lang and Nelson forecast the "Sun Corridor" of Phoenix and Tucson; the "Cascade Corridor" of Seattle and Portland; and three megapolitans in Texas where San Antonio merges with Austin, Houston with Galveston, and Dallas stretches over the border to Oklahoma City. Megapolitans like the Front Range in Denver are especially common in the West, and have come to define the region's population centers. "The rise of megapolitans refutes the notion that Americans live in mostly wide open spaces when compared to Europe and Japan," write Lang and Nelson. "While decentralization might have occurred at a metropolitan scale," they add, the nation as a whole is concentrated in urban areas.[6]

This idea of concentration at the large scale and dispersal at a smaller scale is essential to the Intermountain West. The region lies simultaneously on both ends of the urban-rural spectrum. While Utah and Nevada are among the most urbanized states in the nation, at a large scale, with most of their population packed into metropolitan areas ranging from a half million to two million people, at a smaller scale, urban patterns emphasize space. The culture of these metropolitan areas values things usually associated with the rural, from motorized toys to preferences for large lots.

But a true rural lifestyle is a rather limited choice within our urbanized framework. The opportunities for a rural lifestyle in today's world of climbing energy costs and globalizing economics are becoming smaller and smaller. As one architect puts it, "By and large, rural life is not an alternative to living in an urban system unless one pursues frugal self-sufficiency and monastic isolationism."[7] Life in the rural West is often sustained by the New West tourism economy fed by people traveling out from these same American megapolitans. The results of trying to go rural within one of the West's megapolitans is usually a thinly veiled suburban lifestyle. As Carl Abbott writes, "Much of this superficially rural West has been centralized into the daily and weekly economic orbits of the major cities."[8] But the Great Basin, like much of the West, is holding onto the rural. In a place like the Wasatch Front, whose history and identity is founded on notions of working the desert into a garden—and where there is seemingly so much space—the idea of the rural is hard to let go.

Urbanism is a tougher choice, but to harmonize our built environment with our natural geography and regional economic patterns, urbanism must happen in the American West. Out in the sagebrush valleys, it's still possible to find the "frugal self-sufficiency" of a true rural lifestyle, but it's increasingly rare. After all, the western city is the clearest example of what geographer Paul Groth calls the "new city," horizontal, predictable, land-value-focused and a finished product—in contrast to the "old city" of verticality, density, complexity, walking, and evolution. The result, as we saw in Syracuse, is a desire for the physical feel of the rural but the economic realities of the urban. In an environment regulated by limits and prone to illusion, this incongruity is an impediment to becoming a functional, sustainable city. Places like Tooele County, physically separated from the rest of the Wasatch Front but closely connected economically, still have the choice. We live in a crowded and changing place. Urbanization continues to dominate the region, and the transition to the truly urban will be, for Intermountain westerners, a leap of faith.

Getting Back to Rural

Cold Springs Valley, already a laboratory for life in the Great Basin, has also become a boxing ring for the city versus the country. As the serpentine shape of the City of Reno expands into the open desert that many consider their getaway from the city, the notions of urban and rural have come to the punches of politics and the state legal system. Washoe County, in the process of crafting a plan for the North Valleys, considered a clustering approach that would boost the area's average density from three units per acre to four units per acre while preserving more land for schools and parks. The North Valleys Citizens Advisory Board didn't like the suggestion. "A lot of people don't want density transfers," said a board member, adding that rural character means more than putting parks and schools in the open space; it also means leaving open space in people's yards.[9]

Others took the city to court. Early in 2005, a group of residents calling themselves "Citizens for Cold Springs" sued the City of Reno for annexing seven thousand acres in Cold Springs Valley to the north of them, most of it owned by Lifestyle Homes. Lifestyle and ten other property owners approached the city about the annexation, which would encompass fifty-seven hundred new houses, because much of the county's zoning would allow only one house per forty acres.[10] The new houses might need to import water from Honey Lake fifty miles away in California by building a giant pipe from one basin to the other. "It's enormous," said one Honey Lake area resident in early 2007. "I don't see how any precipitation can keep up with the water in that pipe."[11] The suit alleged that the city went outside its sphere of influence legislated by the Truckee Meadows Regional Planning Agency, the area's regional planning body.

Citizens for Cold Springs consists of residents living in the area just to the north of the White Lake playa. In the soil horizons of modern Cold Springs Valley habitation, this area is the layer below Woodland Village. It sits sandwiched between White Lake and the Lifestyle Homes construction site, a neighborhood of ranch houses and mobile homes, of no sidewalks and irrigation ditches, of cottonwood trees dropping thin yellow leaves on rarely swept streets. The neighborhood, along with the whole valley, used to be part of unincorporated Washoe County, and received its services from the county sheriff and its water from wells and used septic systems in place of sewers. Although most residents worked fifteen or twenty minutes away in central Reno, the city was over the hill, out of sight and mind. Peavine Mountain dominated the horizon, but it was a different side of the mountain than the urbanites saw. The lawsuit they filed was not just about the City of Reno going outside its jurisdictional bounds but also outside its moral right. It was about deeper feelings of rural freedom of and urban encroachment on the people of Cold Springs. "I moved out here seven years ago to get away from rooftop to rooftop," Tony Midmore, the group's leader, told the Associated Press at the time. "It's a peaceful area. You can see the stars at night. We don't have traffic up and down the road. We don't have noise and pollution."[12]

On another clear fall day, I get a different view of Cold Springs Valley, courtesy of Tony Midmore. Midmore is driving me in his pickup up a fifty-degree slope on Petersen Mountain, the long ridge that hems in Cold Springs Valley to the west, and runs north to near Pyramid Lake. Riding with Midmore embodies the allure of Reno's rural life. He had skirted around a gate on two ruts in the sagebrush past a trailer with a rusty basketball standard, then pushed uphill, briefly considering taking a moderate switchback to the top of the ridge, then deciding against it with a grin.

"I was in Search and Rescue for fourteen years," says Midmore, who is thirty-nine and wearing crisp dark blue jeans, Blade-style sunglasses, and a freshly mowed flat-top.[13] He's an avionics technician for the Air National

Guard at Reno-Tahoe International Airport and a lifelong resident of the Reno area. He settled in Cold Springs when he and his wife split up, moving from the house they owned in Sparks to the manufactured home in a Cold Springs subdivision that had been built in the late 1970s.

When we get to the top of the ridge a few seconds later, we get out and face what Midmore wants to show me: Cold Springs Valley, rural paradise. We see the valley in its stages: the ancient lakebed, the access road on its west side, houses like Midmore's on its east side, Woodland Village and similar developments beyond, and the hilly territory slated for more Lifestyle houses. "You can tell by the trees where the existing homes are," Midmore says. It's true, but other than the trees, it is difficult to pick out many differences between the territories of Citizens for Cold Springs and Woodland Village. But to Midmore, it's a different world. "We still have ditches and it's kind of a rural area," he says. Everybody is on a community well system. But it's not just that. "We are still backwoods here," he says. "The North Valleys are typically lower income. We're regular folks, not a lot of attorneys and not well-schooled." And yet, Cold Springs is also fifteen minutes to downtown. A place like Cold Springs is the best of both worlds, what first prompted the nineteenth-century railroad suburbs in the first place—access to work in the city and a respite in the country.

Midmore's house is located on a cul-de-sac, on a pie slice–shaped lot where the tip meets the street. His backyard is currently bare, he says, because he's tired of dealing with it. But that's the nice thing about what he calls the "rural code": It's flexible. The neighborhood is actually something of a lapsed suburbia. It used to have CC&Rs, like provisions for no trees blocking people's views, but they expired because no one cared about them enough to enforce them. Now, rusty engine blocks and ham radios are strewn about the Cold Springs yards. Midmore's neighbors have five old cars in their yard. "You put up with it until it's really bad. You try to sell your house, and it's devalued by your neighbors," he says. "It's freedom."

One of Midmore's neighbors moved to Reno two years ago from San Jose, and her vision of the place, like that of many others, was as a more pastoral foil to the Bay Area but with the burgeoning employment opportunities of the Nevada economy. Once in Reno, she sought to live somewhere that marked the difference between California and Nevada. "I didn't move from San Jose so my dog couldn't run around," she says. "The thing is, I already came from suburbia, in San Jose." Moving back to Cold Springs was a way to get back to her rural Michigan roots. "I have a third of an acre," she says. "I have twenty-three trees in my front yard, nineteen in back. I have horses in the backyard, which I love, because it's one-acre lots behind me." Like Midmore, she relishes the freedom. "There's a mutual let it slide," she says.

People in Cold Springs like Midmore, as opposed to the people moving into Woodland Village, see themselves more as salt-of-the-earth people of the land. They converse with both the ecology of the basin and the void beyond. They run their dogs on White Lake when the water dries up and notice when their stepping stones sink in the alluvial sand. They ride their all-terrain vehicles (ATVs) and dirt bikes out into the BLM land beyond, and no one tells on them if the bikes aren't registered. They talk about the hydrology of the Cold Springs basin, how "no water comes in and no water comes out." They lament that Lifestyle Homes has added much more impermeable surface to the valley, where water can't infiltrate the water table into their well systems, and insist that Woodland Village has so much drainage infrastructure and open space because the old-timers made them do it.

But they do wonder how White Lake could be better put to use. They'd like to see Lifestyle Homes dredge out a lot of it, so it's good for something like waterskiing or for buildings. "In the middle of the playa, if someone wants to build, there's probably more value to that," Midmore says, staring out into the enigmatic glare of the lake bed. "Otherwise it's just a spot in the middle of the valley."

Reno, Urban Growth Machine

Looking back toward central Reno, where he drives every day for work, Tony Midmore sees an issue of logic. "Reno was on the river; it was a crossroads," he says. "It was a logical place to have industry and a city."

Since then, however, Reno has been thwarting logic as its tentacles have stretched outward. Many urban geographers have argued that ever since the mid-nineteenth century, industrial and residential growth did not grow neatly in a concentric ring but jumped around erratically. Richard Walker describes that in the Bay Area the biggest factor of decentralization of manufacturing was "industrialization itself . . . the force of technical and market change in capitalist accumulation," where industries can "erupt in quite unexpected venues."[14] In the modern Great Basin, this process is aided by additional land and resource constraints and Reno's new identity as a recreation capital. The extreme example is Winnemucca

Ranch, a piece of land twice as far from the city center as Cold Springs, that Reno has proposed to annex in order to allow a developer to build eight thousand houses in a "recreation-oriented" subdivision with trails for hiking, cycling, and horses and a "dude ranch."[15]

"Who is in charge of our city? Is it the urban-growth machine?" wrote one *Reno Gazette Journal* reader about Winnemucca Ranch. "Drive up to Winnemucca Ranch and ask yourself: Should it be urban/suburban sprawl all the way out there, out where the antelope and sage grouse live?"[16]

Midmore feels the same about Cold Springs. "It's not a logical extension. If the city was expanding like a balloon, you could see it coming. Out here they made this big snake thing." He objects to the zoning of land between the U.S. 395 freeway and Peavine Mountain as industrial, preferring "estate housing" in the foothills. "Why are you building twenty miles outside of the city when there's so much land inside the city?" It isn't just the concept that Midmore objects to. He sees the city as out of control, salivating over growth, corrupted by money, and cowering in the shadow of the litigious threat of developers. The only thing he sees in density is greed.

The line between sprawl and the rural lifestyle that Citizens for Cold Springs live is blurry, though. Midmore isn't for building more transit to Cold Springs, and he has a hard time with the hard line of an urban growth boundary. And one of the main reasons projects pushing Reno's edge are selling is the same as why Midmore is trying to stop them: the attempt to make urbanization rural.

Reno city planners see Cold Springs as an opportunity within the economic and natural constraints of the city and region. "Other areas of potential expansion will not likely provide the amount of unconstrained land that could support industrial and business park uses," a 2006 planning staff report concluded. "The Cold Springs area is located north and south of the freeway, has direct rail access, existing public water and sewer systems to expand upon, a fire station, an elementary school, and the availability of unconstrained property that is suitable for light industrial/commercial uses which provide employment."[17] Even "rural" development like Cold Springs, because of its mere presence, can be the rationalization for more urban development.

Reno City Council member Dwight Dortsch, who represents the district encompassing the North Valleys, says it is unrealistic to leave an area like Cold Springs Valley, with Woodland Village, to the supposedly rural county. "Woodland Village had already been approved, and it was pretty dense. You're going to need services there that the county doesn't provide. You can't build the restaurants and other commercial needed there in the county," Dortsch tells me. "When the county approves all those homes, it's not rural anymore."[18] I had asked Midmore if he would like to have places to shop within walking distance, if he got tired of going two valleys over for groceries. "I don't plan out shopping trips, so of course I'd love to have someplace nearby," Midmore says. "But that's not why I'm here."

Why he's here is slipping away, just as quickly as the definitions of what is rural and what is urban in the changing landscape of Cold Springs Valley. "We're a subdivision but with ditches and no sidewalks, and the expectation of doing whatever you want," Midmore says. "Suburban these days is getting down to CC&Rs. There's urban, there's suburban and rural, but there's something missing there. That's what we are. That's what we used to be."

A Process of Refinement

If not at Cold Springs Valley, then where does Reno end and the fierce emptiness and supposed rugged individualism of the Great Basin begin? East of the incorporated city, chains of houses and jobs reel out into the Great Basin. These have been some of the fastest-growing places in the United States, bolstered by open space and the booming economy of the last few decades.

Truckee Meadows, which comprises Reno, Sparks, and the adjacent built areas of unincorporated Washoe County, ends abruptly at the Virginia and Pah Rah mountains. But like the Wasatch Front, modern metro Reno pushes through the ranges into the basins beyond. With this larger frame of reference, the City of Reno's "snake" out to Cold Springs that Tony Midmore describes is only the beginning of a Medusa's head of growth. According to the Nevada state demographer, the six counties of Washoe, Carson City, Storey, Douglas, Lyon, and to some degree, Churchill, form a network of commuting, to jobs originally concentrated in Reno but which subsequently have erupted along its edges.[19] These jobs have pushed the metropolitan fringe and brought the Big Open into the urban shadow.

From 2001 to 2005, the job base of Storey County, which lies directly to the east of Reno, increased by 60 percent. Storey County and Lyon County, the next county over, combined to add nearly thirteen hundred jobs over the same time period.[20] On the corridor formed by the Truckee River, Interstate 80, and Union Pacific and Burlington Northern railroads, several industrial parks are under construction; these include collections of large distribution centers and factories at Fernley in Lyon County, where Amazon, Sherwin Williams, Quebecor, and MSC industrial supply distribution have built sprawling facilities.

The king of them all will be the Tahoe-Reno Industrial Center, which, at 102,000 acres—roughly the size of five San Franciscos or Parises—hopes to engulf half of Storey County to become one of the largest industrial parks in the United States.[21] "Vast and promising. Strategically superior in every sense," exclaims the TRI Center's broker on the project's Web site. "A sprawling testament to the adventurous spirit of the West. Visionary development. Unrivaled transportation advantages. Opportunity as far as the eye can see. If you're ready to expand your company's horizons and stake your claim on the all-important western frontier, there's only one place to do it: Tahoe-Reno Industrial Center."

The jobs combined with the space have created the opportunity for more people to live out in Storey and Lyon counties. In 2005, Lyon County became the fastest-growing county in Nevada and the seventh-fastest-growing county in the United States.[22] The zoning for much of the valley is one house per five acres. "It's going to look like a sea of houses," a Lyon County planner says. And a sea of septic systems. Planners are becoming concerned about the septic density leaching out nitrates into the watershed, and the overappropriation of water rights in the valley, where each landowner often drills his or her own well.

But Lyon County is not even the edge of metro Reno. Or, if places like Fernley, Tahoe-Reno Industrial Center, and the Carson River Valley are the edge of Reno, then its hyperedge is Fallon and Churchill County, where many residents work in Fernley, whose industrial growth is itself possible because of the resources and workforce of Reno. A quarter of the county's residents in 2000 had moved from out of state in the last five years, the vast majority coming from other western states. From 1990 to 2000, the percentage of people working outside of the county nearly doubled, going from 8 percent to 15 percent.[23] The chain of jobs and houses runs out into the Great Basin, farther than anything that appears to be urban.

Unlike Lyon County, Churchill County's planners still consider it rural. But while agriculture jobs are more plentiful in Churchill County than in the United States in general, agriculture only comprises 3.8 percent of jobs in the county.[24] And the urban mentality is saturating Churchill County. People moving to the Reno area from California may have lived only thirty miles from work in California but it took them two hours, one planner explains. Here, it's the opposite. It's sixty-three miles to Reno, and you can get there in less than an hour. Some residents make that commute, but many others work in the new industrial jobs of Fernley: The jobs and houses of metro Reno build off one another out into the seemingly endless space of the Basin.

Churchill County's growth piggybacks on affordability and space; unlike Lyon County's ranchette rage, the typical scenario here is a manufactured house plopped on a treeless lot. In Churchill County, manufactured is almost assumed, unless it's advertised as "stick-built." Such developments rarely require any entitlement process. This far out, it's not the Lennars and Pultes of the world but also local people who are cashing in on the arrival of metro Reno to Churchill County. "We still have a good ole boys' system," a planner told me. "If you want to do something, it just takes money."

The point of this series of stories is to grasp the long gradient of urbanity stretching out into the space of the Great Basin. Places like Cold Springs, Fernley, and Fallon provide the jobs, the housing, and perhaps most important, the space that is the catalyst for the jobs and quality of life that are the urban Intermountain West's strongest pull factors. And yet each of these places is more taken with its own ruralness than its urbanness. Within this gradient are many different hues of rurality, from the junky freedom of Citizens for Cold Springs to the ranchette haven of Lyon County, to the real agriculture of Fallon. The farther out one goes, the more the urban ideas of Reno and Salt Lake City begin to interact with the ideas of the Great Basin of the last 150 years: space, waste, ruggedness, solitude, and doom.

But the rural ideal keeps reeling out into the Basin. Perhaps the most prominent developer in Churchill County is a man named Mick Casey. Casey's world stretches over his ranches, over Fallon several times, and out into Fernley and Reno where many of his buyers work. Casey, who is from Fallon, has developed some thirty-five subdivisions, ranging in size from 5 to 140 units, most with manufactured houses.

Casey has developed a magic touch to turn rural ag land into urban land for housing with the help of the Holy Spirit. By asking around I find him at his ranch out beyond Middlegate, at the foot of the Clan Alpine Mountains. You can't see the ranch as you drive down the washboard road that turns off the highway until you're upon it, a scattering of mobile homes, horse trailers, and semi-truck cabs in a gentle ravine where the country opens up to the rolling sagebrush. He runs two thousand cattle on a million acres watered by six inches of rain a year. When I show up, he's feeding cattle but, asking me if I really want to know the stories of his conversion of ag land to urban land, tells me to get out of the cold and into his truck.[25]

"I was raised Catholic," he tells me when we're sitting in the bench of his pickup cab, Casey having removed his black knit balaclava to reveal a thick, weather-scarred face. "You had to be sinless from Sunday to Sunday. I couldn't do that. I never took communion and felt right. I thought when I die, I'll just go to this black place. And I didn't want to go to heaven because I wouldn't know anybody there. If they let me in there would be all this sin and I'd pollute the thing." A friend from the Seventh Day Adventist Church asked Casey if he'd ever had a God talk. He said, no, we've never had a God talk. He told the friend he'd like to meet God. "So I started a relationship with God," Casey continues. "I said, 'I want to know you and be known by you.' I started to hear God and have dreams. I'd see visions as clear as this," Casey gestures out to the open basin on the other side of the windshield. He had a dream with a house with a roof made of abalone shells but dark inside and a fence made of railroad ties and hog wire. He was walking outside around the ranch one night and he asked, "Why don't I hear from you, Lord?" Then he heard a voice: "Because. You. Don't. Listen." Casey had a relationship with God like that.

"One thing God told me was that whatever you put your hand to will prosper," Mick Casey says. By that time, he was a player in the Churchill County real estate market. He had first bought forty acres at age eighteen, then another forty, which was a ranch in Dixie Valley, over the mountains from the valley he lives in now. "I watched other people do it. It seemed like an easy way to make money. You didn't have to labor for it. You just took a risk." A friend said he was losing his ranch because of foreclosure; he wasn't making the payments. Casey had some land, but he owed a lot of money. It was about 180 acres on the northwest side of Fallon. Casey went out to the ranch and said a prayer and poured a few drops of olive oil on the ground. He said "Lord, I want the ranch, but not if it's going to be harmful. If I'm going to have it, you have to make a way." A bank lent him the money and when the auction opened at the Fallon courthouse, Casey was the only one there. He bid $100 over the price and got the ranch. He cut it into twenty-acre parcels and sold them. The ranch was taken out of agriculture. "It was a poor piece of ground," Casey tells me in the truck. "I made $100,000." Another day, he saw a nice piece of property. He got out the oil and said a prayer. Again he said, "Lord, I don't want it if it's not your will." It was owned by another friend of his and he was selling it for $250,000. At the last minute he got the money and got the land. He cut that land up into 34 one-acre lots. He sold the lots to a builder and they put stick-built houses on them. So he built up his confidence. The next ranch was ten-acre parcels. He said if I drill the well, you have to put in the septic tank as the down payment. His buyers were locals from Fallon. He told them they could buy a single-wide trailer for $100, and for another $300 a month, they could own the land. "Now they're landowners and they feel good about themselves," Casey says. "The Holy Spirit is a down payment for an eternal life."

These days, Casey doesn't use the oil as much as he should. Maybe it's because he doesn't feel very good about what's happening in Fallon. He doesn't like that the farms are chopped up. But it's not his fault: He builds where the zoning tells him. As for the Californians, he's glad that at least it's the ones who are dissatisfied with the California lifestyle who move here. And Casey spends most of his time in Clan Alpine, ranching cattle on what he calls his one hundred–mile ranch. It's not his land but the American public's, managed by the BLM. Don't bring up that distinction to Casey. He claims these are his grazing rights and the federal government is circling his wagon. On one side is the U.S. Fish and Wildlife Service, trying to list the sage grouse as an endangered species; on another is the Army Corps of Engineers, trying to declare the accumulation of runoff in the bottom of his valley a wetland. On another is the Nature Conservancy, the group he calls the purchasing agent for the federal government. It buys land from ranchers under the guise of keeping it free of development, he accuses, but is really intending to sell it to the federal government in order to pad the collateral for the national debt. However, ranching is not profitable, for Casey or for anybody in Churchill County anymore. Casey made his killing building the city. With ranching, you're fortunate to get a 3 percent return. For Casey, running cattle is just a way of life, or a hobby, a rehashing of the past.

I ask him about the mountain range on the other side of the valley, the rather large Desatoya Range, which tops out at ten thousand feet directly across from us. I think of William Fox's comment about how the clear air of the Great Basin creates optical illusions and disorientation for the viewer surveying the landscape around him. Today, the sharp winter light of late afternoon articulates the Desatoyas, their fingered foothills, and their frigid blue ridges and snowfields. "They're a lot bigger than they look," Casey says. "I probably know those mountains better than anyone else alive." For fifteen years he made a living trapping bobcats in the high country above the ranch. He was paid $1,000 per bobcat pelt, and he caught enough bobcats to get a new four-wheel-drive truck every year.

I ask Casey how long he plans to stay out at Clan Alpine. But we're not thinking on the same scale, the same means and ends, the same size of the world. Casey's continuum isn't the city and the country but his ground and the heavens above and the hell below. "*This* is not my home," Casey says, wrinkled eye sockets encasing watery eyes staring out beyond the Desatoyas. "This is a refining process with God. I'll keep refining and refining. Then I'm outta here." The space we see in the clarity and abyss of the Basin is, indeed, an illusion.

Tooele Valley: Future City of the Great Basin

From the end of Mick Casey's one hundred–mile ranch, it's only a little over two hundred miles until you hit the edge of the Great Basin's other advancing, celestial city. Between Churchill and Tooele counties are only three Nevada counties. This is what the real rural Great Basin jurisdictions have been reduced to. At an east–west cross section of the fortieth parallel, only three Great Basin counties are free from the urbanization associated with Salt Lake and Reno—Lander, Eureka, and White Pine. Their combined population is 15,000 and declining.

And it's not entirely accurate to compare Tooele Valley to an empty Salt Lake Valley. Tooele Valley, like Lyon and Churchill counties with their naval stations, energy production, waste dumps, and ranches, is scattered with 150 years' worth of different American ideas of the Great Basin, already forming the layers upon which the growing metropolis will build. Whatever city rises here will be truly a Great Basin city, one range and one basin removed from the comforting Wasatch and its water. Does that mean it will adapt more to nature's constraints of water, energy, and topography?

It hasn't yet. The most popular idea in Tooele Valley these days is of unfettered freedom of space. Everything is big here. When you order a meal combo at the Iceberg Drive-Inn, you get a thirty-two-ounce soda— that's the size of the original Big Gulp. When I drive into Tooele Valley a decade after Drew Hall, I see the same emptiness, but it's filling in with growth. The attraction of Tooele Valley is the blank canvas of the open space. Much of Tooele County's growth has occurred along the base of the Oquirrh Mountains between Tooele City and Interstate 80, in the township of Erda, which contains about twenty-three hundred people. Refugees from the town of Tooele and Salt Lake Valley have discovered what Drew Hall discovered and have taken up residence on five-acre lots. They want an extreme degree of the freedom and informality Tony Midmore valued about his rural neighborhood. They want to "stay rural," even though there isn't much agriculture here anymore. Tooele's ag industry is paltry. Only half a percent of Tooele County's jobs are in agriculture, and a job in Tooele County is half as likely to be an ag job in comparison to the nation as a whole. It is quickly losing the few ag jobs it had.[26]

Yet Erda is obsessed with the legend of the farmland that it once was, the Mormon alfalfa and winter wheat, and of the ten families who settled here, including the Droubays, after whom the area's main north–south road is named. As early as the 1950s, the farmland was subdivided into five-acre lots, but no one built on them until the early 1990s.

More than anything, I notice how stark and alone the houses look. There is nothing in the built landscape binding them together. No trees. They are connected by roads, not streets. I am struck that in the Great Basin, in an open landscape naturally uncomfortable to humans, that we have built a place that is so collectively place-less.

"This was always farmland," one Erda homeowner tells me in front of her pink stuccosaurus house. They bought their five acres for $25,000 with water; now it's worth over $100,000 without water. Water rights staunchly modify the value of so many acres. For example, homeowners purchase one acre-foot for their culinary uses but need four acre-feet to irrigate the five-acre spread. One homeowner reserves two acre-feet for the house and three acre-feet for the land. They are constantly drilling deeper. One resident drilled a 150-foot well, and then, when a neighbor's well started to sputter, drilled another 100 feet.

The talk here is horses: The newcomers are taken by the notion that everyone else has them. "Almost everybody here has horses except us," says one resident. "That's kind of the big attraction." Another new property owner says his wife and daughter want horses, but he's not so sure. The neighbors have sheep and a llama and horses; he says they can just look at them. "Originally, the attraction was the horses," another says. "Now it's about people having space."

And residents look for ways to use their space. "We got lots of toys so the kids can play around," says one resident with a four-car garage. One new homeowner, who just completed a sixty-three hundred square-foot colonial-style house, is trying to figure out what to do with all the land. He is considering planting natural wild grass, which attracts wildlife. Others use their land as a doorstep to an even bigger spread: the BLM land in the Oquirrhs. "I can just go jump on my four-wheels and go," one resident says. "We almost have too much space," says another five-acre owner.

But another resident says, "Houses are packing in. It's bad. It's getting more and more congested. We thought it was rural when we moved here. It's still rural but it's getting encroached upon." Says another, "It used to be there was never any traffic out here. Now if you're on SR 36 at the wrong time you might as well be anywhere in Salt Lake." And despite the pastoral life sought by so many Erdites, they have to buy groceries somewhere. Out in the unincorporated county, there aren't a whole lot of options, and most people get most everything in the new Wal-Mart Supercenter, which was likewise glad for the room to spread out. "The evil corporation is where most people shop," one homeowner admits.

Many of Erda's colonizers aren't thinking that they'll stay here. "We'll downsize when the kids go to college," says one homeowner. "We just bought some land in Montana so we can go back to rural when we retire. In ten years we'll be there."

Nicole Cline is Tooele County's planner and is charged with making sure that the county remains rural at all costs. The people Cline calls "the custom-home crowd" don't want to be incorporated because they want the rural flavor. The county's elected officials, meanwhile, didn't know how to react to the county's growth, so they have tried to preserve the closest thing to the past. The county's vision, Cline says, is to try and remain a rural county.[27]

The county's old plan was "kind of a coloring book," according to Cline, about sixteen pages long. It didn't address any of the relevant questions about growth. During the general plan process earlier in this decade, the county had to ask itself whether, with all the urban growth it was receiving, it wanted to become a county that, like Salt Lake County, would provide a level of service almost equal to that of a municipality. But to elected officials, rural meant longer wait times for police and fire, no curb and gutter, and roads resurfaced not as often.

Most important, it meant larger lot zoning. "What people want is rural character, some elbow room between you and the guy next door," Cline says. "The idea is, people on larger lots are more independent. Those who live on smaller lots bring urban expectations with them." Indeed, one Erda couple told me about their struggle for large lots like they were guarding a border. "We're resistant to anything under five acres. We've been very aggressive about keeping it five acres. Every week we have challenges, like when property owners across the street want to subdivide into quarter-acre lots," they said.

Are large lots sprawl? "Yes, they are," Cline says, "but the planning commissioners have it stuck in their heads that that means rural." And despite the space between the houses, the aquifers below are becoming congested. Residents know how much pressure development is putting on these water resources and recount their own wells drying up, and worse, producing undrinkable water. At a county planning meeting in the other unincorporated area of Lake Point, Cline explained that, like many Great Basin communities, Lake Point has its own aquifer and recharge system that is separate from the rest of the groundwater under Tooele Valley. It feeds directly from the Oquirrhs and has been slower and slower to recharge with all the new development sucking more and more water. With the aquifer lacking recharge from mountain snowmelt, the saline water from the Great Salt Lake had begun pushing into the water table. Now, Cline reported, the water in many parts of Lake Point was too salty to drink. Several residents had told Cline that they could not even use the water to irrigate their lawns because its salinity burned them.[28]

As an alternative, Tooele County planners presented the notion of "conservation" or "cluster" subdivisions, residential developments that employ smaller lots in order to create larger communal open spaces. Planners had suggested clustering and conservation subdivisions as an alternative to the five-acre matrix, where lots would be smaller and the extra land, as much as 40 percent of the total, concentrated in a communal open space to be managed by a homeowners' association.

Cline is a supporter of conservation subdivisions and their clustering concept. As a refugee from the Wasatch Front to Tooele herself, she understands why residents want the space between them. But Cline sees through the veneer of calling this lifestyle "rural" or "agricultural." The reality is, one needs much larger pieces of land than five acres to make agriculture more than a conceit or a hobby—even Mick Casey had 100 miles of ranch and it was a hobby for him. As another county planner pointed out, the rural residential and agricultural protection zones pursue completely different objectives. The rural residential zone with a minimum lot size of five acres (RR-5) "is aimed to promote a rural feel in a way that supports single-family zoning. The A-20 zone is intended to protect agriculture and to preserve greenbelt open spaces. The RR-5 zoning district really does neither of these."

"You never saw John Wayne riding on five acres. He had a much bigger spread," Cline says. "Fifty years ago, people wanted large lots here because the intent was agricultural operation. But now, only 5 percent have horses. Ninety-five percent can't afford horses or their job is too demanding. An eight-hour day becomes a ten-hour day. When are you going to have time to do horses? The reality is, people moving in want to *see* horses.

"By altering subdivision design, we can give them that," Cline continues. "People just want to live where they feel like their neighbor's not breathing down their throat. So let someone else [run horses]. A conservation easement held by someone else. Make it more of a public resource, something that creates a feeling of distance between neighbors."

But Tooele County citizens often see clustering as a threat to the rural way of life. Erda prohibited cluster subdivisions in its master plan, and in July 2006, the Tooele County Planning Commission asked Lake Point residents for their input about banning cluster subdivisions. People who came to the meeting liked the idea. They associated clustering with the forces that were undoing the rural character of their neighborhood, despite the goal to create larger, more beneficial pieces of open ground. Clustering also meant infringement of property rights: a homeowner "did not want clustering in the area and the landowner's privileges taken away." It meant infringement of freedom: another "moved from South Jordan because she did not like all of the restrictions that were in place there she likes the rural atmosphere in the Lakepoint area." It meant a break from the sacrosanct past: one woman was "afraid that their lifestyle that is here now will change," while another man "likes the open space in the area so that his children can have the lifestyle that he had growing up [and] wants it left rural." It meant domination by the urban developer Goliath over the rural landowner David: someone did not "want the developers to be able to come in and take over the area and not be able to have what the landowners want."[29] The people of Lake Point believed their stated goal of preserving the "character" of the area could only be accomplished by extended amounts of privately owned space between houses, and not by a public resource. At one level, the idea of open space is clear: unbuilt land that relieves the congestion of urban areas. People in Tooele County seem to believe that a "rural lifestyle" can combat everything that is bad about an urban lifestyle. Many see their efforts of defending sprawl as thwarting sprawl. One homeowner characterizes her efforts as "trying to keep it a greenbelt between Stansbury and Tooele."

At another level, these proceedings make one realize that exactly what open space *is* is unclear. As a term, it is vague: It's not "play space," "gathering space," "wildlife space," as if the very vagueness of the void is the important part. Tooele County planners have found that all the interests involved have different ideas of what open space is. Officially, to Tooele County, open space takes on a decidedly superficial meaning. The county general plan, which puts a "high value" on open space, gave three definitions for open space: (1) an area where ranching can occur, but land still appears as open space; (2) an area where crop lands are accepted but appears as open space; (3) lands that provide an identity, such as foothills and vistas. All three focus on only the appearance of the land, not the use, ownership, or scale. Open space, for example, can be used, looked at, or simply dwell in one's mind as a place that exists. It can be public or private. These aspects are significant not only for the space itself but also for the spaces around it.

Such definitions obscure the lack of discussion about what open space is actually used for—and the appropriate scale for those activities. Tooele County planners, though, have been trying to answer these questions. One planner reported to the planning commission and concluded that "a private resident does not get a private benefit from an open space area."[30] Cline concentrates on the synergy of scale and use of open space. Instead of the more-is-better approach, Cline urges a look at how the use of the land should influence its scale. Pieces of property of five, ten, or even twenty acres border on moronism, Cline says. "It's not enough land to do something, and too much land to do anything. You mow it once, you've had enough of that. You don't have the water shares for it. It's not viable for anything. Then your buddy brings out his old car. It becomes a nightmare." In other words, these pieces of land, while open space, are not meaningful space.

An example of what she's talking about might be found at a place like the Village Homes subdivision in Davis, California. Designed and built primarily in the 1970s, Village Homes was a revolution in suburban subdivision design in its time. The project's concept, apart from a focus on community and a semicommunal lifestyle, is efficiency of space: Lots are small; streets are narrow, and, like the conservation subdivision idea of Tooele County, 40 percent of the total land is dedicated to open space. Village Homes' open space, though, feels different than that of other suburban parks. The space is so efficiently allocated that every patch is being put to use for something: playgrounds, grape vines, citrus, gardens, and large recreational fields. Ironically, with this urban mentality of meaningful space, Village Homes manages to take on rural character.

On the other hand, open space could be just the opposite. To Cline, open space has another meaning entirely: The openness of open space means the possibilities of its future use. The misconceptions of rural character and open space have a large impact on planners. "Future planners are going to come under extreme pressure to do infill. That's poor planning. Remember, this is an area that's supposed to be kept rural. Septic absorption wells will compete for water. It will be a continual race to dig deeper. So then you put in water lines, but it's not efficient in cost," Cline says, before adding, "Nobody's going to damn you for having left them an option. They're going to damn you for not doing so."

If Cline's thought train sounds less and less suited for a county that's decided to "remain rural," that's because it isn't. It's an urban way of thinking: a thought pattern of efficiency, of thinking about what will work within a large whole, and of building around public resources. It comes down to the basic notion of how one's household fits into the metropolitan picture. For Cline, the best way to keep the character of today's Tooele County is to adopt an urban way of thought.

Ted Knowlton, of Envision Utah, who was a planner at Fregonese Calthorpe Associates in Portland, Oregon, saw such a synergy between the rural and the urban in Portland's development over the last thirty years. Portland is well-known for the urban lifestyle it has been able to foster, but Knowlton believes what set the stage for Portland's urbanity was a desire to preserve agriculture and other rural uses. The love of urban places, he observes, was fostered by a love of what was outside the city, and the type of lifestyle necessary for the majority of the residents to live to preserve it. "They have an ethic throughout the population that their farms matter and their forests matter," Knowlton says. "When I talk to people about farms here, they don't care as much."

But Tooele doesn't want to hear it. "We'll die with the gun in our hands over the rural issue," Cline says. "We're not going to admit we're urban."

Overlake

Drew Hall, the Seattle developer, meanwhile, proposed a different kind of relationship between the rural and the urban. By the time Hall prepared to develop his twenty-seven hundred acres, it was apparent that Tooele would not become a ghost town with the closure of the Army Depot. By

In Tooele Valley, Erda's rural of space (above) sits side by side with Overlake's rural of place (below).

the late 1990s, the large national and local developers were filling out Stansbury Park, and the City of Tooele was preparing to annex the rings of land around it. In 1990, Tooele was building twenty homes per year, and by 2000, it increased the pace to eight hundred houses per year.[31]

The deficit between the perception of Tooele as "hell and gone" from Salt Lake and its convenient location for commuters had evened a little. By 2000, 43 percent of Tooele residents worked outside the county, up from 15 percent in 1990. By the mid-2000s, a consulting firm hired by the county estimated that three quarters of county residents commuted to jobs along the Wasatch Front. Tooele was becoming the new affordable housing market. Hall's notion of the metropolis that defies geographical barriers was becoming a reality around the Oquirrh Mountains. Naturally, Hall decided to target his development toward Salt Lake Valley workers who wanted affordable houses to own.

He approached architect and planner Mark Simpson of Seattle firm Bumgardner Associates for help in designing the project. Simpson says that Hall made some good pitches on why that location was good for residential development, noting Tooele Valley's easy auto commute into Salt Lake Valley and the low cost of its land relative to the rest of the metro area. "Of course, it did have the nation's largest stockpile of mustard gas," Simpson adds. "That seemed like a negative."[32]

Simpson took the job. His firm had designed adventurous projects in Seattle, such as mixed-use residential buildings with grocery stores in their bottom floors, and he offered Hall a chance to hitch himself to the bandwagon of the new urbanism and traditional neighborhood design, which, in the mid-1990s, was a much smaller wagon than exists today. Simpson took Hall on a tour of existing traditional neighborhood projects like Disney's Celebration in central Florida, Kentlands in Maryland, and Harbor Island in Memphis. Hall also scoped out the oldest parts of Salt Lake, the Avenues, Harvard/Yale, and Sugar House areas, admiring their front porches and the connectivity of their streets.

The pedestrian idea especially resonated with Hall, who is originally from a small town in Washington state called Carnation. He has fond memories of his town, population 325, where, as he describes, "everything was in walking distance" and he would "drink a fountain cherry coke almost every day after school" at the local store. Hall was nostalgic for the elements of Carnation that he remembered as a kid, such as accessing the entire town by his bicycle. "I thought back to my childhood on my bike. That was when I gained my freedom, by being able to go anywhere," Hall says. "I think we take away our kids' childhoods by not [allowing them to feel] like they can move about their neighborhoods." Simpson, meanwhile, recalls visiting neighborhoods in Salt Lake Valley while doing research for the project. "People kept saying they hated their neighborhood and just wanted to get out," Simpson says. "Even in these gated communities, everyone was so afraid of [people they referred to as] 'them,' whoever 'they' were."

Hall also romanticized the concept of the neighborhood market. "Forty years ago nearly every small community in America had a neighborhood market," read Hall's promotion materials. "Parents would send their children to pick up a quart of milk and the grocer would write the price on the family's tab. The town market was also the social center for the community; neighbors would often visit and get to know 'new-comers.' Not only did town markets provide a sense of community, but they also helped keep children out of trouble by providing them a place to go with friends."

This line of thinking gravitated toward the rural. Hall also noticed that "people in Utah have a sense of needing more space and land." Much of the growth in Tooele was being caused by Salt Lakers seeking not only affordable housing but also affordable places to stretch out, a mountain range away from the busy economic center. Hall could relate to the pastoral desires—after all, he came from tiny Carnation.

But Hall and Simpson's solution wasn't the "rural atmosphere" of large lots, rural infrastructure like wells and septics, or horses standing next to every house. Despite the same romantic glorification of the past that Hall's notions share with the Erda or Lake Point notion of rural, an important difference emerges. While the Erda approach eviscerates the collective public realm and forces the community into a position where the only options are six-lane highways and Wal-Mart, Hall is building around the public realm. His nostalgia concentrates not on escape and isolation but on gathering and connections. It was the town, not the country, he wanted to reproduce.

It was going to be a challenge. Hall and Simpson talked about what would work and what wouldn't work in Tooele. They concluded, for example, that studio condos wouldn't work because families tend to be large. They recognized that affordability was important and that the shift to public transportation would be slower than in other, larger cities. They concluded that it was important to build around schools, that the schools should be two-story buildings to conserve land, and that students of those schools should be able to walk to them. They analyzed the collective resources that the development could use to its advantage, like views, which benefit from a 3-percent grade down to the Great Salt Lake. And, they planned the meetinghouses of the Mormon congregations known as wards and stakes into the privileged positions at the intersections of the important street axes. They always analyzed the project as a piece of the whole of the metro Wasatch Front.

Hall and Simpson recognized the spectacular open views of the Great Basin, but they also recognized that those views needed a community framework, through the occasional concentration in the open desert. They created an innovative street pattern that worked within the framework of the old Mormon farm grid. Diagonal collectors (or "connectors") ran between the corners of the grid squares, creating important intersections both on the "main" old grid streets, like 2000 North, and within the squares. There were important public spaces planned into each kind of street and intersection. Intersections of grid arterial streets, like 2000 North, would harbor mixed-use commercial-residential development, while the centers of the old grid squares focused on civic spaces like parks, schools, and churches (see fig. 4.1). The scheme, with its recognition of external commercial neighborhood arteries with internal quiet neighborhood streets and pocket parks, evokes the classic "Neighborhood Unit" created by planner Clarence Perry in the 1920s.[33] At completion, Overlake would be as big as the existing town of Tooele, a more urban vision of the future abutting the old Mormon town.

Hall included a golf course amid his houses, and he put it to work. With water resources thin in Tooele Valley, he and the city devised a system that treated wastewater, created open space, and took care of nonculinary water uses. The Wastewater Treatment and Reuse Project would collect wastewater from the city, convey the water through gravity to a treatment plant, and then discharge the water to storage ponds between fairways.[34] It would reduce the demand for culinary water by forty-six hundred acre-feet, enough to supply almost ten thousand non-Erda households.[35] Perhaps most important, we see a "meaningful space." The space of the golf course and its ponds, carefully carved out of the neighborhood, is layered with uses: recreation, views, elbow room, water resources, and wastewater treatment.

Finally, Hall made sure his development would include a neighborhood market. Hall traveled across the United States with Simpson to find "the perfect town market." They found it in Belmont Forest, Virginia, where Hall walked through the door and "saw several of the locals

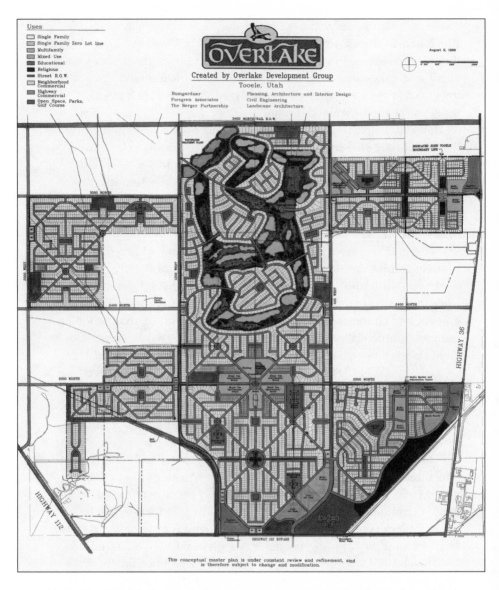

Figure 4.1. Overlake's master plan intertwines commercial and mixed-use development (larger darker lots) along the old Mormon farm grid of Tooele Valley with a diagonal grid connecting houses, parks, schools, and community places like LDS wards and stake buildings. (Adapted by author; image courtesy of Tooele Associates)

sitting at the counter, eating hamburgers and laughing with the cook." Hall named his store Jack's Market and sought to convey "a small, country store type feeling" with a "steeply pitched gable roof, covered front porch and surrounding veranda." The proprietor would even live above the store, and at 5 p.m. each evening, someone named "Colonel Chuck" would dine at the market's café.[36] Hall knew he wanted the name of this project to relate to Great Salt Lake because of the views, and the name of the hospital where his kids were born came to him. Looking down at the silvery basin, he decided what he would call the new project: Overlake.

In the late 1990s, Hall began building Overlake, a process that would unfold over several decades. He built Jack's, he built townhouses around it, and he built small starter houses by the future LDS stake house, leaving the more intensive development to future phases. Local developers drove by in their Ford F-250s to look at Hall's roundabout on 2000 North. Hall says that, as he expected, 70 percent of people buying at Overlake commute to Salt Lake Valley. Most are buying out here because of affordability: Two thousand to thirty-two hundred square-foot houses sell for between $185,000 and $200,000. The community is active: In a few instances, the neighborhood association rose up and fought Hall because he wasn't being hard enough on homeowners lagging in their compliance with the covenants. It is becoming a neighborhood with far more than its share of kids. In 2006, an Overlake Mormon ward set a record for most sets of twins in an LDS ward at 13, all below age 18.[37]

When one begins to embrace the ideas of connection and the public realm of efficiency of space, of Tooele Valley as part of the Wasatch Front metro area, interesting possibilities surface. Some in Nevada's Churchill County see agriculture not as a way of preserving false rurality but of making the real urbanity work. Farmers in Churchill County are experimenting with new crops, like cantaloupes: The high–low range of the area's temperatures produces an especially sweet cantaloupe, and farmers are now trying the same idea for grapes. Planners there see the management of nature as part of an urban whole. They point out that the agriculture around the canals and the naval air station actually complement each other because cows and crops don't care about the jet noise. Space becomes more meaningful and layered.

A cityscape that supports urban life doesn't have to be tall towers. It could be a more medium-density mix of houses, apartments, and commercial buildings with enough intensity to support transit and commercial services while also taming the alien scale of the Great Basin into human-scale places—all strung along a common transportation corridor like Route 36, defining a new shape of Tooele Valley. With such a scheme, transit, and hence, walking, would make sense as a dominant means of getting around. Researchers studying the relationship between land use and transit have found that ridership increases most dramatically when land use is taken from low density, such as quarter-acre lots, to medium density, 12 to 15 dwelling units per acre, which could be accomplished with single-family houses.[38]

Houses and open space, though, are only part of the equation. The other vital part of the urban future for metropolitan edge areas like Tooele County is jobs. Tooele County has the chance to wean its growth from providing bedrooms for Salt Lake Valley by adding more employment, creating the opportunity for its new residents to lessen their commutes and experience more of the urban energy of living and working nearby one another. And the creators of these jobs are likewise attracted to Tooele County's space and affordability. In 2007, CNN Money.com recognized Tooele County as one of 25 top counties in the United States for job growth in the first part of the decade.[39] Even in the recession, economic growth in the county has continued.[40] "They're still going to town here," Nicole Cline told me. Planners like Cline will face similar challenges to planning for housing developments in integrating these new plants and offices into an urban conception of space.

Cline, though, has her own idea about the key to Tooele Valley's urban future. Joking, I ask her about the possibility of a train over the Oquirrhs to transport Tooele residents to jobs in Salt Lake Valley. But she's serious when she answers yes. Kennecott, the mining company which has drilled copper and other ores out of Bingham Canyon, on the other side of the range, for one hundred years, has bored an extensive system of tunnels through the mountains to move ore. The company will likely stop mining in the next decade or two, and Cline has begun the process of putting dibs on the six-mile trans-Oquirrh rail tunnel. "The day they quit mining, what I've asked is, leave some of that rail," Cline says. "Then we've got the rail we need to get to West Valley City." Once in West Valley City, the rail could connect to the new Utah Transit Authority Trax light-rail lines that will be built on the valley's West Bench. On the Tooele side, the Kennecott rail could be connected to the Union Pacific rail to State Route 28. Cline says a retrofitted system would face the problem of subsidence, of a fault rupturing and the tunnel filling up with water, but that would be much cheaper than carving a new tunnel.

Providing Tooele Valley with a mode of rail transit that connects to the city where many of its residents work would, like Overlake, help change the valley from not merely urbanized but fully urban, fulfilling the potential of physical connections created by the economic ones. It lowers auto dependency, and thus energy dependency, and takes advantage of an existing resource.

To Cline, rail transport, not five-acre lots, is freedom. "Getting on public transportation to go to Tooele would be the most urban thing, but it could have rural elements," she says. "Why not have the train stop at trailheads? In this country, public transportation has always meant lower socioeconomic status. When Americans start to think along European lines of efficiency, it starts to go somewhere." Pulling off Cline's vision would take a miracle of bureaucratic cooperation involving at least four or five major agencies and corporations. Public support is questionable. "But," says Cline, "we'll have all sorts of support at eight dollars a gallon. In that time, a lot of these issues become moot. We'll have to be in an urban environment. Only those who really know how to work the land will live a rural lifestyle. You can't just run thirty or forty miles a day into work."

That day is a ways off in Tooele Valley, where urbanism struggles along. On a blustery day in October, I visit Drew Hall in his office, which is located above Jack's Store, where the inclement weather has apparently prevented the little league team from sitting out with ice cream cones on its veranda.

The streets of Overlake are mostly empty, as if Hall were manning a remote outpost like Mr. Kurtz. Inside Hall's perch, the mood is similar to the weather outside. "We have not been anywhere near as successful as I'd like to be," he reports, "because we've met stiff resistance from the City of Tooele. They view it as people coming over to take over their city."

In 1998, the Overlake development agreement Hall signed with the City of Tooele was a campaign issue because of its density. Hall began a long dispute with the city's mayor over aspects of the development agreement. The mayor wanted to limit residential growth in Tooele, so he did not fulfill the city's agreements with Overlake in regard to providing culinary water, Hall argues. The city also instituted a steep increase in impact fees for residential developers. Overlake was also promised secondary water, Hall alleges. Hall and his partners sued the city over the alleged mismanagement of development impact fees paid by Overlake to the city.[41]

On Hall's wall is a map of the intriguing diagonal street pattern he and Mark Simpson planned for Overlake. This, Hall tells me, has been changed. The City of Tooele widened Overlake's streets to a width that Hall believed would let cars go too fast. "Street hierarchy is important," Hall says. "Residential streets need to be calm. That concept has been missed by Tooele." The city also objected to the connectivity, forcing Hall into a cul-de-sac design. And the school district "didn't want anyone telling them what to do," so the two-story school became one story. By 2007, Hall had built fewer than a quarter of the four thousand housing units he planned to build by that year. Even if Overlake is allowed to build out according to its original plan, it still faces the problem of difficult connections to the rest of Tooele and the rest of the region over the Oquirrhs. Overcoming this will require more than just one forward-thinking developer, but leadership and consensus among public officials working together.

"It's a funny rural attitude," Hall says. "I'm sick and tired of fighting."

Many Tooele officials sadly agree with Hall, such as the city engineer, who tells me, "I think it's fantastic to plan the city like that." But, adds another city staffer, "It's hard to convince the city council what we need when it's beyond our lifespan."

Philosopher Marshall Berman notes the "paradoxical reality" that "in modern society, only the most extravagant and systematic 'thinking big' can open up channels for 'thinking small.'"[42] Creating a fine-grained urbanism in urbanizing places like Syracuse, Tooele County, Cold Springs, and Lyon County requires big thinking. It requires the acceptance that the economy has created the regional pattern of urbanization, but it's up to us to define how we live within that urbanization.[43]

Unlike the Mormon pioneers who determined the form of Salt Lake Valley, Tooele Valley has a place to learn from, an antitemplate in the valley next-door. But some are not optimistic about thinking big. "I say, go over and look at what they did wrong," Hall says gloomily from his outpost above Jack's Store, gesturing over the Oquirrhs. "You have an opportunity to not repeat the mistakes. But they're bound to do it. They're bound to do it and it makes me sick."

Public Land, Private Politics

Finding a New Urban Realm in the Great Basin

> It was never the West as landscape she resisted, only the West as
> transience and social crudity. And those she might transform.
> —Wallace Stegner, *Angle of Repose*

In South Jordan, Utah, in the southwest corner of the Salt Lake Valley,
up at the end of 11400 South Street and at the crest of a bluff overlooking
the great big bowl of this basin, is an apron of spent land marked by
decades of mining activity. The mining company that owns the land,
part of the largest unbuilt holding in the valley, is turning it into a place
to live and work. This place is named Daybreak because once you have
risen above the South Jordan populace on the entrance parkway, with its
giant copper-colored capital letters DAYBREAK set on a stone mount,
and cleared the bench, you can turn around and—depending on the time
and the season—watch the sun rise over Lone Peak, Twin Peaks, Mount
Olympus, the Pfeifferhorn, or Thunder Mountain, the sun like a molten
snowcone on the silhouette of any one of the Central Wasatch giants.

Salt Lake Valley may seem an evenly filled-in oval from maps and
some vantage points, but most of the development lies on the east side of
the valley. Most of the houses with views lie on the East Bench, the name
given to the table of higher ground against the Wasatch Mountains. In
Salt Lake City, the East Bench starts at around 1100 East Street—11 blocks
east of Temple Square—with the short, steep rise of the Wasatch Fault
and the climbing of brick bungalows up the slope. Going farther east and
higher up is like taking a course in twentieth-century architecture. Frank
Lloyd Wright makes an appearance past 1300 East, and then Abraham
Levitt. The farther you go up the East Bench, the bigger and more taste-
less the houses get, until the majestic edge of the valley, where massive

stucco, steel and concrete boxes cling to eroded slopes. The Wasatch wall hangs above these monsters and, apart from the weather sweeping across the valley and the sunsets, the view of the bleak Oquirrh range and the gray puddle of Great Salt Lake can be a tough sell.

Daybreak is pioneering the West Bench. It has taken the sunrise metaphor gleaned from the views to craft a message of new beginning in the valley. Until now, the West Bench has been empty because it has been a fallout zone for the nearby Bingham open-pit copper mine, that nearly mile-deep Great Basin earthwork that is one of the largest open-pit excavation sites in the world. The Kennecott Utah Copper Corporation, since bought out by international mining giant Rio Tinto, owns almost the entire west side of the Salt Lake Valley and much of the Oquirrh Mountains as a buffer for the mine, a spread twice the size of the District of Columbia. Some time ago, realizing that it would stop mining over the next few decades, Kennecott hatched an exit strategy from Salt Lake Valley: Plan a city on the west side of the valley, better than the one that's on the other side, build it, sell it, and leave.

That ambition is evident even in the first few completed phases of Daybreak, the first project of Kennecott Land and Salt Lake County's West Bench Master Plan, which plans eventually to house one million people. I've come here, cresting the hill up to the bench on a sparkling fall morning to walk Daybreak's model streets with Nathan Francis, a planner with Kennecott Land. So far, only about two thousand of the thirteen thousand homes have been built. The rest of the houses, plus 5.2 million square feet of office space, 2.4 million square feet of retail, and 1.5 million square feet of industrial space, will be built over the next fifteen years.[1] That's equivalent to the downtown of a medium-sized city, dropped on the West Bench. It is also another pod of houses and jobs that has moved out into the Great Basin on the surf of the booming economy earlier in the decade,[2] but Daybreak regards itself as a break from that pattern of sprawl. Like Overlake, it is the importation to Utah of new urbanism, a school of city planning, design, and development that recommends building cities made of walkable, diverse neighborhoods. This approach can mean smaller single-family residential lots with houses that greet the sidewalk with front porches instead of large garages; greater varieties of housing options; the mixing of these residences with stores, services, and offices so residents and workers can walk to many of the places they need to go; streets made for walking and bicycling and not just autos; and, perhaps most important, a variety of good public spaces. The goal of new urbanists is to make more complete, enjoyable neighborhoods that are themselves tied into the greater regional metropolis by balances of jobs and housing and easy access to transit systems. Unlike tiny Overlake languishing in Tooele Valley, Daybreak has emerged onto the landscape with much fanfare, as a heralded Step in the Right Direction, a collaboration of worldly West Coasters and locals, an embodiment of the Daniel Burnham "make no small plans" directive that has forged the West and of the out-of-town mining money that has bankrolled it.

New urbanists also like to pick from local history and geography, and Daybreak's designers found plenty of grist for their mills in the Salt Lake Valley. Nathan Francis and I had toured the first Daybreak "village" by car but are now walking through the second village, a pleasant, if empty, tousle of houses and streets with freshly poured asphalt, newly planted trees, and replica antique lampposts with yellow "Eastlake" banners hanging from them.[3]

Having come out to South Jordan to see Daybreak, I find myself face to face with replicas of the types of houses found in the turn-of-the century Salt Lake City neighborhood where I grew up, the Avenues. The Avenues is one of many older areas along the East Bench that have become fodder for Daybreak's house designs. Along the Daybreak streets, I see brick foursquares, shingled bungalows, even the Tudor revivals that were popular in the 1920s and 1930s. I see alleyways and sidewalks lined with young trees. Then I see aspects of Daybreak where Utah necessities mix with new urbanist standbys: three-car garages hidden on the sides of houses, bioswales that filter dirty stormwater on its way into the watershed, a secondary water source doubling as a recreational lake. The austerity of the pioneer-style brick houses standing on the barren West Bench manages to stir up hardscrabble Brigham Young, "This is the Place" sentiments, but one needs only to glance at the horizon of the bench where diligent city building is taking place to realize this is part of a calculated master plan brought by a prosperous society.

It all makes Daybreak feel like a laboratory. Many writers have likened new urbanist–influenced developments to Disneyland, for superficial copying and oversimplification of past styles ("a fantasy of a perfect order that never was," as Michael Sorkin writes).[4] While Daybreak exhibits many of the worn chops of one of America's most notable purveyors of new urbanism, Peter Calthorpe, the streets and houses being built on the West Bench also have a fresh ambition to them. Here in South Jordan, they feel experimental. Less a theme park than a Petri dish, circled by scientists monitoring the behavior of the organisms. "When Daybreak opened you had to drive way up here," Nathan Francis is telling me. "It was kind of a mystery. It was a new subdivision concept."

I wonder if he means that the mystery was Kennecott's property or the new urbanist concept. I am guessing, to South Jordanites, both. We are looking down a street that seems to be careening into the spectacular hazy-blue wall of Lone Peak. He tells me that Kennecott made a few tweaks to the plan for the second village: a different pattern of mixing the builders; adjustments to the sizes of the cottages clustered around a "green court"; bolder colors, like the eggplant purple of a hip-roofed craftsman bungalow.

Looking out over the valley, the fresh-faced Daybreak seems to be saying to the tired East Bench, we'll take what we want from you, mix in some other stuff, and do it better. "Transportation will be better going east–west, and more diverse live-work, so fewer trips," Francis recites. "More walkability and trails. And, we say, on the East Bench, million dollar homes, but on the West Bench, million dollar views. The east side was piecemeal and this is drawn out." Some piecemeal projects have begun to develop in the eastern part of Salt Lake Valley that will mix and intensify land use in existing centers of activity, such as the Cottonwood Mall project that plans to replace the demolished mall with a mixed-use neighborhood. Such projects show the potential for the infill and transformation of the "dysfunction density," especially near rail transit stops.

Daybreak is not the only part of Kennecott Land's scheme—if a benevolent or progressive one—to get out of the mining business. The West Bench plan is even bigger than the West Bench: It views itself as a part of a larger movement to change the way Utahns build their towns and cities—to come to terms with the region's explosive growth, reverse the harmful effects of the last 150 years on the built and natural environment, and make Wasatch Front cities more urban and metropolitan places. Daybreak is the outgrowth of one of the quirky institutions of regional planning that has developed in the Great Basin. One of these, a group known as Envision Utah, is the closest thing the state has to a regional planning body. A nonprofit put together by political and business leaders in the 1990s, Envision Utah has evolved into the state's clearinghouse for "smart growth" ideas. The coalition, which is based in Salt Lake City, actively promotes well-known planning concepts: interlocal coordination, walkable centers, and residential and employment density along transit corridors. In Reno, meanwhile, the Truckee Meadows Regional

Planning Agency (TMRPA) has taken a different path toward growth management. It owes its existence to the Nevada legislature, which issued a mandate for the area's cities to work together. TMRPA has teeth: Local plans must comply with the regional authority.

Underneath the obvious differences, Envision Utah and Truckee Meadows Regional Planning Agency serve a similar type of often-thankless mission: preaching growth management in regions where—at least on the surface—this idea counters the dominant political momentum. Utah is the most Republican state in the nation. Its citizens are known for resisting land-use planning, a trend which has stretched across most of the Interior West for the last forty years. As the official history of Envision Utah describes, "Local control is revered and a move toward the establishment of another layer of government in the form of a regional power would be easily defeated. . . . In some political circles, words like 'planning' or 'growth management' are considered 'four-letter-words.'"[5]

At the same time, regional planning is sorely needed in this part of the country. There are few other places in the United States where regional planning makes as much sense as it does in the urbanized valleys at the edges of the Great Basin Desert. They are clearly defined island metropolises: They are fast-growing, contain a proliferation of jurisdictions, and have precious little water to serve new—and existing—growth. And while each planning body necessarily started as a disinterested peacemaker in regions with doom imminent, each has become a champion for smart growth. These efforts scratch at something deeper than the bureaucracy of planning. They have attempted to create physical urbanity in the Great Basin, but also they have had to touch on a trickier kind of urbanism, the tension of what is public and what is private. They have had to balance *Gemeinschaft*—community—and *Gesellschaft*—individual self-interest—in society: what is civic and what is sold.[6]

"The surrounding neighborhoods are known for putting walls around them," Nate Francis says at Daybreak, gesturing down the West Bench to the City of South Jordan's more typical subdivisions. Where, I wonder, are Daybreak's walls?

New Regionalism

Traveling at the Great Basin's edges, I had seen the growth of cities filling with people and jobs and houses. I had come to see that most people just want their own sanctuary from the urbanizing world. You can't blame them. But what happens when this idea covers an entire metropolitan area? Self-interest of people and cities has been a major factor in leading to the sprawl that pervades America.[7] Often within metropolitan areas, a few municipalities hoard the most desirable land uses, such as sales tax–generating retail, foisting less desirable land uses, such as the homes and apartments to house these stores' poorly paid workers and the services to serve them, onto other jurisdictions. Or, cities at the edges of metropolitan areas may have fertile and scenic agricultural land that is worth far more money as executive housing. Viewed alone and through the narrow lens of self-interest, the chain of decisions that have led to the dominant development pattern makes a lot of sense; sprawl is a cruelly rational way of accommodating our individual lives.

But the need to plan and govern cities at a regional scale was recognized long before sprawl could be conceived of as an idea. In the late nineteenth century, Scotsman Patrick Geddes proposed a planning system of overlaying a region's natural resources over its built resources and considering the two in tandem. Geddes influenced Lewis Mumford, whose own writing pushed forward pioneering efforts like the Regional Plan of New York in 1929. Yet local governments remained wary of letting go of their power to control land use and tax their citizens and companies. The 1970s brought forth a new generation of regional cooperation under the theory that a government whose boundaries include the entire region will be more likely to consider the external effects of local decisions and will therefore plan for more equitable, less segregated, and more efficient land use.[8] One famous contemporary example of this movement, of cities sacrificing—or being made to sacrifice—their self-interest for the betterment of the region's economic and environmental goals, is the Portland area's directly elected Metro government, which sought to control growth and preserve agriculture and open space. Leaders in the Minneapolis–St. Paul area, meanwhile, sought to reduce economic polarization in the region by forming an alliance between impoverished central cities and impoverished inner-ring suburbs to pass legislation mandating revenue sharing among its constituent cities.[9]

Even the interior West has had regional planning efforts and proposals—and not only that of the Mormons. In the 1878 report he prepared following his famous exploration of the land surrounding the Colorado and Green Rivers in present-day Wyoming, Utah, and Arizona, John Wesley Powell recommended an overhaul of the way land was distributed and irrigated in the West. Powell proposed replacing the mile survey grid with a system based on watersheds, instituting a survey that classified unclaimed land according to its highest potential use, and distributing land to settlers who would organize in collective irrigation districts.[10] But Powell's system was not adopted, and real regional planning such as that in Portland and in the Twin Cities continues to be the exception rather than the rule.

Regional planning naturally relates to neighborhood planning. The success of regions depends on successful neighborhoods and districts, just as successful neighborhoods and districts often benefit from a successful regional framework. The last century has also seen similar, closely related trends at the neighborhood and community scales. In 1899, British court stenographer Ebenezer Howard promulgated his "Garden City" as an ideal mix of the best parts of "Town" and "Country." Howard, often described as the most important influence of modern planning,[11] proposed a Garden City of thirty-two thousand people living on one thousand acres, surrounded by a permanent agricultural greenbelt. Each Garden City would contain residences, shops, industry, and several parks and would be self-sufficient and easy to get around.[12] These ideas were interpreted in the United States by the designers of Radburn, New Jersey, in 1928. But the next residential building boom, after World War II, ignored many of Radburn's ideas of walkability, centrality, and park space, instead catering to the automobile and creating a supportive environment for individual households with little attention to community-building.

And, like regional planning, some of Howard's ideas and those evident in walkable neighborhoods like Radburn were embraced in the 1980s in the new urbanist movement. The movement was a blend of this neotraditionalism and an environmental slant of compact cities to conserve and preserve natural resources.[13] New urbanists such as Florida architect and planner Andres Duany contrast urbanism not with ruralism but suburbanism. The richness and complexity of a neighborhood-focused pattern, they argue, lead to the conservation, efficiency, and overall quality of life missing from the suburban pattern.[14] New urbanists also have created regional frameworks that inform the character of neighborhoods depending on their location within a metropolitan area.

Reform has been active at the region and the neighborhood levels because these are the scales that matter. The neighborhood is the natural unit of everyday interaction among people, and the region is the framework for the availability of resources most important to society, such as jobs, recreation, and water. The common theme among all these ideas

is a sense of urbanism, of living together. During the age of industrialization, Americans experienced the destructive effects of urbanization,
such as overcrowding and pollution, and looked to the suburbs as the
solution. But many planners have come to see suburbanization as the
destructive agent of the day because of the products of the escape from
industrialized places: the auto dominance that distorts the human scale
of the neighborhood and the disconnection and blandness of the new
built environment. The fix would be to reestablish urban priorities in
architecture and planning.[15]

The center of this mission is the development of the public realm, a
vague term for a broad idea—but one that is the heart of any great city.
The balance between the public and the private realms of every city helps
to give it its essential character. The public realm is the core of urbanism
because it embodies the essence of cities and citizenship,[16] of difference,
not sameness, of people coming together to talk freely where everyone
sees and hears from a different perspective.[17] The public realm means public spaces. It is the streets, sidewalks, plazas, and parks[18] that have been the
building blocks of cities from Athens to New York. Under the suburban
prototype, some claim, open space has become "merely residual,"[19] filling
the gaps between private places of residence and work. Movements such
as new urbanism attempt to re-create public places as the centerpieces of
neighborhoods and to improve the transitions between public and private
space—even if it means a smaller house, less private vehicle access, and
more time spent in public places.

But the public realm is not only spatial. It's also the relationships one
has with others throughout the metropolitan area and what gives urban
regions a sense of cohesion.[20] The regional public realm is the give-and-
take that makes the whole region a better place to live. In the United
States, this notion is best embodied in the Twin Cities region's approach
to revenue sharing, where some individual cities give up some of the
tax revenue they generate to help poorer cities, or in Portland, where
intensity of development is considered a regional decision. Under these
systems, individual or private city burdens and windfalls become shared,
or public.

In recent decades, writers have lamented the fall of the public realm.[21]
The rise of the automobile as a dominant form of transportation over
more public modes, such as the train or walking, accelerated this trend;
now some cities even have private freeways linking people from private
homes to private offices.[22] While writer Mike Davis likens America's new

public realm to a "fortress,"[23] Michael Sorkin's metaphor is a theme park. And as the physical public realm has eroded behind gated communities and unwalkable arterial roads, some have argued that a "public" realm has emerged on the Internet, where individuals can "talk" in a forum from the comfort of their own homes without sacrificing any privacy. But these virtual agoras are usually not public at all but are run and controlled by private corporations. As one college student who recently had a group page removed from the social networking giant Facebook said, "Increasingly, our society is moving online and when private companies own these very public places, how can we make sure that people can legitimately speak their minds and discuss political issues?"[24]

Personal Liberty and the Public Realm

The cities of the Great Basin seemingly play right into this privatization of America. In a region whose main attraction is escaping from other, overcrowded, crime-infested parts of the country to a vast, sunny mountain-protected paradise—where one, in turn, escapes the city to the real attraction, the mountains—the message of an urban public realm faces challenges. The original Salt Lake streets and parks were never conceived as a public realm for different walks of life to meet but for a specific religious group to achieve its celestial goals. Once the Saints became one group among many in the modern Wasatch Front, and the church internalized its nineteenth-century social planning into the confines of its ward and stake buildings, its members often opposed aspects of public city planning in deference to what they believed was the correct political orientation for church members. Former Utah Congressman Jim Hansen liked to remind his constituents that the G.O.P. was the party with righteousness on its side, and at one point, a church spokesman had to say that it was OK for church members to vote Democratic.[25] The obedience so strong throughout church history, once used to encourage public planning, now served to oppose it. One referendum for urban renewal in downtown Salt Lake City in the 1950s was defeated because small business owners expressed the "Latter-day Saint idea of personal liberty and loss of God-given inalienable right to own property."[26]

By the late 1960s, Salt Lake City was taking on its present urban form—and political orientation. The expanding East Bench suburbs seemed a fitting new habitat for a church whose members were becoming known for large families, high incomes, ultraconservative politics, and a desire to embody stars-and-stripes America. Meanwhile, the downtown, where the church had maintained its headquarters for 120 years, was depressed. The city's inner neighborhoods, many of them platted by Mormon pioneers, were decaying. Writer Charles Sellers, in a 1968 article in *Dialogue*, a magazine for discussion about the LDS Church, noted that church members, because of their aversion to urban federal aid or institutional preference for rural lifestyles, wanted little to do with the public act of shaping the city. "This is a field that should have intrinsic appeal for land use and social relation–minded Mormons," Sellers wrote. "What is so surprising is that as individuals, a people who once pioneered urban planning and city building are now so little involved."[27]

Without revered public spaces like the Boston Common, the nerve centers of the urban Great Basin—downtown Salt Lake City and downtown Reno—struggle against co-option by the private interests that built them. Reno's traditional iconic downtown of the Biggest Little City in the World was by and large constructed in the 1970s and 1980s when blank casino façades and winking tourist traps wiped out the last vestiges of a walkable central business district. As one local architect put it, "When the casinos opened up, they didn't want benches. They didn't want shade. They wanted people in the casinos." The public realm can be collective history: In demolishing the Mapes Hotel at Virginia Street and the Truckee River in 2000, Reno city officials destroyed a central public monument to its gambling heyday.[28]

The dominance of private interests over the public realm in Salt Lake City is less obvious but more damaging. The traditional downtown centerpiece, Temple Square, is now a walled, private space. Although the public is welcome to enter, it must do so at the whims of the church and behave in accordance with church rules. In 1999, the Salt Lake City council sold the stretch of Main Street between Temple Square and the church headquarters block to the church for $8.1 million, creating a church superblock in the middle of downtown. The church turned the street into a pedestrian plaza, which a church architect advertised as "A Little Bit of Paris" in Salt Lake. But many wanted it to remain a little bit of Hyde Park, too: Behavior on the plaza was tightly controlled so that no one other than the LDS Church could proselytize, only church music could be played, and speech could be controlled. Despite the sale, the federal circuit court ruled that the city retained a public right-of-way, but that, too, was purchased by the church. It ended in an opinion by the circuit court that Salt Lake City's central block of Main Street was "no longer a public forum."[29]

At the same time, the thousands of acres of public land that surround cities of the Great Basin offer a different kind of public realm. In most of the United States east of the 100th meridian, the longitudinal line west of where annual rainfall usually dips below twenty inches, land is predominantly private, whether residential, commercial, industrial, or agricultural. Public space in this part of the country is concentrated in towns and cities—the places that people in Indianapolis go to recreate are those created and managed, whether regional trails or community parks. At the center of older New England towns is a village green; New York was wise enough to set aside, design, and build Central Park. The public realm defined these older cities. They were places where people from the hinterlands congregated to buy, sell, converse, and play.

Cities in the West turn this notion around. In the map shown in figure 5.1, public lands look like a frontal storm system moving across the western United States, with the center focused smack on the Great Basin. Much of the land in the West that is not publicly owned is owned by either large corporations such as Rio Tinto/Kennecott Land, which owns nearly the entire Oquirrh mountain range, or billionaires like Ted Turner, who owns large swaths of several western states. So cities are islands of private property in a sea of public and corporate land. The Wasatch Front and Truckee Meadows are surrounded by land managed by the Forest Service and the Bureau of Land Management. In both metro areas, public land directly borders densely populated places. So much public land, most of it managed by the federal government, has created a circle-the-wagons mentality. Of the public land in Nevada, 84 percent is managed by the federal government. Local governments are unable to tax this federally and state managed land, and decisions made in Washington have strong effects on local economies. The philosophy is most easily seen in rural areas such as southern Utah, where property rights–oriented values conspire with federally managed land to concoct a hatred of the federal government and jealous guarding of anything private.

But the result in the cities, especially as the western economy has transitioned from natural resources to services and recreation, has been that the public lands offer an endless playground. Hikers, backpackers, cyclists, skiers, and rock climbers, four-wheelers, snowmobilers, water-skiers, and dirt-bikers—all find a respite from city on the public lands just outside of it. Forest Service and BLM visitor days for recreation increased from 225 million in 1983 to over 400 million in 1997.[30] The Wasatch Range encompasses some of the most heavily used National Forest recreation

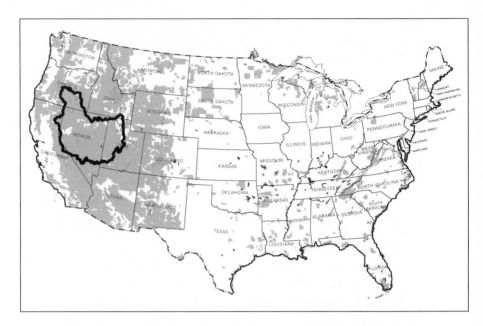

Figure 5.1. Federally managed public land in the United States is heavily concentrated in the West, with the highest concentrations in Utah and Nevada. The black line is the approximate extent of the Great Basin.

areas in the United States. In 2003, the Wasatch-Cache National Forest received twice as many visits as Yellowstone National Park. One poll found that 29 percent of Salt Lake County residents visit the Wasatch canyons five times or more per year.[31] The public lands that border Reno and Salt Lake, such as Peavine Mountain and the Wasatch Foothills, are connected to miles and miles of wilderness. Leaving downtown Salt Lake up City Creek Canyon, one could walk for weeks through the foothills and then the mountains without seeing anyone. These publicly owned mountains crowd Salt Lake and Reno to the point where one feels that people are a limited commodity and land is an infinite resource. Topography dominates buildings. Homes often seem little more than staging areas for two-stroke engines, or ramparts against the encroachment of the mountains. The urban Great Basin's public realm is not here but out there, and it seems like it goes on forever—even more incentive to buy land not in the center but at the periphery. To conservative intermountain urbanites, the recreational possibilities of the land often balance out

distaste for the federal government. Still, the perceived surfeit of land
leads to its devaluation as a public resource. In 2005, for example, the
BLM contemplated selling 325,000 acres in the Smoke Creek Desert,
ninety miles north of Reno.[32] The Truckee Meadows Regional Planning
Agency's board of elected officials has instructed its staff to look at ways
to convince the federal government to sell the BLM-managed land so it
could be developed.[33] This has "worked" for the agency before: The sale
of BLM-managed publicly owned land provided the ground for many of
Las Vegas' edge subdivisions at the beginning of the 2000s.[34]

The challenge faced by metropolitan areas in the Great Basin and
throughout the West is making their regions' large reserves of public land
part of the urban public realm, to accord them the same respect and
role one would give the Boston Common, to integrate them with transit,
make them walkable from neighborhoods, and connect them to smaller,
urban public spaces. If what people want is open space to play in, to give
themselves space and peace of mind amid the congestion of the city, there
is no shortage of it just outside the city. The trick is to pull it into the
pedestrian orbit, to remove the automobile from the equation, to replace
the nasty arterials and McMansions at the periphery with denser, human-
scale places where walkable streets and small parks and plazas transition
to the great American commons. For example, starting in downtown Salt
Lake today, you can take the Trax light-rail to connect with a bus heading
across the valley and up Little Cottonwood Canyon, disembark at Alta,
ski tour up the north side of the canyon to the summit of Mount Superior, ski down five thousand feet to Big Cottonwood Canyon, and board
another bus that returns you to the valley—all without having to get in
a car. And yet, here at the mouths of the Cottonwoods, the epicenter of
where the city meets spectacular public lands, the awful street network
and segregated land uses make this some of the most difficult terrain in
the valley to traverse on foot.

In the 1990s, it became evident that the surge of private growth was
creating a new public realm in the city: environmental externalities.
Transportation officials green-lighted a $1.4 billion, seventeen-mile
widening of Interstate 15 to twelve lanes, and state lawmakers planned
another, parallel freeway along the Great Salt Lake shorelands to alleviate
the bottleneck between Salt Lake and Davis counties. Salt Lake Valley's
air quality succumbed to its geography; in the winter, when high pressure parks above the valley, pollution particles sink and, with no wind,
stay, putting Salt Lake's air above the Environmental Protection Agency's

(EPA's) health limit on many winter days. In the Truckee Meadows, the jurisdictions of Reno, Sparks, and Washoe County were growing so fast that they often duplicated unnecessary infrastructure. Water providers were wondering where the resources were going to come from.

But especially in Utah, discussion about managing the growth was out of the question. "We couldn't have an open dialogue, it was a taboo," says Ted Knowlton, the planning director of Envision Utah, about the political climate surrounding growth in the 1980s and early 1990s. "If you talked openly about the idea of spending public money to protect open space, you were painted as a liberal or against property rights."

South Jordan: Hyper-Utah

Today, the dominance of the private over the public and the need for better regional and neighborhood planning are visible in Utah's fastest-growing cities such as South Jordan. The city began as a collection of crude mud huts along the Jordan River housing pioneer families who chose to settle "over Jordan" until they could dig irrigation ditches and build farms in the uplands. Using picks, shovels, and water buckets as levels, they carved out a system of trenches that diverted water from the Jordan River and ran parallel to it in order to flood water over their newly tilled fields.[35]

The mud huts are gone now, but the irrigation ditches remain. Barely visible between blocks of houses, they are one of the only remnants of the city's pioneer history. As Ricky Horst, the South Jordan city manager, admits, South Jordan doesn't have a lot of historic presence.[36] That would be true if, by "historic," Horst meant before 1990 or even before 2000. In 1960, South Jordan had 1,354 inhabitants.[37] In 2000, the city's population was 29,000 people, and six years later, it was 48,000. The city has been growing at up to 9 percent per year[38] and estimates its buildout at 120,000, as if time was just another metric by which the city was understood.

Now, South Jordan's most notable physical features are the walls that Nathan Francis had spoken of, which surround neighborhoods, and in some cases, home compounds. They are mostly made of stone, or concrete etched to resemble stone, sometimes with metal spikes on top of them. These, combined with the remaining equine fields and the proud windbreak poplars, give a fiefdom effect, like a contemporary Fortress Jordan. The city's median income has risen to one of the highest in the state—$75,433 in 1999. A total of 95 percent of residents have graduated from high school. Less than 1 percent of its families live below the poverty level. Nine out of ten of households own their home. Some 95 percent of South Jordan's residents are white, and the average household size is nearly four.[39] While people of other faiths live in the area, very few other religious congregations hold meetings within the South Jordan city limits other than the Church of Jesus Christ of Latter-day Saints.[40] While Utah is, in general, wealthier, better-educated, more home-owning, whiter, and more Mormon than the rest of America, South Jordan is even wealthier, better-educated, more home-owning, whiter, and more Mormon than the rest of Utah. It's a hyper-Utah.

Ricky Horst is from Florida, though he went to college at Brigham Young University, in Provo, and is ambivalent toward the built form in his jurisdiction. On one hand, he is proud of the design standards that the city demands, such as stucco, with rock and brick on the bottom for every house, of buildings "that are worthy of our affection," and of the welcoming arms with which the city embraces developers. But the city also mandates sprawl: It requires thirty-six hundred square feet of livable space, and most houses take up forty-five hundred to fifty-five hundred square feet. The city does allow developers to build multifamily buildings but only in lower-value dumping grounds, like land next to freeways where the apartment blocks are really just more walls to protect the large houses.

Even so-called small-lot communities have eviscerated the public realm. Jordan High Pointe, a new subdivision just below the Daybreak bluff that offers five thousand to seven thousand square-foot lots in the vein of the pioneering project to the west, requires that "each site must have an enclosed garage for at least two cars, emphasis should be made in home design to provide for additional third car garage or storage behind the conventional two car garage. . . . An additional area for at least two guest parking spaces shall be provided, typically in the driveway or the area between the driveway and the side property line. . . . Absolutely no overnight on-street parking will be permitted in South Jordan High Pointe by the Owner, their lessees or guests."[41] That's required space for at least five cars in front of the house by my count, with the street cleaned out of any parallel parked cars of outsiders, which can protect pedestrians from traffic on the roadway.

Pushing the public out of these neighborhoods has further coarsened and divided them. "The problem," Horst says, "is that we have all these gated communities. We've built a city of cul-de-sacs and forced large collector streets." At a city council meeting in 1998 during which residents of a subdivision did not want their neighborhood connected to a new subdivision, a council member said, he "has been on the City Council for several years and now sees many mistakes and subdivisions that were not linked. . . . The circulation issue is critical to the growth of the City. He said if he does not vote to connect the roads in this subdivision because there are people he cares about in the area, he does not know how he can make the next subdivision connect." He then "apologized for the pain this issue has caused people."

As the city has grown over the past few decades, it has struggled to provide public space. At a 2000 South Jordan Planning Commission meeting, a planning commissioner expressed concern about a lack of parks in South Jordan. The city planner present replied that the city's dearth of open space was due to the city council being, despite the city's high incomes and rising property values, "unable to afford it." If they had really wanted parks, the planner added, the city would have required a zoning of smaller lots that mandates them.[42] Developers at another meeting claimed that they were "told by the City Council that they didn't want [parks]."[43] The city, meanwhile, receives requests from citizens to gate the parks it does have.

The extreme not-in-my-back-yard position, known as NIMBYism, gives Ricky Horst a headache. "Being a citizen means you share each other's burdens," he says. "We don't want to share anyone's burdens."

Quality Growth and Good Choices

Envision Utah has helped pioneer a new kind of regional burden sharing. The edict comes not from above but from within each decision made by local government, like a nagging conscience. The coalition has achieved a degree of regionalism along the Wasatch Front through two related strategies, both of which have catered to the region's conservative politics and zeal for private property. First, it organized not around a goal, like Portland or the Twin Cities, but a process, which involved a broad swath of the region. "Envision Utah showed the broad public consequences of long-term strategies and then trusted [the public] to make a decision," Envision Utah planner Ted Knowlton says of the first strategy. "We do this by saying, 'This is a broad tent, it's not advocacy.'"

The second strategy was the voluntary implementation of policy. This strategy has come to be known as "new regionalism," and according to new regionalist writers, the economic fate of cities and suburbs is so interdependent that suburbs will voluntarily aid ailing central cities,[44] a theory which doesn't always play out. For the founders of Envision Utah, this approach wasn't so much a choice as the only viable option in the political climate. It had to accomplish growth management with as little regulation and red tape as possible. And so, Envision Utah is something of a model of efficiency: Instead of forming a new organization, the idea piggybacked on an existing organization formed not to control growth but to create it. The organization, called the Coalition for Utah's Future, had come together in 1988 in response to a recession. Its mission was to promote the state as a location for business, but it began to be interested in issues of housing, neighborhood and community, water, air quality, and transportation.[45]

At the same time, the state wanted to present a positive image to the rest of the world when it staged the 2002 Winter Olympics. The Games, which also made public funds available to Olympic-host jurisdictions, enticed state and local government entities to think creatively. Progressive, cosmopolitan ideas like light-rail transit, which met resistance in the late 1980s and early 1990s because of Utah's culture and postwar auto-oriented layout, became possible with the persistence of the Utah Transportation Authority and Olympic funds. When the Trax system opened in 1999, it carried a ridership of sixty thousand people a day, four times what planners expected.[46] One of the reasons was that UTA presented a version of the public realm that, unlike the existing bus system, didn't sacrifice Utahns' notions of prestige. As one city official says, "Trax is classy, a bus is not."

The Coalition for Utah's Future took this tack when selling its ideas to the public and political leaders. Instead of portraying growth control like Twin Cities' regional advocates had, as a way to bring regional equality and limit the power of wealthy communities over poorer ones, it was a way for everyone to keep living the good life—an appealing notion for anyone with any power in the state. This approach relied upon a central regional identity for the Wasatch Front, and of Utah, as a place with a unique quality of life, of family, of clear air on mountain peaks, of safe neighborhoods. In a later Envision Utah study, the coalition hired a psychologist to evaluate what residents like about their home region, and she repeatedly found the idea of "peace of mind." Ironically, the identity existed in part because of many of the challenges Utah faced: development constraints like mountains, lakes, and deserts, and the Mormon church-influenced conservative culture. Despite the political fractals of the Wasatch Front, it brought its leaders together around the quality of life, whether a reality or an illusion. The coalition coined the idea "quality growth," spawning a Quality Growth Steering Committee in 1995.[47]

The nascent steering committee employed already-powerful voices. Robert Grow, an engineer and attorney, was the chief operating officer of Orem-based Geneva Steel when he emerged as a leader of the Quality Growth Steering Committee. In later years, Grow would assume the position of Envision Utah chair, and he would be succeeded by an even more powerful Utahn, future governor Jon Huntsman Jr. The Coalition for Utah's Future also approached Utah's current governor, Mike Leavitt. The group asked Leavitt for his support in forming an official growth commission. Anything that smacked of state land-use planning, which the governor strongly opposed, was of course off the table, but the governor's creation of a subcabinet study group led to a "Growth Summit." The summit happened in late 1995, and the governor publicized the event enough that the four major local TV channels broadcast it two nights in a row for an hour. The coalition put special emphasis on educating the notoriously conservative Utah Legislature about regional planning. They presented their research about how places like California and Portland have addressed—or not addressed—growth within their regions, and what the consequences have been. The Legislature responded by appropriating $250,000 to the creation of "Quality Growth Education Tools," and $100,000 annually to spread them around the state.

The key to the Envision Utah's strategy was its inclusion of a wide range of people, but it was more complex than the folksy "big tent" idea. The group consciously included people who might have opposed the effort if they sensed it was a liberal planning agenda, such as Governor Leavitt, future Governor Huntsman, and Utah Jazz basketball team owner, auto dealership mogul, and real estate developer Larry H. Miller, all of whom were present when Envision Utah officially came together in January 1997 at a kickoff event at the Delta Center arena, the home of the Utah Jazz. Robert Grow, Governor Leavitt, and Larry Miller gave a press conference to introduce the new public-private project. It was seeded by a private grant from the Dolores Dore Eccles Foundation. An actor impersonating Brigham Young told the audience about the proud legacy of planning in the state that the coalition hoped to revive.

The heart of Envision Utah's early work was to allow Utahns to evaluate and choose from among several long-term growth scenarios for the

Wasatch Front.[48] The commission used public input gained from a series of workshops held in 1998 and 1999 and run by planners John Fregonese and Peter Calthorpe, marked areas where they did not want growth to occur and delegated chips to areas where they did. Envision Utah put together four scenarios of the Wasatch Front's future. They ranged from a base scenario assuming that the region's dominant large-lot suburban development (averaging over a third of an acre per lot) would continue, to what might happen if development took place on smaller lots and within existing urbanized areas, as well as around "town centers" where residents would live, work, and recreate. Envision Utah didn't want to scare anyone off—the average lot size from the base case to the ambitious fourth scenario shrank to a very comfortable size of about a quarter acre. But the scenarios gave the public an idea of the different directions they could go. Viewed side by side with each other, different development approaches offered alternate visions of the Wasatch Front's future. While the areas projected for development over the next several decades under the base scenario ballooned the metro area out to a bloated shape, the areas identified for redevelopment and infill offered a lean urban vision of a city slimmed-down around transit lines.

Yet there was a tension between the necessary openness of the process and the narrowness of what many hoped the answers would be. Envision Utah was comfortable allowing Utahns to choose the agenda of the coalition because, like many activists, they thought that once the public had the facts it would make the right decisions. Robert Grow was fond of saying, "We believe if we give good people good information, they will make good choices."[49] Those choices included seeing aspects of urbanity like density and transportation in a different light. Knowlton, for example, points out the fallacy of the connection between antigovernment and low density. "Zoning has gotten in the way of the private sector. There was an unmet market for townhouses and duplexes," he says. "Envision Utah's notion of mixing uses is not adding more regulation—it's reducing regulation of use and increasing regulation of design." It's true: Developers, even in Utah, love to build at higher densities because they make more money, and many understand land economics better than many elected officials. Davis County's Adams Company, for example, recently built a townhouse project called Clearwater on a piece of land on Main Street in Kaysville that was less than a mile from one planned commuter rail station. Stuart Adams says the company decided to build townhouses because of the downtown location and because the presence of Homes Creek (the same stream that flows through the Great Salt Lake Shorelands Preserve) made the site tough to develop large-lot homes. Adams designed Clearwater in the same mountain lodge style that dominates the rest of the new houses along the Wasatch Front, with steep gables and large garages, but the townhouses are clustered together and walkable, with pleasant, accessible common spaces along Homes Creek. The density was ten units to the acre, Adams sold the units for about $200,000 each and, of course, the neighbors stormed city hall, claiming it would become the province of hookers and drug dealers. But there was clearly a market for Clearwater, and it wasn't criminals, it was grandmothers. "We say newly wed or almost dead," Adams says. One man I found at Clearwater told me that after his father died, the development lured his mother. Now, he says the stretch of Homes Creek behind her townhouse is the site of summertime gatherings. "I tell her, she can borrow my shotgun, because there are ducks that come through there," he says.

And Utah cities were clearly amenable to regulating design, as we have seen with the requirements for brick, rock, and stucco in many of the suburban jurisdictions. But in addition to resistance to alternate development types, the skepticism of the coalition was based more on deeper notions of control and hegemony. City officials and their constituents were skeptical of the group's intentions and its promise to allow local jurisdictions to keep land-use control. "It's easy to see how it worked now, but there was a lot of nervousness," Ted Knowlton says. "We thought, maybe people would just pick the current trend, that they would say, 'We don't care about air pollution, and want medium-density subdivisions.'"

They didn't, at least when asked the questions in a survey. From eighteen thousand surveys collected and talks with elected officials from ten different counties, the preference was for smart growth, or smarter growth, which contrasted with the current reality of the Wasatch Front. While 70 percent of respondents preferred single-family homes, 79 percent of participants agreed that "housing within a neighborhood should be designed for a mix of ages and incomes," and 85 percent agreed that "government should encourage mixed-use development and reduced auto dependency." Most people wanted development to occur near transportation corridors and were reluctant to replace farmland with development. In this way, Envision Utah's inquiries brought out the Tragedy of the Commons gap between the private realities of citizens and the shared, civic realm they imagined. But the result of this process, says Knowlton, has been that, "it was no longer taboo to talk about density. . . . It opened the gates."

Instead of pushing for reforms at the state level, or the creation of a regional government, Envision Utah fashioned itself as an information clearinghouse, albeit a proactive one. This is the most common role taken on by regional governmental bodies in California, called councils of governments (COGs): For example, the Association of Bay Area Governments, California's first COG, approaches its regional mission by undertaking research, analysis, education, and outreach. Envision Utah representatives making presentations to local jurisdictions emphasized that they were not removing local control.

Envision Utah developed a "toolbox" of about two hundred strategies with which local governments could accomplish the goals set forth by workshop and survey participants. The coalition says it has reached staff members of 90 percent of cities and presented the tools to them. Envision Utah has also provided the manpower and know-how for the creation of local plans, acting as a pro-bono consultant for regional plans such as the Davis County Shorelands Plan (with the added bonus of knowledge of how other Wasatch Front jurisdictions are planning). Meanwhile, planners like Knowlton have become deft at using the language of conservative America in the context of smart growth. "It relies on appealing to the regional patriotism of elected officials," Knowlton says.

These approaches have worked in some places. According to Envision Utah, 60 percent of cities have implemented at least one of the organization's strategies. Most of the implementation has been piecemeal, in neighborhoods and downtowns. The most popular tools have been cluster subdivisions and walkable centers. "Almost every city wants [one]," Knowlton says. "They don't want to change their overall development path, but at least have a heart."

Envision Utah has also catalyzed a change in the way Utah residents and city governments perceive transit. In the early 1990s, public transit was largely viewed as only for those who couldn't drive. Envision Utah's workshops showed how transit, largely in the form of light-rail or commuter rail, is a key to realizing the widely supported concept of quality growth. The construction of the Wasatch Front's first light-rail line illustrated for Utahns that riding transit could be fast, cost-effective, and "classy." Now, cities almost universally see light-rail as a major amenity, and some like Draper and Midvale have rewritten their zoning codes to support walkable development around light-rail stations. And Envision Utah became a power player: When planning the Mountain View Corridor freeway in western Salt Lake Valley, the Utah Department of

Transportation joined the coalition in its own collaborative land-use and transportation planning approach with the local jurisdictions, which Envision Utah believes narrowed the freeway and created more opportunity for future transit along it.

But many city and county governments are loathe to buy in wholesale to the coalition's ideas. As one city manager puts it, "Envision Utah is a tool. We don't take what they say carte blanche." One of the more ambitious "pioneer" plans Envision Utah has helped put together is the Davis County Shorelands Plan, which gathered leadership in the cities in Davis County along the Great Salt Lake with the intent of protecting the rare natural resources of the shorelands. The plan set out an overall land-use framework that included strategies like cluster housing in sensitive areas to preserve bird habitat. Yet, as always, the measures were optional, and it's questionable whether the shorelands regional plan will figure into any local plans, despite being formally recognized by all the participating governments. City officials in Syracuse, the city with perhaps the most developable land remaining along the shorelands area, put in their most recent general plan provisions for an open space and agricultural buffer along the lake, an idea that came from the Davis shorelands plan. As part of a large sanitary sewer plant, the city purchased land to add to the buffer. At the same time, Syracuse has made clear it will not let go of its control over its development bonanza. "The city isn't too willing to make itself part of a regional plan," says one Syracuse city official. "It doesn't accept the [Envision Utah] principles. [The city leadership] just doesn't understand how it all fits together. . . . Envision Utah in the past has been like a red-headed stepchild in Syracuse."

Envision Utah does have one notable powerful ally: the LDS Church. Emeritus LDS Church general authority Alexander Morrison has become a vocal advocate for the group and quality growth in general. He sees the church as closely related to its geographic context. "I think there is a certain amount of self-screening by people who come to Utah to live," Morrison once told the *Deseret News*. "Many of them come here because they like the lifestyle that's here. That's not just religious lifestyle; they like the mountains, the open spaces. They like the way people live here."[50] And Mormons have a responsibility to protect this way of life, Morrison said in a speech:

> Intrinsic to the faith to which I cling is the principle that all of human-
> kind who dwell on earth . . . are but tenants, with a steward's sacred

responsibility to look after our earthly home. . . . There is broad and growing consensus . . . that our modern way of life is, in many respects, environmentally unsustainable. . . . [Envision Utah] is designed to assist Utahns to deal effectively with growth-related challenges, while preserving Utah's quality of life for future generations. One of [Envision Utah's] greatest strengths has been its desire to effect change through education and promotion, rather than top-down, heavy-handed regulatory actions. In this approach—a grassroots, bottom-up model of public engagement for regional planning—Envision Utah reflects Utahns' preferences for local government and private property rights.[51]

One strong thread in the culture of Mormonism, from the beginning, is the idea of obedience to the church's priesthood—whether it be one's father, the ward bishop, or the president of the church. It is the same thing that made regional planning work for Brigham Young. As First Presidency member James E. Faust wrote in 1999, "Obedience helps us develop the full potential our Heavenly Father desires for us in becoming celestial beings worthy someday to live in His presence."[52] The idea drove Salt Lake City's famously jack-Mormon liberal mayor, Rocky Anderson, crazy. "The culture of obedience is a dangerous place to be," Anderson warned on a radio talk show in 2006. But has this same provincial attitude helped along urbanism on the Wasatch Front?

Daybreak

You can find an optimistic synthesis of nearly all of Envision Utah's ideas at the beachhead of Salt Lake Valley's West Bench. Daybreak's particular genesis is neatly laid out in the development's marketing office at the far end of the little traffic circle at the lip of the West Bench. Everywhere are blown up photographs of cute kids and the development's motto: "This is getting good." Here, Nate Francis is waiting for me. Francis, who grew up in Davis County, is clearly good Utah stock. He's wearing a red button-down shirt tucked into jeans and a pair of work boots. He apologizes for not being more dressed-up.

We go straight to the relief model that takes up much of the marketing office's far end. The development is such a testament to Envision Utah toolbox ideas that the ideas are articulated in museum-like fashion in the glassy marketing office. Clearly visible in the relief model is mixed use, a village center, plenty of open space set aside, a pair of alternating

South Jordan's modern walls and castles (above) mix with fields and steeples (below) to create one of Utah's wealthiest cities.

Looking west over Daybreak yields an imposing view of one of the world's largest mines (above), but the views toward the east to the Wasatch Range are the real attraction (below).

Daybreak balances dense urban places in its "village centers" (above) with active parks (below).

Daybreak's residences include both pioneer house replicas (above) and streamlined townhouses (below).

Cottonwoods, railroad tracks, steep slopes, four-wheel jeep trails (above) and even bus stops (below) now line the City of Reno's North Virginia Street transit-oriented development corridor. How long, and what form, will TOD take here?

one-way streets (known as a "couplet") bracketing a commercial area and plenty of roundabouts.

At the center of the model is Oquirrh Lake. The man-made pond has a central blob, with an inhabited island in the middle of it, and three arms of varying length with inlets and boat slips that make the models of certain Daybreak neighborhoods look like Fort Lauderdale. "Usually, in planned communities, the centerpiece is a golf course, but ours is a lake," Francis is saying. "Running the numbers, we found that a lake required less water." The water comes from Utah Lake and is filtered, piped, and pumped up onto the West Bench. Kennecott Land stocked it with 250,000 blue gill, bass, and other bottom-feeding fish. Next summer come the trout. There are docks for canoes. They use bubblers to keep the water oxygenated and the visibility at four feet. Oquirrh Lake doubles as Daybreak's secondary water source.

Oquirrh Lake is not yet the beauty that Kennecott Land envisions. As I step outside into the breezy morning, with the mine looming above, it serves to remind me that this is not a greenfield, like so much else of Zion, but an aggressively reengineered and remade place. For Utah, it's a new go at imagining itself in the Great Basin landscape. Despite the artificial lake, there's plenty here that does respond to the surrounding geography in an urban way. It doesn't continue the Saints' trajectory of making the virgin desert bloom but instead adapts more realistic expectations to a human-scarred landscape.

No scar in Utah is larger or deeper than the Bingham mine. In its prime, the mine operated all day, every day of the year. Eight thousand miners dug pits thousands of feet deep, pulling out copper and other ores, smelting the metals and spewing the tailings in creeks and along the West Bench's gentle slopes. Arsenic, cadmium, chromium, copper, lead, nickel, selenium, silver, acids, sulfate, and zinc all found their way into floodplains and aquifers. Sulfate contaminated a 72-square mile plume of groundwater.[53] As with regional growth control along the Wasatch Front, the mid-1990s were a turning point, both for Kennecott's realization of what it needed to do with its property, and what it could do with it afterward. It took until the 1990s for the environmental laws of two decades earlier to catch up with Kennecott: The site was contaminated enough that it was likely to receive the "Superfund" designation given to the nation's most uncontrolled hazardous waste sites by the U.S. Environmental Protection Agency (EPA). In 1995 the company signed a memorandum of understanding with EPA and the state to clean up its site. Now, Daybreak homebuyers must sign an eight-page document disclosing sixteen "issues," one of which is acknowledgment of the site's history of contamination.[54]

Around the same time, Kennecott realized that it was cleaning up the largest contiguous landholding remaining in Salt Lake Valley. It also held the largest collection of water rights left in the Salt Lake Valley, which increasingly determine the extent of growth in the West more than available land. And, the company had merged with London-based giant Rio Tinto, which gave Kennecott the ability to branch into real estate development. As early as 1999, Rio Tinto funded Kennecott's exploration of development of the 93,000 acres along the new "West Bench." The company hired Peter Calthorpe to design a master plan for the holdings. In 2001, Rio Tinto helped Kennecott create a "daughter" company, Kennecott Land, which would manage and develop the property. Kennecott was not the first Utah mining company to trade tunneling and ore for real estate. It was United Park City Mines whose decision to develop a ski resort on top of its closed Wasatch Mountain mines in the 1960s ignited the rebirth of then–ghost town Park City and the rise of skiing to Utah's number one industry—the West's old resource economy giving way to its new face of lifestyle and amenities.

The land where Daybreak is rising today used to be known as the South Jordan Evaporation Ponds. The contamination here consisted of fifty years of sludge spread over one hundred acres, which cost $15 million to consolidate into one pile.[55] A business viability study found that the evaporation pond land presented a nice opportunity: The land was a tab extending from the West Bench toward the heart of South Jordan. It was close to existing sewer and water infrastructure and the Bangerter Highway. It had spectacular views.

Kennecott Land says it wanted to develop its brownfield in a "sustainable" manner. Calthorpe, who had worked with Envision Utah in the late 1990s, conceived of a master plan that would center on amenities like transit stops and a lake, arranging around them denser development than Utahns were accustomed to, as well as mixed land uses. Such a development had to get past the South Jordan City Council, a body representing a large number of people who, like many others in America, had serious fears about living close together, poverty, personal safety, and anything that compromises the ability for an unlimited number of vehicles to go and stop wherever, whenever. "The whole concept [of Daybreak] was foreign to South Jordan and Utah," says Ricky Horst. "People don't understand the value of having the open space combined. It's a different aesthetic." Horst himself had seen nice dense projects while working in Florida. So he was encouraged by Kennecott Land's idea. "Our community was founded on large lot development," Horst says, "but there is a recognition that we need to diversify if we want to be sustainable."

In the late 1990s, the Daybreak site was a large question mark. The city's citizen long-range planning committee found it hard to think outside of large-lot, single-family development, but they asked whether there would be apartments in the area. One city councilor suggested that "it would be helpful to go see the apartments in the valley," adding that "some are terrible, but some are nice." "We have some decisions to make out there," the mayor said. The Kennecott development first appeared on the South Jordan Planning Commission's radar in the late 1990s under the name "Sunrise." According to Horst, city staff broached Daybreak with the city council and the public by telling them that it wouldn't be in their back yard. It would be up on the West Bench, with the six-lane, at-grade Bangerter Highway and a million-square-foot commercial development in between. Also, the overall density, set out in the development agreement, was still only about three units per acre with the open space included. To accomplish this clustered density, the city created a planned unit development (PUD) zone, which took three years. Quelling citizen anger over disruption of their isolation, a city council member said in the late 1990s, "Brigham Young has received posthumous awards for his design of cities, and that is where everyone faced a road. Salt Lake City is viewed as a miracle in planning because of the wide square blocks. . . . The roads were designed to connect, but not designed to be collector streets or major thoroughfares." But another councilman said his "fear is that Envision Utah would like high-density housing," while another said he was "uncomfortable with the direction of Envision Utah. . . . South Jordan is a unique area," and he would "like to maintain a unique character."[56]

Indeed, from the beginning there was synergy between Daybreak and Envision Utah. The coalition acknowledges that Kennecott Land was interested in the concept of a walkable, transit-accessible development from the beginning, but Envision Utah believes it made these concepts more acceptable to the public. "If Envision Utah wasn't here, they still would have done [Daybreak]," Ted Knowlton says, "but there would have been barriers. We lowered the barriers regionwide." Kennecott Land

President Peter McMahon said that public understanding of Envision Utah made it much easier for South Jordan residents to accept Daybreak in context of regional planning.[57] At the same time, the relationship was symbiotic: Daybreak provided Envision Utah with an exhibit of its concepts—in one of the Wasatch Front's most conservative, fastest-growing, auto-oriented suburban cities. Daybreak is "designed to be balanced," admired Robert Grow. "You can live there, you can shop there, and you can work close by."[58]

As if cleaning up a sure-fire Superfund site and entitling a massive development whose central concept was new to the City of South Jordan wasn't enough, now Kennecott Land had to market its new product to Utahns. The fact that two thirds of the Wasatch Front's growth was expected to be internally generated meant that many of these houses would be built for individuals, couples, and families moving from Clearfield, Draper, Orem, or even from down the hill in South Jordan. Envision Utah hoped that the coalition's principles would "pass the ultimate test"—market success.

It's time to take a tour, and we get into Nate Francis's black Audi. "This is how it is when you've got a one-year-old," he apologizes, pushing toddler accessories off the passenger seat. As we drive through Village One, it becomes clear how they are marketing Daybreak. Much like Envision Utah's regional coalition-building, the company's success would depend on speaking the local language, both in design vocabulary and public relations. Like many other new urbanist developments, they hit on a few universally American themes and give them a local spin—all of them seen in the beige-walled castles below but given new forms at Daybreak.

Utahns Like Rural

New urbanists often employ rural archetypes to achieve the urban character of their developments—and rural-sounding words to market them: the wide front porch, the lake, the village green, the town center. Many new urbanists see similarities in the urban and the rural—merging quality versions of both into the "community" type of development, whose foil is "suburban" development. One of the reasons developers and planners do this is to attract the public and local governments to urbanism by distinguishing their product from the urbanization they sought to escape. It is clear that many Utahns like to think of themselves as living in a pastoral paradise, and Daybreak has capitalized on this. The foundation of Daybreak's concept is a rural term—"the village." Kennecott Land aims to build one thousand houses in each of its villages. One million new people on the West Bench will mean, literally one thousand villages—each, says Kennecott Land, with its own theme.

Utahns Like Their History

The Daybreak model villages, perched on the windy bluff, with newly planted trees along the sidewalks, have the odd feel of a pioneer village movie set. Kennecott Land is trying hard to replicate the prewar Victorian and bungalow architecture that defined the early version of Salt Lake City, made for walking and streetcar travel. For the architectural standards, the company studied the "local vernacular" of the Avenues and the Harvard-Yale area. They studied how the house was set on the lot, where the garage was located, the colors, and the building materials.

Utahns Like Prestige

Kennecott Land's other motivation to copy neighborhoods like the Avenues and Harvard-Yale was these areas' classiness, their prestige. In the case of the Avenues, this prestige was newfound: The neighborhood was the first to deviate from the City of Zion–mandated ten-acre blocks, for reasons of economy (land speculators wanted to make more money) and to house an increasing artisan and merchant (and non-LDS) class. The area stayed steadfastly un-Mormon and many of the turn-of-the-century houses fell into disrepair in the 1960s and 1970s, but in recent decades the Avenues has become a tony address, emerging, as the *Salt Lake Tribune* describes, as "a refuge for the urban elite, professionals lured by charming small homes that carry big price tags."[59]

Utahns Like Lawn

Despite new urbanism's environmentally conscious approach, Daybreak has accommodated Utahns' love of green, well-watered lawn in their oasis cities. Most of Daybreak's houses have not only front lawns, but lawn on the "parking strip" between the sidewalk and curb. Even the townhouses that have begun to appear come with large lawns in front of them.

To distinguish Daybreak further from the beige brigades below, Kennecott Land devised a complex system of mixing its product types. It chose eight builders, who would each design twelve house elevations, meaning ninety-six house façade designs. For Village 1, Kennecott salt-and-peppered the builders throughout the neighborhoods, but for Village 2, they grouped each builder by block and encouraged them to go even wilder with the house colors, so that neighbors nicknamed one street "Crayola Street."

Putting it all together was, like Daybreak itself, a calculated experiment. For Village 1, builders interpreted the designs, but they weren't getting them quite right. For example, in the first green court, builders designed houses that were too large for the common lawn area they surrounded. For Village 2, the company created a pattern book with pictures of the Avenues and Harvard-Yale areas that showed how to detail a window and door. "Some builders picked it up really quick and some [still] struggle," Francis says.

And in marketing the aspects of Daybreak that truly make it a smart growth development, such as increased residential density, Kennecott appeals to another well-known Utah obsession: family. Because the members of one's family are in different stages of their lives, Daybreak argues, they need different types of housing. The life cycle and diversity, Kennecott and other Utah planned community developers have found, are good stand-in concepts for the evil density. The products Daybreak is selling range from a standard single-family house to residences with strange names: 1,162–1,515 square-foot "carriage homes"; 1,500–2,100 square-foot "paseo homes"; and "mansion condos," which accommodate multifamily housing units by placing them in a building that looks on the outside like a large single-family house.[60]

It's not fair to judge Daybreak yet by what's on the ground. The place feels, like most new development, a little empty and a little sterile. Most of what's been built is single-family houses, schools, and parks, which, though well designed, don't give the visitor a sense of the denser housing options and the other two key ingredients in the project's mix: jobs and public transit. With the balance of jobs and residences making possible shorter commutes, and the carless connection of Daybreak to other urban nodes throughout the Wasatch Front, Daybreak will evolve over time into an increasingly complex, compelling—and urban—place. Sometimes, real estate professionals talk about a house that has "good bones," a solid fundamental structure that can be built upon. Daybreak is developing good bones.

One of the most interesting aspects of Daybreak that is readily visible from the outset is its incorporation of the Church of Jesus Christ of Latter-day Saints. As with Envision Utah, it was an easy decision for Kennecott Land to include the most powerful cultural and political institution in the state, as well as one of the powerful financial ones, in its project. For its part, the church was eating up the explosive growth happening in wealthy cities like South Jordan, where the land and population created more opportunities for wards and temples. As a consequence, the majority of the "worship sites" scattered throughout Daybreak are LDS ward houses. There will even be a new temple on the edge of the bench, making it the second temple in tiny South Jordan. Not even Salt Lake City has two temples.

The cultural gravity of the temple changed the original design of the development. The original plan for Village 2 has houses oriented north–south because of the potential for solar heating and light. But Kennecott changed the street grid to a radial pattern centered around the "civic space" of the church. Yet planners were really capitalizing on the prestige created by the temple and its orientation on the West Bench, Francis says. The lots around the temple, naturally, will be the development's largest.

Northern Nevada's Regional Stick

Across the Great Basin, in Reno, regional planning appealed to another politically conservative ideal: It would waste less tax money. Northern Nevada is not as politically conservative as Utah, but a similar property-rights mentality permeates.[61] In addition to confronting sin-tolerant individualism instead of sin-intolerant individualism, the Truckee Meadows Regional Planning Agency has a much different origin story than Envision Utah. In the late 1980s, Reno, Sparks, and Washoe County were expanding rapidly to accommodate residential and commercial growth by laying down infrastructure. They fought over boundaries and duplicated sewer and water lines. In 1989, one state senator, William Raggio, a Republican, recognized the waste and pushed through a bill that made these jurisdictions cooperate. The legislative approach had the advantages of an overriding mandate for cities to work together and the capability of enforcement of policies.[62] Envision Utah had sought state legislature support, but it had come more subtly, through cautious research and education funding rather than police power. Though its geographic scope was limited, TMRPA actually had regulatory authority.

Like Envision Utah, the Truckee Meadows Regional Planning Agency has eventually become a voice for smart growth principles, but it has been a slow evolution. The Nevada Legislature's order showed the differences between Utah and Nevada in how each approached its conservative citizenry: While Utah's *enlibra*[63] approach dangled the carrot of collaboration, Nevada's stick was bare and unforgiving, a Wild West approach to planning in another "instant city" of the West. Some of the Nevada Legislature's provisions were somewhat irrational. The 1989 legislation ordered the nascent agency to write a plan within thirty days. It would focus on land use, infrastructure, and natural resources and would contain eight elements. The crux of the agency would be its conformance jurisdiction: Each local plan has to conform to standards established by the regional plan, revised every four years.

From the first approved Truckee Meadows Regional Plan in 1991 to the 2007 plan, the agency has grown into its challenging mission. The first plan was overly broad; it didn't have a lot of teeth. Planners designated separate districts for residential and commercial and other uses. It looked like regional planning, but it didn't do much. It just created more boundaries for the cities to argue over. But in the last few years, the agency has become more about defining the shape of the squid that Reno-Sparks is becoming. It is about finding the place where the city meets the vast spaces of the Great Basin. There has been more inquiry into what the policies can create, not just what they can prevent. Slowly, regional planning in Truckee Meadows, amid the drawing of the lines between private places, has begun defining a public realm.

By 2000, the TMRPA had thrown out the previous plans to work on a new one. It set up subcommittees, and much like Envision Utah and other regional coalitions, spent eighteen months holding some two hundred public meetings. At the end of that process, the agency staff realized there was agreement over 95 percent of the issues, which included infill strategies, infrastructure concurrency requirements, and annexations. The last 5 percent caused the City of Sparks to sue the agency after the 2002 plan was approved—even after one of the Sparks representatives had voted for the plan. "It's been a battle to get this far," Dwight Dortsch, the Reno City council member who is one of the city's four representatives to the regional governing board, told me. The compromising nature of the regional agency and its enforcement power has meant that elected officials are usually unwilling to take regional policies very far. "A lot of policies in the plan, you could drive a truck through," one official says. Often, either a policy has to be broad or it doesn't get in.

But it has helped that the agency is required to make and enforce policies. Unlike with Envision Utah, "encourage infill development" cannot take on the simplicity of sage advice; it must be worked out in detail—where, how, and who. Everybody agrees that infill development is a good thing, regional planning officials say, but it gets down to how you do it, how fast, and where: In Truckee Meadows, as in the Wasatch Front, regional planners could not think in the simple center-and-edge way of traditional smart growth. Truckee Meadows contains steep, unbuildable slopes; many of its existing infill parcels have no water rights. In Truckee Meadows, growth—and urbanism—have to happen where they can.

These constraints, though, offer planners clues about a regional growth strategy. In Reno-Sparks, steep slopes and public lands squeeze development along long, sinewy valleys radiating from the downtowns. And because subdivisions had been built at the edges of the basin, and in other, more distant basins, building in between them, connecting them, was actually infill. The 2002 plan designated these long valleys as "corridors," designating them for denser development to support and be supported by a new bus rapid transit system, in which buses would take on many of the efficient characteristics of rail transport. The scheme formed a big cross centering on Virginia Street and Fourth Street, with a Mill Street corridor branching to the airport. Complementing the corridors were centers, at key points such as the university, the growing Redfield area south of downtown, and the area around the old Stead Air Force base. Using its power of conformance, the TMRPA would wield its stick in dry, hilly Reno, Sparks, and unincorporated Washoe County, forcing the cities to grow according to its concerted vision.

The most intriguing policy of the Truckee Meadows Regional Planning Agency's approach is its North Virginia Street transit-oriented development (TOD) corridor, the northern half of the Virginia Street spine that forms half of the corridor cross. Virginia Street is Reno's prime meridian. Its bridge over the Truckee River was the city's original crossing. The city's first "Biggest Little City" arch spanned it just to the north in downtown. In these blocks, tourist shops and bars cram along its flanks, and to the south, Virginia Street runs through the thick of Truckee Meadows. And, indeed, South Virginia Street is another TOD corridor. Because of its location in the heart of Reno and Truckee Meadows, it is most ready for the bus rapid transit envisioned by the agency.

But the North Virginia Street corridor is the future. The combination of its proximity to downtown and the university and its unbuilt land produces the most possibilities. Where South Virginia is already packed with types of development frowned upon by planners and infill parcels are few and small, North Virginia pierces large tracts that have never seen development. If South Virginia today makes the most sense for the "transit" part of TOD, North Virginia is most interesting for the actual "development." North Virginia Street, connecting some of the city's most important amenities and landmarks, passing through some of its most beautiful country, granting some of its best views, and reaching to some of its highest-growth areas, has the opportunity to become one of Reno's most monumental streets. It connects the string of North Valleys, along with the U.S. 395 freeway, often forming the only link between them. And yet, in many stretches close to the city center, it traverses open land, crosses dirt roads, and passes neighborhoods of mobile homes. Huge condominium and apartment buildings sit on hillsides and ridges between trails heading up into the mountains. This corridor embodies the demographics of Reno's transient, renter-heavy, mobile home–dwelling, recreation-loving populace. "Perhaps nothing indicates growth in the North Valleys like the changes coming to Old Virginia Street," wrote the Reno *Gazette Journal* in spring of 2006, describing how the narrow, two-lane road running alongside a deep ravine, with jackrabbits, magpies, and an occasional coyote in the adjacent sagebrush would soon be converted into a six-lane throughway.[64] Planners included in the North Virginia Street TOD corridor an area that averaged about a quarter mile on either side of the road. In some areas, the corridor balloons out, in others it sucks in, to fit the changing landscape and existing development.

Like Daybreak in Utah, the place feels like a frontier. Virginia Street shoots north from downtown past the Silver Legacy, over Interstate 80, and hugs the western edge of the University of Nevada–Reno. Past McCar-ran Boulevard, Virginia Street curves and enters a shallow canyon parallel-ing railroad tracks and cottonwood trees. It's here where one realizes that North Virginia Street may have the most junk per acre of any designated TOD corridor. In the steep ravines that branch off the canyon, spotted with pine trees and worn four-wheel trails going straight up the fall lines, are old ovens and engine blocks and scattered chewing tobacco tins.

There are people who ride transit here. One will see residents of the apartment complexes along the corridor scurrying across Virginia Street's travel lanes carrying groceries or coming home from work. One resident of the Pinnacles subdivision, which sits on top of one of the hills overlooking North Virginia Street, a crown of red houses and poplar trees, says he chose his house because of its transit access. "I ride because it's less expensive," he says. "I cut down my costs. It's $600 per year as opposed to several thousand a year for a car. I know it's inconvenient but I don't have to work so hard. I can do things I like to do, like read. . . . When I was in a position to purchase a home, I bought this because I liked the neighborhood, it was close to the university, and I had two routes. It's a higher up elevation, and it's close to the backcountry."

As you move up the corridor, though, the majority of folks are trying to get away from the city, not make it more accessible. On Mohawk Lane, a rutted dirt road just off Virginia Street, is a cluster of prefab houses. And typical is the resident carving out his own version of paradise between the highway and the apron of Peavine Mountain. One family had just put their mobile home on the lot, having to remove six single-wide trailers "with Mexicans living in" them. "Out back was nothing but shit," the husband says. "Old dishwashers and crap everywhere." A spiky German Olive tree provided minimal shade. The guy across the street had three peacocks and a donkey. ("Shit, they get on top of your car, they don't care.") To the west, toward the rail tracks, packs of kids broke windows of old cars. He's digging a trench for a fence to stake out his property, and there are long-term ambitions. "My wife wants to make a pond with some waterfall bullshit," he says.

"We don't go anywhere unless we have to," the man continues. "It's one reason we moved out here. To miss the traffic and shit. I'm from Truckee, and if I could live in the mountains I would. It's too expensive." When he does have to leave is nearly every night to work, as a dealer and pit boss for the graveyard shift at the Peppermill Casino. Each night, at 1 a.m., he rumbles his Dodge pickup down the dirt road, hearing the coyotes, rabbits, and frogs.

The most desolate straits of North Virginia Street lie where the road contours along the toe of Peavine Mountain and the rim of Lemmon Valley. There are empty Airstream trailers strewn in chain-link and cyclone-fenced lots, and standing on its own near the intersection with Stead Boulevard, a stout roadhouse bar, the Air Base Inn. It's built with concrete blocks painted red, with a tattered red vinyl booth out in front, which seems neither a design detail nor an accident. There is a rusty metal scaffolding where a neon sign once flashed and a dirt parking lot where a few trucks are parked haphazardly. It is noon, and inside are the names of locals painted on wooden tags hanging from the ceiling: "Bonnie," "Bull," "Chet." They have Budweiser and Budweiser on tap.

The inn is the preferred watering hole for a number of aging local residents in Lemmon Valley and Stead, some of whom are already holding court at the bar and are well on their way. The rather ramshackle structure has proven durable: It started out as a garage in the 1930s but was opportunely converted to a bar in the 1940s, when the Stead Air Force base opened during World War II. The days might be numbered for the inn, however, as the owner, Harold, who lives out back, is eagerly looking for a buyer for the property.

I tell the bartender that the bar lies in a transit-oriented development corridor, that the city wants to put high-density housing, mixed-use buildings, and bus rapid transit along Virginia Street. It's news to her. "I've always thought that anyone who lived along the highway that had some property was sitting on a gold mine," she says. "They're just going to keep building. People call it progress. I don't. They'll probably bulldoze this place, which is kind of sad." And it's news to me that this place is already a mixed-use property: "They couldn't run the bar and live back there, like Harold did," she says.

A guy at the bar wearing a Union Pacific jacket flags down my attention. "Hey, what do you want young fella? You want my money? You a Mormon?"

I tell him no, but he doesn't listen. "I'm one of them. I'm a jack Mormon," the guy says, ordering another drink.

Trials and Errors on the Todd

The City of Reno, which has brought its North Virginia Street transit-oriented development plan through the rigors of regional conformance, isn't concerned with all the junk, however. The city's most pressing concern is infrastructure. Suburban subdivisions have ended up where ground is flat and cheap and water is available. The resulting pattern wasn't a neat concentric circle of central city, suburban and rural, and water systems, sewers, and roads are a patchwork rather than a network. "In our community, places have hopscotched," says Julee Olander, the Reno planner in charge of the "Todd" plan, as Truckee Meadows area planners are in the habit of calling the TOD corridor.[65] "Within the McCarran Ring, it's fairly urban, then suburban out at the edge. But there are places between urban and suburban that are rural."

Many roads are dirt. Sewer pipes were put in twenty years ago but were not set up for urban densities. Few areas even have water lines; most residents have their own water wells, and for new property owners without any water rights, there is no one to turn to. The more interesting problem, though, is how to configure higher-density development near transit nodes within the land and other property constraints. You can't simply apply a quarter-mile or half-mile walking radius here and then build forty units to the acre, because within that distance you're certain to hit public land, steep slopes, or both, and it's unlikely that any of the land will have water rights. And, with neither an attractive transit system nor enough people to warrant one, achieving the TOD will take some growing pains. Virginia Street, for example, will actually become more intimidating, as it is scheduled to widen to six lanes, none of which will be dedicated to a bus rapid transit or light-rail—yet. "Is it the chicken or the egg?" Olander asks. "There will be traffic until we get a higher density and transit comes. Transit will only come if there's ridership there. There will be a lag time."

Reno is starting with the basics. They're asking for the buildings in the TOD-designated area to front the street directly and to provide safe pedestrian access. "We're looking for anything within the corridor to be walkable," Olander says. "Most people come in and say, here's our parking plan. We're saying, how do you walk there?" Much of the district is a compromise, owing to the resistance of neighbors to the idea of more density and to developers who would have to get loans from a financial industry that still has trouble backing mixed-use development, of mixing commercial and residential loans. The minimum density has been lowered throughout the process to eighteen dwelling units per acre, which would likely be manifested as townhouses. The floor-area ratio (FAR) ended up at .25, which means that a one-story building covers only a quarter of its lot; a two-story building, an eighth of its lot.

But the heart of what the regional plan and the city are seeking is the creation of an urban public realm. Among other things, that's what TOD is: a way to get people out of the privacy of their autos and into more interactive modes of transport, such as light-rail, buses, and perhaps most important for the end result, walking. What North Virginia Street offers, like other places in the Intermountain West, is a chance to integrate the public realm *out there*, the raw federal public land residents love so much, with an urban public realm *here*, of walking streets, squares, parks, and transit. Here, the city is trying to learn from its past mistakes in allowing neighborhoods to be so disconnected from each other, streets to be unwalkable, and private development to block access to the backcountry. The city has designated trailheads at certain points along the North Virginia TOD corridor. The trailheads require the city and the developers to work together to design access to public land into their projects and to bring the vastness and expanses into the realm of the urban walking routes of living and working.

"Regional Planning has made an impact in the sense of looking at the big picture," Julee Olander says. "It makes agencies have to comply with someone else besides themselves, so we don't have narrow, within-my-backyard-in-the-city-of-Reno thinking. It brings out the issues. But at the same time, regional planning doesn't have to deal with going to the public forums and hearing, 'There's nothing out here on North Virginia. How can you ask for 30 units to the acre?' That's outrageous to these folks. Regional planning doesn't hear those conversations.

"It's going to be a bit of a trial and error. I think we'll find some problems," Olander continues. "I tell developers, 'You'll be the guinea pig, you'll show us what works and what doesn't work.' It's a challenge. No easy answers."

Public Realms, Private Politics?

Envision Utah, Kennecott Land, Truckee Meadows Regional Planning Agency, and the City of Reno are working to create physical urbanity in the isolation of the Great Basin. It's a tall order, and they have explored ways to mix uses, to define a street with building enclosure, to get people out of their autos and onto the sidewalk, buses, and light-rail cars in the difficult conservative political and cultural climate. But have these efforts led to social urbanism? Have they satisfied the origins and underpinnings of the regional planning and traditional neighborhood movements, of a sacrifice of the private for the public? Most important, have they created a strong regionwide public realm, with public spaces large and small? After all, isn't physical urbanity only a means to the ends of a rich quality of life in neighborhoods and regions?

It's easy to see the theoretical connection between bright concepts like front porches, parks, and greenways and a social utopia of community. It's easy to make the jump on promotional materials. Many urbanists yearn for places where physical and social urbanism dovetail, like millennium-old European cities. As urban designer Jan Gehl points out in his book, *Public Space, Public Life*, whose title enunciates this concept, Copenhagen has found a match between its well-defined public spaces built off a fine-grained medieval street network and its culture of people using these spaces.[66]

In the United States, physical and social urbanism have not met as easy a match. In many cases, the price for good physical urbanism has been a compromised public realm. Strangely, this trend has its roots in the same soil as those revered by the regionalists and new urbanists: Ebenezer Howard's Garden City and Radburn. In fact, one of Radburn's most important contributions might be its innovative form of private government, which became the template for the common interest development (CID) government, more commonly known as homeowners' associations (HOAs). As Evan McKenzie writes in *Privatopia: Homeowner Associations and the Rise of Residential Private Government,* "Some of Howard's utopian vision was retained, other [elements] excised and new elements added as a new kind of residential construction evolved throughout the twentieth century . . . Designers of American CIDs dwell on the physical plan but slight the social-economic structure of the community."[67]

New urbanism, in its attempts to gain ground in the United States, sometimes takes on traits of privatopia. Because physical urbanism goes against the dominant development pattern in the United States, it needs institutional supports. While city codes offer many of these, through design standards, it's often easier to do it privately, through CC&Rs and homeowners' associations. Ironically, a form of development pushed by regional planning coalitions, once realized, itself pushes a type of government on the other end of the scale. Smaller, even, than local jurisdictions, HOA governments push the agenda of a smaller group of people. In this case, in place of one definition of citizenship—a process of liberation from the private sphere of our homes into the public place of community and political life—that given in urban historian Sam Bass Warner's *The Private City* may be more apt: Seek wealth while the job of cities is to be a "community of private money makers."[68]

New urbanist proposals are most vulnerable to these compromises in places such as Utah and Nevada, where they come from left field and need an entrée into acceptability. And as many edge cities in the West have not been able to keep up with the growth, they have relied on the private sector to create, and in some cases manage, the "public realm." It's no wonder that the Utah development community is building new urbanist projects: They carefully market the walkable, old-fashioned concepts endorsed by groups like Envision Utah and shed the gated community stigma, all the while maintaining even more control over the development than if there were walls and gates. And density is often more efficient and profitable for developers and builders.

The concept plays perfectly into the recreational-amenity lifestyle so many are seeking in the Intermountain West. These developments emphasize the values of safety, family, and wholesomeness already associated with the Interior West, combined with the opportunities of the open landscape, and accentuated with a dash of history and cutting edge. At Harvest Park, in Mapleton, Utah, in one of the most conservative counties in America, "the 'neighborhood' means something very different. A planned park-laden living space where it doesn't pay to even start the car. Here you go to church and come home from school. You go to the store and come home from the park and still never leave the neighborhood."[69] On one hand, the statement evokes the pedestrian and complete-community planning goals of Envision Utah and new urbanists, and, in fact, Harvest Park won an Envision Utah Quality Growth Award. On the other, you could pay particular attention to the *go to church* and *never leave the neighborhood* parts of the marketing pitch, and to the homogenous lifestyle to which it alludes.

The Daybreak Homeowners' Association office, for its part, sits across the street from the marketing office in a brand-new, warm, craftsman-style house. The Daybreak HOA manager is experienced in homeowners' associations, having managed them for several years in Reno. He is speaking with a kid wearing a company golf shirt tucked into baggy jeans, a pair of sunglasses propped up on his sweaty forehead. The kid is hunched over the counter going over drawings of a landscape plan with the HOA administrator in minute detail. The sticking point is a waterfall that the new Daybreak owner is intent on installing. The administrator is telling him how the scheme needs to be changed if the plan is to clear the formidable Daybreak architectural review board.

The HOA man is telling me after the landscape kid has left, "The thing about Reno, the recreational opportunities are exactly the same as here. Recreation is always a part of these things." I ask him what is attracting people to Daybreak. "Having a community provide activities for these families is attractive," he says. "There's not as much privacy here, but residents get a satisfaction of participating in a lifestyle that is demonstrative of what their goals are. We're providing them the opportunity to get together with their neighbors." He continues, "You'll see more families walking around here, more kids. Lots of participation. Lots of participation. The project and the activities are successful in Utah because of the family lifestyle here. It's manifesting itself as a real walking lifestyle community."

And, Daybreak is gearing up to be bigger and more powerful than the City of South Jordan. At the center will be the homeowners' association. "The HOA will end up becoming powerful by design," the HOA administrator says. "Cities can't keep up with growth, so developers create amenities attractive for buyers. As a city manager, you're just governing. Here, we have the opportunity to provide activities." In other words, Daybreak not only governs families but also programs their daily lives.

Many of the development's new citizens would tend to agree. "The way one person described it, it's like living on a cruise ship—there's always something to do," one homeowner tells me. It's also like living in a museum, especially for toy-loving Utahns who are known for letting their possessions such as boats, dirt bikes, and swing sets spill out of their houses. Another homeowning couple noted that the HOA was hawkish enough to warn them about their horse trailers the first week they moved in—as with the original City of Zion plan, such things are supposed to be kept in the off-site garage where every resident gets a space. (In one of Tooele's Overlake townhouses, a frustrated resident opened up his garage to reveal a dormant hot tub, a swing set, and a pair of quad ATVs stuffed together.) Most, however, agree that, in the end, the regulation is a good thing. Its importance is not so big compared to the amenities of the development. Many moved to Daybreak from half- or even full-acre lots, and are quick to tout the benefits of a twelve-minute lawn mow.

The whole package has some who are responsible for the greater public a little uneasy. Ricky Horst's city manager office faces uphill to Daybreak's sunny spot on the West Bench, and he figures the effort to integrate the development into the city will have to push up the same slope. "How do we integrate people out there with people here?" Horst asks about Daybreak. "We've got to have a presence there. They will have a large and powerful HOA, and we have to be careful they're part of the city and not a city unto themselves." He shrugs. "In many ways, it's a large gated community." Nathan Francis admits as much. "Because of our branding, people say, 'I'm from Daybreak,' not South Jordan," he says. "We want to change that."

Daybreak is winning for better or worse, but the spoils are not all its own: The influence of its ideas are spreading throughout the city. There are smaller examples of Envision Utah concepts in other new developments but with some reservations. Across the street from South Jordan's City Hall, for example, the Arbors gives residents more tightly packed mini-castles with a narrower street—and a coded gate at the entrance.

Below Daybreak, South Jordan High Pointe, despite its flaws, aims to "make maximum use of land space to provide all desirable elements usually associated with homes built on larger land parcels," and provides access to "trailheads and parks that are planned to interact with neighboring developments and the community as a whole."[70]

Even Ivory Homes has gone new urbanist. The company's Ivory Ridge development in the tech industry–suffused suburb of Lehi in northern Utah County is no meager subdivision but a "master planned community" of which the detached single-family house is only one option. Ivory Ridge will also include townhouses and live-work lofts. Of course, this development was advertised as "something big—something really BIG—from Ivory Homes . . . a country club atmosphere with a community feel to it."[71]

If urbanism is a goal worth pursuing by means of a public realm that is engaged by private development, what is the most effective way to do this in the Great Basin city? A historically derivative subdivision? A patched-together badlands? A consensus-seeking, carrot-toting coalition, or a powerful, stick-wielding peacemaker with limited vision capability? Up on the West Bench, the answers are decades away. The sun has already set over the Oquirrh Mountains, which are much closer and more imposing than the Wasatch. I'm walking around the large man-made lake that will be near the middle of Daybreak. It's windy as hell, and a few plucky residents are reconsidering their decision to take a canoe on the lake. There aren't any houses yet built on the western side of the lake, so the copper mine looms over us. I realize that the million-dollar views toward Lone Peak at sunrise aren't the most important ones here. It's the slightly ominous views up the hill. This vista hints not at the sprawling out into imagined space but at the revising of the urban Great Basin landscape to fit the realities of our time and our place: not what people come here to escape from, but what we are starting to confront.

The Depot

To Zion, To Aztlán

You could identify Temple Square as the center of Salt Lake City, Utah, and not be wrong. But you might not be 100 percent right. Four blocks to the west, two buildings at the edge of downtown make a strong claim to the historic gravity of the city: the railroad depots. These buildings, separated by a few blocks along the north–south trajectory of the rail line, are both spectacular and intact. Today, they are time warps, legacies from a much different period of Salt Lake's history, when the city's existence seemed more prone to chance. The red-brick façades, steep mansard roofs, the mural of Brigham Young and two trains of wagons and bulls high on one of the walls of the Union Pacific Depot, and the sixty-foot-high hall "lighted by three immense arched windows on each side through green opalescent glass" that "gives the room a dignified quietness," as the *Salt Lake Tribune* described the Rio Grande Depot just after its construction in 1910, create auras of sublimity.[1] Walking through the depots today offers solemn sanctuary from the modern landscapes of consumption that surround them. Hard-soled shoes click and echo in the rooms' space.

The intent of this architecture was not as noble as its form, but just as awesome. The depots are remnants of this Great Basin city's early industrial arm wrestling. They are the result of the jockeying by the railroads to gain control of Salt Lake, and thus the West. The Union Pacific (U.P.), owned by Edward Harriman, having completed the transcontinental railroad link at Promontory Summit in northern Utah in 1869, dominated the transportation business in Salt Lake Valley in the late decades of the nineteenth century. But George Gould, the son of financier Jay Gould, created his own railroad, the Western Pacific, from San Francisco to Salt Lake. Gould realized that the Denver and Rio Grande was building a line from Denver to Salt Lake and thus Salt Lake became the linchpin of the two lines that would compete with the U.P. Gould needed an impressive train station to lure passengers away from the U.P. and challenge Harriman's monopoly. And so the depots are clear symbols of Salt Lake as western city of naked capitalist ambition, as opposed to those of Salt Lake as Mormon utopia a few blocks away, a notion that Utah historians Thomas Alexander and James Allen articulate as, "in its uniqueness, a study of community planning and cooperative enterprise. In its sameness, a study of urbanism in the American West."[2] In contrast to Temple Square's orderly vision of an urban utopia, this, you could argue, is the heart of Salt Lake's real urban history, of capitalist competition, and multiplicity.[3] Without the infusion of this capital, these buildings and the people who worked in and around them, the Great Basin Kingdom would never have achieved the prominence it now holds.

Back from the edges of the urban Great Basin, from the castles in culs-de-sac and pods of sprawl, saltscapes and green dreamscapes, Mormon pride and California ambition, I have landed where I began but not quite. On a day when a frontal storm moving across the west desert threatens to wreck the warm sunshine and blossoms of an early spring, I take Trax from the East Bench to downtown, where Crossroads Mall is being demolished across from Temple Square. But I don't stop there, continuing west on the light-rail to the terminus at the Delta Center, recently renamed EnergySolutions Arena after a nuclear waste storage and processing company. I walk through the Union Pacific Depot—now with a popular music club in one wing—to the Gateway Mall, the bright yellow product of the 1990s where spurting fountains are marked by the 2002 Olympic Games' giant snowflake logo and the gaudy Olympics theme anthem plays intermittently; here, as I shoot photos of the street scene along Rio Grande Street, the two young rent-a-cops guarding the southern flank of the mall from the homeless encampments across 200 South approach me and say that I can't take pictures here without permission from the mall. I ask them whether this is a public street, and they shake their heads. "Not anymore," they say. Then I walk south through crowds of homeless people lined up for the shelters on Rio Grande Street to the front doors of the Rio Grande Depot. In one wing of this building is the Rio Grande Café, a city institution where I sold tequila and taco combinations for two summers as a waiter and bartender. I've come and gone from this building hundreds of times but have rarely entered its main hall and never really admired it. Like the U.P. depot, it's empty and feels pristine, its dignified quietness still presiding. Though trains don't stop here anymore, its doors still open westward, and I walk over that way to check out the view.

This book has been about measuring the Great Basin metropolis as it expands outward rapidly into the high desert, about urbanism as a mediation between people and a seductive, unforgiving landscape. We have seen how old and new ideas about the Basin, for better or worse, are shaping the remaking of the Intermountain city—its embrace of the possibilities of the landscape and its chances to conform to the landscape's limits. As we have seen, today's frontier is not an outward one of an endless horizon but an inward one of building a good city.

In any good city, the center must relate to the edge and the edge must relate to the center. Here, in the Great Basin, this is happening, slowly. The meadows and forests of the Wasatch Mountains have invaded the roofs of the Mormon headquarters as the Great Salt Lake shorelands becomes a city for birds. Peavine Mountain is circled by the concerns of half a million city dwellers while the Truckee River washes recreators and transients through a new downtown. The concerns of the inner cities are broadcast to the exurbs, and the junk-strewn stretches of Virginia Street may become the city's new backbone. All of this, I hope, has led to what will be the true urbanism of the Great Basin, and that is the comfortable meeting of people and their ideas, those at the center and those at the edge.

Salt Lake's depot buildings, in addition to marking capital infusion, are also symbols of the city's role as a meeting place in a once-thought-barren landscape. Downtown Salt Lake's center needs to be the place where multiple ideas of the Great Basin's experiences, meanings, and possibilities overlap with one another and create a city. Salt Lake is Zion, but as a modern city it embodies the ambitions, opportunities, and possibilities of other faiths. In the physical isolation of the Great Basin, with the global age upon us, Utah's cacophony is one of its greatest assets.

Today, the Rio Grande Depot's grand windows look westward down a bleak stretch of 300 South toward what the City of Salt Lake believes will be its new portal to the future: Salt Lake Central Station. Here, the City has put forth a vision for commuter trains, light-rail, buses, bicyclists, and walkers to converge on a central hub around which will rise a neighborhood of rowhouses, townhouses, and condominiums housing twenty thousand people.[4] New streets would carve up the historic ten-acre blocks into smaller blocks. Property owners and designers have dancing visions of European urbanism. A designer hired by the Salt Lake

Redevelopment Agency envisions a version of Barcelona's Las Ramblas on 300 South; a property owner hopes to build a version of Copenhagen's Tivoli on his block.[5] A 1998 rendering of a future "Depot District" weaves the historic depot structures with a colorful urban fabric; a massive park occupies the space between a consolidated railroad corridor and I-15.[6]

The Depot District will be Salt Lake's "most urban" neighborhood. While malls need high-end department stores, the Depot District would take a finer-grained, more neighborhood approach to its commercial, luring a grocery store, coffee shops, and smaller stores and galleries. While the City Creek Center will be for old folks and Mormons, younger, edgier residents will like the "grittier" Depot District, with its historic warehouses and railroad tracks, a mayoral aide told the *Salt Lake Tribune*.[7] "An urban neighborhood evokes images of a broad mix of experiences, activities and uses," a 1998 plan for the area stated. "The strongest, most important, diverse and enriching element in the mix must be homes for people of all incomes, backgrounds, ages and interests."[8]

The city has targeted this diversity for a place that has traditionally supported it but has also been cleaved off from the rest of the city for some time. According to historian John McCormick, the area emerged as a distinct district after 1870, when the railroad arrived in Salt Lake and divided the city in half. In the previous two decades, the area had grown in a similar manner to the rest of the burgeoning Mormon city: small one- or two-story adobe houses set back on the large lots platted by Joseph Smith's City of Zion plan. True to Brigham Young's ambitions for the settlement, almost all the residents of 300 West, 400 West, and other streets west of the Temple blocks were farmers, and they rode out every day to their fields on the outskirts of the city.

The railroad's access to national markets made the large blocks attractive for industry. By 1890, the intersection of 300 West and 500 North was crowded with a stockyard, two breweries, and two tanneries. The result was an industrial district whose bizarreness is visible even today, with leftover houses fronting onto the wide streets, Mormon setbacks, and fruit trees overlaid with helter-skelter capitalist ventures. While the Avenues was emerging as an upper-middle-class artisan and merchant neighborhood above the smelter haze, with nice views and connected by a streetcar system to downtown, the railroad isolated the West Side from the rest of the city. The combination of the isolation from mainstream Mormon society and access to the railroad and its related industrial jobs created a neighborhood that became home to the often-Gentile and

Salt Lake's "most urban neighborhood" will grow between depots past (above) and present (below).

often-immigrant working classes. Greek Town was from 400 to 600 West; Italians settled around the depot; Japantown was in the present location of the Salt Palace on West Temple and 100 South; and Armenians settled behind the depot. "Little Syria" was the area surrounding 300 South and 500 West because many Syrian immigrants were employed at the nearby Utah Fire Clay Company. They lived side by side with unpleasant industries like pounds, dumps, and crematoriums. The American economy split the Zion blocks with narrower streets and alleys to pack in more worker residences and factories. The new interior streets were free from regulation and degenerated into "crowded back alleys of squalor."

By 1971, two thirds of housing on the 125-block area of the West Side was rental property. Three quarters of housing in the district was "blighted." The disconnection and isolation of this area became city policy. As in most American cities, the tool of isolating some properties to remove nuisance and protect other properties' values, known as "zoning," first happened in the West Side in the late 1920s, when Salt Lake City removed any provision for residential use in the district. A 1941 plan maintained that trend, keeping only a few isolated blocks for housing of the entire "Gateway" area from West Temple to Interstate 15. A 1978 plan, meanwhile, called the inner West Side a "gray area" and a place where "a veritable maze of strikingly incompatible uses scars the landscape." A group carried out a door-to-door survey and found that people did live here, but they seemed remnants of an earlier age. The "typical household," the study found, was a one-person household that was over fifty years of age, unemployed, and living in a masonry house also over fifty years old. Only 8 percent had gone to college, 41 percent were below the poverty level, and 80 percent rented their homes. The image of the area was troubling: "The Gateway district is a propos the 'gate' to the city," the plan noted. "Yet there is no sense of entry into the city, nor any indication of welcome for the many guests the city beckons. The picture that is thrust onto the visitor . . . is that of hapless and dismal abandonment." As recently as 2004, the *Salt Lake Tribune* pointed out that the future Depot District is often called a "no-man's land."

At the same time, the West Side became a meeting place for different walks of life and an alternate—more urban—version of the Great Basin Kingdom. Even the foreboding 1978 plan recognized that 42 percent of residents walked as their transportation, 29 percent took the bus, and 23 percent shopped within two blocks of their residence. The plan found that the Gateway was "by no means a run-of-the-mill blight area" and that it had "lots of potential" in having "the best public transit in the city." It offered recommendations that the city create amenities, such as a tourism center and museums, but also a differentiation between pedestrian and vehicular circulation, accessibility of the central parts of blocks, defined commercial streets, and coordination of alleys. The inner West Side became home to gathering places of those outside the cultural mainstream: the Trapp bar, one of Salt Lake's first gay bars, opened by a former San Franciscan in the early 1990s; and Centro Civico Mexicano, the Mexican cultural center that not only hosts the traditional *bodas* (wedding celebrations) and *quinceañeras* (fifteenth-birthday celebrations) but also rents out to Tongans, Samoans, and Pakistanis.

Indeed, in the last three decades, ethnic minorities like Latinos, Polynesians, and refugee groups have claimed Salt Lake's aging neighborhoods between downtown and the industry spreading out into the open desert—and have remade them in the image of both opportunity and newfound struggle. Head west from downtown, over the railroad tracks, and over Interstate 15, and you'll land well into the western street digits. These neighborhoods—Glendale, Poplar Grove, Rose Park, and Guadalupe—are the thin layer of green trees and humanity tucking in Salt Lake from the Great Basin beyond. With its inexpensive neighborhoods, good transit, and proximity to the job base of the central city, the West Side offered much to newcomers, becoming what scholar Timothy Davis calls a "hand-me-down landscape." Here are the auto-oriented, inner-ring suburbs and strips of commercial spaces that every American city built on its way out of town in the mid-century, where, Davis writes, subsequent generations of ethnic minorities "are quietly converting barren and forsaken automobile-oriented wastelands into vibrantly humanized and strikingly heterogeneous places."[9]

Latinos in particular have revived Salt Lake's West Side neighborhoods, having packed into the district's houses and apartments. As in Los Angeles, Mexican immigrants push carts selling *helados* (ice cream) and *elotes* (corn) through cul-de-sacked inner-ring suburbia. They have filled retail spaces with small *tiendas* (stores) and *mercados* (markets) for daily needs like grocery shopping and wiring money back to Mexico. Occasionally, the influence of the new West Side inches into downtown, such as the taco carts that moved into a Sears parking lot at 800 South and State Street. The vendors quickly multiplied and undercut each other. The tacos went from 99 cents to 50 cents. David Rosas, owner of Tacos Don Rafa, was one of the first. "I am a pioneer," Rosas told me once. "When I got here, I saw people used big tortillas. I said, 'Those aren't tacos.' In Mexico, we use small corn tortillas and fry them in oil. Often people ask for sour cream, butter, cheese. Cheese! Real tacos need only salsa, cilantro and onions. That's how we eat them over there."

It's one aspect of what some call "Latino new urbanism," a new twist on *the* new urbanism. While one tries to create a more urban environment for suburbanized people, the other does the opposite: the natural consequence of forcing people used to walking, taking transit, spending time in public places, and shopping at small stores into an American suburban environment.[10] The way of life in Latin American cities is in essence new urbanism, without the regulations. The concept of people living within walking distance of shops, schools, places of work and entertainment, and easy access to mass transit is all that many Latino immigrants have known before coming to this country, and they often feel trapped when they arrive here because of the car dependency. They complain that here everything is far away. Latino new urbanism's critics argue that the concept romanticizes the conditions of poverty many Latino immigrants face, and most immigrants would take the American suburban landscape and lifestyle if given the choice. But supporters say they view new urbanism as a way out of impoverished conditions, and they argue that upwardly mobile Latinos often opt for cars and a house in the suburbs because it is their only option in suburban America.[11]

The challenge for Salt Lake's West Side, however, is fitting in with the city across the railroad tracks while maintaining some cultural integrity. And this goal has not been easy to achieve, even for those who have come here precisely because it is the Mormon Zion. Despite the economic opportunity, the neighborhoods of the West Side have fought prejudice, discrimination, and ultimately, isolation and violence. Rose Park's Latino population more than tripled from 1990 to 2000, growing from 11.6 percent to 37 percent of the neighborhood. By 2000, languages other than English were spoken in 37 percent of Rose Park households. Yet despite riding—and, in another respect, driving—the state's economic engine, the residents of the West Side neighborhoods didn't benefit from the boom as much as the rest of the Wasatch Front. The median income of Rose Park increased by only 5 percent from 1990 to 2000, adjusted for inflation, compared to 34 percent statewide. Latinos, especially, were left behind. A research team from Georgetown University in Washington, D.C., visited Salt Lake in 2002 and noted that despite the bilingual resources of the LDS Church, it fell short of offering biculturalism. One of the researchers said that immigrants with whom they spoke were disappointed with the lack of understanding underneath Utahns' friendly faces. "People here are silent about their neighbors," she said. "That's disturbing."[12]

Latinos aren't against fighting back. Complaints from nearby businesses, including the Taco Time across the street from the taco vendors in the Sears parking lot, led the Salt Lake City council to ban taco carts south of 600 South, but it later reversed its decision. "We would have fought *mucho, mucho, mucho*," David Rosas, the owner of Tacos Don Rafa, told me. "But if they would have said no, I guess we would have gone to the Capitol and sold tacos there." Gilberto Rejon, meanwhile, was arrested during a 2001 Immigration and Naturalization Service sting on the Salt Lake International Airport called "Operation Safe Travel." The federal government was ready to deport him to his native Jalisco, Mexico, but allowed him to shepherd his U.S.-born children through school first. In the meantime, Rejon became a minor celebrity, appearing on an ABC News special on illegal immigration and writing and recording songs such as "La Redada" (The Raid) and "Persecución" to voice his disapproval of U.S. Immigration policy and enforcement. "There are lots of possibilities for our children here," Rejon's wife, Esperanza, said. "In Mexico, there are a lot fewer." The children were already acculturated in the United States. Rejon's eleven-year-old spoke mostly English at home. She must go, but the older siblings planned to stay behind. His nineteen-year-old studied at an alternative high school and worked at Taco Maker. "I don't want to go back to Mexico. I don't have any friends there." Rejon added: "Utah embraced me when I got here. Utah gave me a job. Utah enabled my kids to get an education. I definitely want to come back."[13] In 2006, when immigrants and their supporters protested proposed changes to U.S. immigration policy, Salt Lake City held one of the nation's largest marches, attracting an estimated fifteen thousand people.

Pacific Islanders have also made Utah their unlikely Zion. Thousands of natives of Tonga, Samoa, and other South Pacific islands and their Utah-born offspring have a long history in Utah, much of it grounded in the LDS Church. Islanders make convincing Mormons. The reverence for family and authority in the Tongan and Samoan cultures is matched only by the church, their mean household size of almost five people outdoing the state average. In fact, Mormon missions to the South Pacific began before the church's move to the Great Basin. In 1844, church missionaries visited Tahiti, and when, in the late 1800s, Hawaiians, Tahitians, Tongans, and Samoans began to immigrate to the Great Basin at the promise of spiritual salvation and a better life, cultural conflict led the church to establish a colony for the islanders in Skull Valley, fifty miles out into the Great Basin over the Stansbury Mountains from Tooele Valley. The seventy-five islanders named the place Iosepa—"Joseph" in Hawaiian—after Joseph F. Smith, a nephew of the church's original prophet, who served his mission in Hawaii. They irrigated and farmed, planted fruit trees, and became famous for their yellow roses. But Iosepa was a rough go for islanders used to the bounty of the tropics. Irrigating the dry country, and trying to grow traditional foods such as seaweed in briny reservoir water, was hard work. They suffered from the harsh winters and endured an outbreak of leprosy, and almost all of its surviving residents returned to the South Pacific.

In the mid-twentieth century, Polynesians began to immigrate to Utah again. They created their own Latter-day Saint wards and stakes and spiced up the normally bland Sunday services with their tropical flower leis, *lava lava* skirts, and sandals. They formed brass marching bands, played rugby and cricket, drank the intoxicating island beverage made from kava root powder, and received the king of Tonga on visits to this new outpost. This time, though, they faced a more urban existence and a different kind of isolation. "I thought it would be a place for just Mormons," one Western Samoan immigrant who came to Utah in the 1980s and who now runs a Boys and Girls' club on Salt Lake's West Side told me. "I was so naive." As his plane from Hawaii descended into Salt Lake International Airport, he noticed that "everything was so brown and looked dead." They also joined and formed street gangs. The surge of Polynesian immigrants to the Wasatch Front mirrored the rise in gang life made popular in Los Angeles in the 1960s and 1970s. Like other kids, Tongans joined gangs for self-defense and the addictive rush of money, drugs, and weapons amidst poverty, eventually starting their own. A youth advocate at Glendale Middle School, on Salt Lake's West Side, told me that the two greatest influences on Polynesian kids now are church and gangs. Despite their numbers, and the turning over of generations who are born as native Utahns and American citizens, many Polynesians remain isolated in places like the West Side.

The most recent groups of people to seek salvation on the Wasatch Front, meanwhile, are those with experiences of an even steeper level of violence. Refugees from countries in serious conflict—Bosnia, Sudan, Somalia, Afghanistan—have been agglomerating into Salt Lake's West

Side alongside the other newcomers. Resettlement agencies have chosen Salt Lake for the same reasons as previous waves of migrants: It was safe, family-friendly, affordable, and full of jobs. Consequently, the blocky apartment buildings near the intersection of North Temple and Redwood Road have become a landscape of cacophony. Out on the periphery of the city's livable places, this 126-unit complex is a hub for Salt Lake Valley's refugee resettlement programs. Likely due to its proximity to the Salt Lake International Airport, but providently enough for the refugees, this place is called the Landing Point. After overnight flights originating in Nairobi or Bangkok, new refugee families plop down in empty apartments, the $600 cost of the two-bedroom units at first subsidized by the resettlement agencies; then, as the refugees find work and learn English and the ways of life in Utah, they pay more of the rent themselves.

In the Landing Point's parking lots before dawn, pairs of tired headlights fire up, bound for many of the least desirable jobs the Wasatch Front has to offer. Parents with young children work opposite shifts so they can watch the kids, spending a half hour a day together eating a meal in a tiny apartment. When I visited one day, I met a thirty-one-year-old Sudanese who told me he worked in a freezing meatpacking plant that made him sick. He talked about a friend who lived in the other side of the complex, with whom he grew up in a small town in Sudan before moving his family to Khartoum and Cairo. He was a Christian and told me he refused to talk to the Muslims in the Landing Point. "This is my house," he said. "I get up, I go to work, I go to school, I come home, I eat, after I take a shower, I go to sleep. I go to church, I play soccer. I have no problems." One Somali Bantu refugee spoke four languages, none of them English, before he, his wife, and three young children were brought from Kenya to the Landing Point. The Bantu are the lowest caste in a country ruined by civil war. He told me he had escaped from Somalia when he was fourteen, having walked and run for a week with no sleep to reach the nearest major city, and having eaten grass, leaves, and clay to stay alive. His first night in Salt Lake, he said, he lay awake until morning, expecting someone to break into the empty apartment. I talked to an Afghan family headed by an eleven-year-old who said the Taliban had "stolen everything we had"; a couple who work opposite shifts at a nearby McDonald's, whose parents won't go to their wedding because one of them is Mexican and the other is Guatemalan; and a fifteen-year-old Bosnian girl who hung out at the Mexicans' barbeques while she translated their Medicaid forms. Always, the parents wanted to return and the kids wanted to stay in Utah. The Bosnian girl, suspecting a move back to the Balkans, told me, "I want to stay so badly. I wish that, oh my God."

Imagine again the Great Basin bowl along the Wasatch Mountains that came to be known as the Salt Lake Valley. A valley cut off from navigable water but pushed up against large mountains, fed by snowmelt of the high country, and possessing its share of mineral ore in the Wasatch, Oquirrhs, and beyond. Imagine that Bernardo de Miera y Pacheco had convinced Spain to build a city here, which, instead of becoming Salt Lake City, had become another Mexico City—not far-fetched, since the cities share similar high-elevation, mountain-surrounded, prone-to-air pollution locations, and until the Mexicans lost interest in the region and lost the war with the United States, it was part of Mexico.

Or, imagine that this valley was, in the first place, the very kernel of Mexico City, of Tenochtitlan, the city conquered and built along Lake Texcoco by the Aztecs only to be conquered again by the Spaniards. In Mexico, Aztlán is a concept referring to the origin of the Aztec people. Various versions of a story describe people emerging from the bowels of the earth through seven caves and settling on an island called Aztlán, translated as "place of the egrets" or "place of whiteness." Aztecs, and modern mestizo Mexicans, have been searching for Aztlán for almost six hundred years, since Aztec leaders burned the picture books that recounted the migration to the Valley of Mexico. More than a few scholars from different places in the United States and the world have tried to prove that the location of Aztlán is, in fact, Utah. A Belgian researcher pinpoints Aztlán on Gray's Mesa above the San Juan River in the red rock country of southern Utah. A Nebraska doctoral student is swayed by geologic features in the eastern part of the state. A Mexican cosmologist is intrigued by pictographs in Sage Canyon north of Green River in central Utah. And a University of Utah professor named Armando Solorzano feels Aztlán right in the Salt Lake Valley. He tells of arriving in Utah in the 1990s from Guadalajara and seeing the Wasatch Mountains and the Great Salt Lake. "I said, 'My God, this is Aztlán.' I felt a spiritual unity with the land, something I had never felt before outside Mexico." Solorzano compares the concept of Aztlán as a sacred land of harmony with that of Zion in the Mormon tradition. The similarities, he says, show that both cultures are searching for a common goal. Solorzano calls his Utah adaptation of Aztlán "Utaztlán."

The origin story we all know about this particular Great Basin valley, of the Mormon Zion, exists in parallel with stories such as that of Aztlán, which, around the depots and into the neighborhoods of Salt Lake's West Side, have been occupying the margins of metropolitan growth alongside the Saints since the city's inception. As newer waves of hopeful new intermountain residents move into the city, a project like the Depot District is relevant not only for how it could open up an isolated district like the West Side but also what the West Side can teach it—and the whole region. In what city leaders are planning to be Salt Lake's "most urban" neighborhood, West Side immigrants' stories and their landscapes should inform the development of conscientiously "urban" places like the Depot, for they, perhaps more than anywhere else in the Great Basin, show us the process and the fruits of urbanity. Here, these ideas at the margins, at the edge, can be brought to the center. Salt Lake Central Station will sit shoulder to shoulder with institutions like Centro Civico, each with its own rich histories of life at the margins of Utah society as well as of a crossroads of people.

For now, the West Side neighborhoods unceremoniously end at the noise walls of the new and improved I-15, through which only a few major streets penetrate. But the city's plans are trying to give identity and definition to this area, between the freeway and the west edge of downtown, and boosters for the new Depot District say they hope the new neighborhood helps erase these barriers. Van Turner, the Salt Lake City councilman who has a vision for the urban neighborhood, grew up in Glendale and remembers walking home from downtown through Japantown and along the railroad tracks. "Train service dictated what this area was all about," Turner told the *Salt Lake Tribune*. "The west side was developed as a kind of a service center." But with rail transit, Turner said, "this neighborhood is about to change. It will change dramatically. . . . These old railroad yards are where we can build the city we want to be."[14]

Walking south on 600 West across 200 South toward the future site of the Salt Lake Central Station, I step around a bunch of high school kids loading instruments out of a van into Club Sound, and I pass the UTA crews blasting the trench for the Trax extension. Things are happening here. The station will sit at the meeting of 600 West and 300 South, across from a picturesque brick refrigeration facility. Preliminary plans for the station call for "a public plaza, delis and maybe a bowling alley, 24-hour diner or year-round fresh-food market." An architectural rendering of the hub shows "a flashy multi-level building arranged around a curved plaza." One City of Zion block eastward, the back of the Rio Grande Depot looms, making this stretch of 300 South a link from past to future.

On this day, this intersection is quiet. The only portion of the station that is built is the Greyhound bus station. There is a man in a cowboy hat and a Starter L.A. Kings jacket sitting on the low wall around the station waiting for a ride, and a taco stand across the street. I walk over to the stand, where a few old guys chat with the doña behind the grill, and order a few tacos. Opportunity lies at the heels of every load of passengers into town: "I asked the station manager if there is any food, and he said no, so I asked if I could set up here," she tells me.

After eating, a little tired and full of tacos, I plop down my bag and sit against the wall, next to the guy in the cowboy hat, who is still waiting for a ride home. Here and now in the once-and-future center, I decide it is time to start sketching what the future might hold:

I am awoken by a gentle hand on my shoulder. I turn around from my seat against the wall and see that the hand belongs to a thin black man in a gray suit.

"Excuse me," he says, "but there is a train leaving north in ten minutes and I suspected it might be the one you're waiting for."

I look at my watch. He's right. I clear my eyes and look back around to thank the man, but he's gone, into a crowd of suits moving from the taco stands across 600 West to the ticket window of Salt Lake Central Station. There must be a convention or something, I think hazily. Will they be on my train? If it leaves in ten minutes, I still have time to stretch my legs before boarding.

The late afternoon sun shines in the horizon to the west, the threat of the storms having cleared. The pink blossoms on the allée of dogwood trees along 300 South are spared from a blast of spring snow for now. Above them, the giant cottonwoods tower like guardians of the walking street of 300 South, or Broadway, as it has become known again. It's quite a street. I steer through the crowds at the intersection of West Broadway and 600 West that has been cobbled in a giant, variegated beehive, criss-crossed by the rail tracks. The intersection is a chaos of slow-moving cars dropping off passengers, yellow, green, and red taxi cabs, buses lining up for the transit mall along the curb, and people walking in every direction. On the southeast corner is the lobby entrance of the new Hotel Utah, built from the renovated cold storage building with a glassy, twenty-story tower added behind it. I stroll into the lobby, a high-ceilinged hall where the sound of a piano ballad lolls under the din of conversation of old men in high-backed chairs. I move on through, out a back entrance to a leafy outdoor courtyard where I can see the soccer fields behind the hotel in the center of the block. These are part of the new Centro Civico. The nonprofit had found it hard to say no to a generous offer for its land by one notable Utah developer, so it took the money and bought a brownfield two blocks south, used city redevelopment money to clean it up, and its own capital plus transient occupancy taxes and tax credits to build a new mixed-use building on 300 South, becoming a nonprofit housing developer in the process. Above the new meeting space and *salon de baile* (ballroom) are three- and four-bedroom housing units in a tower above. Ironically, even as the city has become over 50 percent Latino, with the Hispanic birthrates crushing the non-Mormon DINK (Dual Income No Kids) professionals who have taken over the other half, less than 50 percent of the units are occupied by Latinos themselves; instead, these units have been snapped up by large refugee families from Holland, Japan, and California who, true to Basin tradition, sought refuge in the high country, this time from the rising seas in their countries.

Back out on West Broadway, next to the Centro Civico, I see Ivory Homes' latest project. Having long moved away from the mountain lodge look of the 2000s, Ivory Homes, in conjunction with Envision Utah, returned to its roots of infilling built-up areas of the Wasatch Front. On the other corner is the result of a near disaster for the state: the Skull Valley Casino. When the owner of the property at the corner realized the Skull Valley Goshute Tribe was serious about importing spent nuclear fuel rods to its reservation west of Tooele Valley, the owner's family and the Salt Lake Redevelopment Agency cut a deal with the tribe: Drop the nuclear plan in exchange for several acres of prime land in the new Depot neighborhood over which the tribe would retain sovereignty. At first, like other Indian nations, the Goshutes opened a casino as they built up the rest of their new land, but they soon gained enough revenue from the housing in the towers above the casino that they agreed, under pressure from the Utah Legislature and the City of Salt Lake, to convert the ground-floor space into a Trader Joe's.

Midway through the block is the façade of a recent architectural innovation: the urban ward. With only a five thousand square-foot parcel to work with, the newly formed Depot LDS ward wanted all the things that American suburban wards usually have: a spacious sanctuary, a gymnasium, meeting rooms, miles of hallways, and plenty of parking. A

Salt Lake architect was able to stack this program vertically, and now the urban ward is being replicated in Provo and Brigham City. The first-floor basketball gym's floor-to-ceiling windows allow passers-by to see "ward ball" in action. Some Saturdays, the Mexican kids from Centro Civico come across the street and take on the Mormons, and sometimes the Mormons play soccer on Centro's fields.

The best thing about West Broadway is the street itself. Very little of its 132-foot right-of-way is dedicated to either motorized vehicles or paved surfaces. Nine-foot lanes are pushed to either side of the street, leaving over one hundred feet for the public activity of the neighborhood. The street has been reconstructed as a series of squares, each one of them different. There is one square of grass, an intensely used oasis, since private lawn is now illegal in Utah and Nevada. There are two new, smaller streets intersecting the old Mormon block in each direction, cutting the block into nine smaller ones, a district in itself, and one much easier to walk around. The square across from the train station is a giant beer garden, with a small stand serving up pitchers to outdoor tables on an extension of the intersection's cobblestone.

The central square, believe it or not, is a man-made playa, a kind of desert retention pond for stormwater and floods, with a wetland at the edge fed by wastewater. In the winter, it's a skating rink. The water flows into this central space via runnels along the sidewalks. The water works its way among new species of greasewood and iodine bush bred to tolerate not only salt content but also urban runoff pollution. The water is cleansed and then filtered back into an engineered soil in the large seasonal lake in the middle of the street. At the end of the street, the old Rio Grande Depot still stands, resplendent and dignified in the evening light. Tables from the expanded Rio Grande Café spill out in front of the old depot.

Standing in the beehive intersection, I realize that the onset of Friday evening is a good time of the week to be in the depot because everyone is descending on the place. Urban single-track reels in from the classic foothill rides in Perry's Hollow and City Creek through the large blocks and converge at 300 South, and muddy mountain bikers line up for pitchers at the beer garden. Since the Utah Department of Transportation put the downtown section of I-15 underground, in combination with a giant, sloping platform over the railroad tracks, the West Side melds into the new neighborhood, with lines of maturing street trees along the uncovered streets shading wide sidewalks and the boutiques of the long-ago gentrified district.

But time is running short, so I walk back to the station through the glassy hall of the Salt Lake Central Station, where a tennis court–sized digital screen displays names of places, times, and durations of trips, the words and numbers shifting and flickering constantly to adjust to incoming trains, late flights and time moving along. I see, for example, that I can take a 7:15 light-rail Trax train to Foothill Station at the mouth of Parley's Canyon, transfer to a Little Cottonwood Canyon train, and be at Alta at 7:55. I see that I can board Trax to Daybreak, transfer to the Trans-Oquirrh Express, and emerge in Tooele Valley. The station has become, true to the vision of the tenacious generation of civic leaders, a true hub of the city, with travelers making their way into the city from southern Idaho, workers from Utah Valley passing through on their way to jobs in downtown Salt Lake, and shoppers who live in downtown taking the free Trax over to hang out on West Broadway.

My ticket already in hand, I move through to the platforms, where the FrontRunner train is humming in anticipation of its journey north. I board a middle car and find the man who had woken me sitting with an empty window seat next to him. Still wanting to thank him for allowing me to catch my train, I take it. His name, it turns out, is Ngindo Ooji Makua, and he's a banker in Sandy on his way to visit his parents and brothers in Brigham City. Ngindo tells me his parents came to Utah from Somalia in 2003, and a few years later he was born in Salt Lake. He's going on about how, thanks to the new university there, Brigham City has become the kind of left-wing commune it used to be, but I am looking out the window at the blur of scenery rushing by, the removed gas refineries, the new Costco, the removed Legacy Freeway.

At Layton Station, I must switch trains, but Ngindo is staying for the long haul to Brigham; so I thank him again and look out the windows as the train slows into downtown Layton, the neon tubes reading "Doug and Emmy's Family Restaurant" turned on above the old "Layton, Elev. 4358" sign. Beyond them, along Main Street, stores soak in the bustle, and the five floors of residences above them sit aglow in the late spring sunlight of seven o'clock. I step onto the Layton platform, walk over the tracks and along the pedestrian path that lines Kays Creek, past the stately First National Bank building, and turn the corner of Main and Gentile streets just as the G line streetcar backs into its turnaround. The streetcar whirs out westward along Gentile Street, past the fields that have been consolidated for a new kind of urban agriculture where melons, winter wheat, and tomatoes are grown on six-acre fields in the middle of ten-acre blocks, surrounded by the backs of townhouses facing south out to the shorelands, providing views and food for the whole block in the summer. These blocks are periodically interrupted by swirls of freshwater wetland receiving the runoff from both the agricultural fields and the urban area above.

And then we're here: The Bluff, the end of the line, as slight and meaningful as it ever was, the old emigrant trail northward. The streetcar slows as the roadway of Gentile Street changes from concrete to rails running through bunchgrass, its sidewalks becoming paths of red paving blocks on either side. The car screeches to a stop and I step off it onto the path and see people from other parts of Syracuse taking their evening walks. I see houses made of reused steel beams and corrugated metal panels, stacked on one another terracing westward. I see the world in these buildings—Amsterdam, Tijuana, California—and I see the Great Basin in them, too. The paths widen and run along rows of small neighborhood stores, the markets and dry cleaners doing brisk business, and then part on either side of the upland fields, where ibis dig for worms, and I see the shorelands. Past the last house, where a family pauses from its barbeque to watch the sunset over the lake, the path turns to pebbles and then, over the Bluff, to a boardwalk curving into the wetlands. At the end of the boardwalk, the surface of the brackish water still, I look out over the wind waving through the grasses and reeds, toward the uncaring blotches of juniper and gray-green sage and withdrawn greasewood, how it always was, and back at the new contours of the Wasatch Front, of the concentrated humanity circulating in hard production and joyful consumption, in oscillating harmony of center and edge, and I realize that we are, now, a city of the Basin.

Epilogue

The recession that began in 2007 enveloped the Great Basin as it did the rest of the United States and the world, tamping the buoyancy and exuberance and slowing the pace of growth that had been helping to shape the region's cities. The economic downturn exposed once again the differences between the metropolitan areas on opposite sides of the Basin. Northern Nevada, historically more susceptible to the boom-and-bust cycles of the mining, entertainment, and tourism industries, was among the areas hit hardest in housing-price declines and unemployment: By the end of 2009, the median sale price for single-family houses in the Reno area had declined by 50 percent from the peak of about four ears earlier, and over 12 percent of the labor force was unemployed. Far-flung Lyon County was one of the nation's most spectacular busts, going from being Nevada's fastest-growing county in the middle of the decade to actually shrinking by 2008 and reaching 15 percent unemployment by mid-2009. Utah, on the other hand, with its low-profile but usually stable economy, slowed to a lesser degree. The Wasatch Front experienced housing-price declines that were minor relative to the rest of the United States and unemployment several percentage points below the national average.

Overall, the populations of the Great Basin's metropolitan areas still grew quickly relative to the rest of the United States. With its high birth rates, Utah became the fastest-growing state in the nation. Nevada was more affected by the economy and slowdown in immigration but was nevertheless eighth fastest growing. The slowdown in growth, population, real estate, and jobs offered local, regional, and state policy makers a chance to step back and formulate strategies for addressing the next wave of western growth and urbanization.

And the Great Basin's burgeoning urbanity lives. In the depths of the market downturn across the United States, it became apparent that the real estate that remained the most attractive to buyers was compact, mixed-use development, often built near to rapid transit. In its *Emerging Trends in Real Estate 2010*, the real estate industry's Urban Land Institute noted that "next-generation projects will orient to urbanizing transit-oriented development. Smaller housing units close to mass transit, work, and 24-hour amenities gain favor over large houses on big lots at the suburban edge."[1] Americans increasingly want urban—especially those belonging to my generation who are beginning to make their first home purchases and will carry the weight of demand in coming decades. The places of varying shades of urban in this book have found some success in the awful market. Daybreak, the large-scale, consciously new urbanist, master-planned development of diverse houses, jobs, parks, and transit was selling about a house a day in the spring of 2009.[2] Although the future of the long-term West Bench Master Plan is vague, Kennecott Land actually increased the number of houses it planned to build in Daybreak from thirteen thousand to twenty thousand, as builders put up higher-density townhouses filling the need for smaller, less expensive residences in the downturn. It is filling in with a mix of houses, townhouses, and condos, and under construction is a shopping street called, fittingly enough for Utah's sweet tooth, SoDa Row. And Daybreak's populace is multiplying like cells: In Daybreak's online forum, a poster noted that in the year and a half she had lived at Daybreak her Latter-day Saint ward had split "3 or 4 times and will need to split again before the year is over."

Woodland Village in Cold Springs Valley, with its new neighborhood grill, is "a bright spot" in Reno's otherwise slow new housing sales according to the *Reno Gazette Journal*. In Tooele County, Overlake won a $20 million judgment against the City of Tooele, and the victory may help to enable the narrower streets and better street connectivity laid out by its original plan. In downtown Salt Lake, the Church of Jesus Christ of Latter-day Saints is building the City Creek Center. Condominium towers have begun to rise alongside the Temple spires and conference center conifers, signaling the next, mixed-use era of the Mormon headquarters. A realtor reported that most of the condo sales so far were from LDS Church members who were willing to pay almost $1 million for a view of the Salt Lake Temple.[3]

I returned to Reno one hot July Saturday to see the havoc the economy had wreaked on the city's downtown. Gary K. Estes had told me that the

Residences at Riverwalk had sold most of its condos before the downturn, but the last few were being auctioned off. The Montage condominium tower was finished, but many of its units sat empty. For many residents, the Montage stood as the testament to Reno's ever-unfulfilled potential; downtown's vaunted revitalization had run into another obstacle. The blocks around the Montage were deserted, the depressing casino walls silently baking in the summer heat, but toward the river I glimpsed people with giant inner tubes slung over their shoulders dashing across the downtown streets. I followed them and emerged at the River Walk, where I discovered that hundreds of Renoites were occupying this public space. There were groups of teens cannonballing into the Truckee's eddies, and dads making a go at bodysurfing the whitewater. There was the brunch crowd in sundresses and heels and large Latino families picnicking. There were salty old dudes with big headphones, lying in the grass on one elbow. Investments made in the public realm during flusher times, it appeared, were paying off in the recession. The private downfalls were, for the afternoon, absorbed in the collective experience of the concentrated, riparian green and the summer sunlight bouncing off the cool water. I sat in the river, surveyed the scene, and looked up to the tall cottonwoods above, the waiting condo towers beyond, and then to the river's origin in the high mountains above and its destination in the dry country to the east. Urbanism! For now, at least, there is far too little of it in the Great Basin.

Notes

Preface

1. See Brookings Institution, *Blueprint for American Prosperity: Mountain Megas*, Brookings Metropolitan Policy Program, 2008.

Chapter 1. Of Sin and Salvation

1. From speech given by Turner at Chicago World's Fair, 1893, http://west.stanford.edu/cgi-bin/pager.php?id=25.

2. Alicia Barber, "Reno's Silver Legacy: Gambling on the Past in the Urban New West," in *Imagining the Big Open: Nature, Identity and Play in the New West*, ed. Liza Nicholas, Elaine M. Bapis, and Thomas J. Harvey (Salt Lake City: University of Utah Press, 2003), 204.

3. Deidre Pike, "Leaving the Comstock," *Reno News and Review*, May 20, 2004.

4. Interview with Gary Estes, by author, Reno, Nevada, October 19, 2006.

5. Susan Voyles, "Downtown Projects Push City's Evolution," *Reno Gazette-Journal*, March 12, 2007.

6. Susan Voyles, "Layering the Foundation for a Great Downtown," *Reno Gazette-Journal*, March 30, 2005.

7. Interview with Eldon Cannon, by author, Reno, Nevada, December 19, 2006.

8. See the spatial juxtaposition given by D. W. Meinig in "The Mormon Culture Region," *Annals of the American Association of Geographers* 55, no. 2 (June 1965): 212.

9. The *Doctrine and Covenants* is a Church of Jesus Christ of Latter-day Saints scripture that is "a collection of divine revelations and inspired declarations given for the establishment and regulation of the kingdom of God on the earth in the last days." See http://scriptures.lds.org/dc/contents.

10. Heather May, "A Real Blockbuster," *Salt Lake Tribune*, October 4, 2006.

11. William L. Fox, *The Void, the Grid and the Sign: Traversing the Great Basin* (Reno: University of Nevada Press, 2000), 10.

12. Thomas R. Harris, William W. Riggs, and John Zimmerman, *Public Lands in the State of Nevada: An Overview*, University Center for Economic Development, University of Nevada, 2001.

13. Calculations by author based on data of the U.S. Census Bureau, "Census of Population and Housing," 2000, http://www.census.gov.

14. Richard V. Francaviglia, *Believing in Place: A Spiritual Geography of the Great Basin* (Reno: University of Nevada Press, 2003), xiv.

15. U.S. Census Bureau, "Census of Population and Housing," Summary File 1, 2000, http://www.census.gov.

16. There are different measures for Las Vegas' growth from 2000 to 2005, since its census-designated metro area changed between those years. Some reports put Las Vegas' five-year growth at as high as 17 percent.

17. U.S. Census Bureau, "Census of Population and Housing," Summary File 1, 2005, American Community Survey, http://www.census.gov.

18. Carl Abbott, *Metropolitan Frontier* (Tucson: University of Arizona Press, 1995).

19. Barber, "Reno's Silver Legacy," 205.

20. Thomas Michael Power and Richard Barrett, *Post-Cowboy Economics* (Washington, DC: Island Press, 2001), xix.

21. Utah Foundation, *Utah Water Use and Quality*, Research Brief, August, 1, 2004, http://www.utahfoundation.org/reports/?page_id=331; see auto ownership rates from 2000 U.S. Census in later figures, http://www.census.gov; American Lung Association, State of the Air, 2009, http://www.stateoftheair.org.

22. John D. Reps, *Cities of the American West: A History of Frontier Urban Planning* (Princeton, NJ: Princeton University Press, 1979), ix–xi.

23. Bradford Luckingham, "The American Southwest, an Urban View," in *The American West: The Urban West*, ed. Gordon Morris Bakken and Brenda Farrington (New York: Garland, 2000), 261–62.

24. William G. Robbins and James C. Foster, eds., *Land in the American West: Private Claims and the Common Good* (Seattle: University of Washington Press, 2000).

25. John Findlay, *Magic Lands: Western Cityscapes and American Culture after 1940* (Berkeley: University of California Press, 1992).

26. Kevin Starr in William G. Robbins, "In Search of Western Lands," in *Land in the American West: Private Claims and the Common Good*, ed. William Robbins and James C. Foster (Seattle: University of Washington Press , 2000), 6.

27. Luckingham, "American Southwest," 263.

28. Gunther Barth, "Demopiety: Speculations on Urban Beauty, Western Scenery, and the Discovery of the American Cityscape," in *The American West: The Urban West* (New York: Garland, 2000).

29. Leonard J. Arrington, *Great Basin Kingdom: An Economic History of the Latter-day Saints 1830-1900* (Cambridge, MA: Harvard University Press, 1958), 24.

30. C. Mark Hamilton, *Nineteenth Century Mormon Architecture and City Planning* (New York: Oxford University Press, 1995).

31. Frank C. Robertson and Beth Kay Harris, *Boom Towns of the Great Basin* (Denver: Sage, 1962), 19.

32. Michael P. Conzen, *The Making of the American Landscape* (London: Routledge, 1991), 197.

33. Cecilia Parera, "Mormon Town Planning: Physical and Social Relevance," *Journal of Planning History* 4, no. 2 (2005): 165.

34. Robbins, "In Search of Western Lands," 6.

35. Much of this summary of Reno history is based on Barbara Land and Myrick Land, *A Short History of Reno* (Reno: University of Nevada Press, 1995); and Alicia Barber, *Reno's Big Gamble: Image and Reputation in the Biggest Little City* (Lawrence: University Press of Kansas, 2008).

36. Land and Land, *Short History of Reno*, 38.

37. Land and Land, *Short History of Reno*, 43.

38. Barber, *Reno's Big Gamble*, 89.

39. Jeff DeLong, "An Ambitious Goal: Get Nevadans Out of Cars, On the Bus," *Reno Gazette-Journal*, December 18, 2005.

40. Josh Johnson, "County Commission Overturns Brothel Permit," *Lahontan Valley News*, April 7, 2006.

41. U.S. Bureau of Labor Statistics, "Location Quotient Calculator," http://data.bls .gov:8080/LOCATION_QUOTIENT/servlet/lqc.ControllerServlet (accessed February 2007).

42. The Milliken Institute, "2005 Best Performing Cities," http://bestcities .milllikeninstitute.org/bc200_2005.html.

43. See Tim Sullivan, "A New Breed of Ski Bums Is Anything But," *High Country News*, November 8, 2004.

44. Mike Gorrell, "Three Outdoor Companies' Decisions Bring 1,335 Jobs," *Salt Lake Tribune*, January 30, 2007.

45. Abbott, *Metropolitan Frontier*.

46. Robbins, "In Search of Western Lands," 6.

47. U.S. Census Bureau, "Census of Population and Housing," Summary File 1, 2000, http://www.census.gov.

48. Envision Utah, *The History of Envision Utah*, http://www.envisionutah.org/ historyenvisionutahv5p1.pdf (accessed October 2006).

49. See Hal Rothman, *Neon Metropolis: How Las Vegas Started the 21st Century* (London: Taylor & Francis, 2003).

50. Barber, *Reno's Big Gamble*, 208.

51. Eric Dieterle, "Five Minutes to Midnight in Cold Springs," *Watershed* 1, no. 3 (2006): 14.

52. "Radio West," KUER, Salt Lake City, October 6, 2006.

53. "Radio West," KUER, Salt Lake City, October 6, 2006.

Chapter 2. Scaling the Basin

1. Hannah Arendt, *The Promise of Politics* (New York: Shocken, 2005), 201.

2. Stephen Trimble, *The Sagebrush Ocean* (Reno: University of Nevada Press, 1989), 59.

3. Peavine Mountain Project, 2006, http://www.unr.edu/journalism/peavine/files/ index_content.html.

4. A geocacher is some one who takes part in a treasure-hunting game commonly played with a Global Positioning System (GPS).

5. Raymond Williams, *The Country and the City* (New York: Oxford University Press, 1973), 8.

6. Interview with Glenn Rogers, by author, Shivwits Paiute reservation, April 2003.

7. John McPhee, *Basin and Range* (New York: Farrar, Straus, and Giroux, 1981), 49.

8. Trimble, *Sagebrush Ocean*, 10.

9. Trimble, *Sagebrush Ocean*, 12.

10. Hugh Mozingo, *Shrubs of the Great Basin: A Natural History* (Reno: University of Nevada Press, 1987).

11. Naturalists Stephen Trimble and James McMahon have devised this outline; see Trimble, *Sagebrush Ocean*.

12. Richard V. Francaviglia, *Mapping and Imagination in the Great Basin* (Reno: University of Nevada Press, 2005), 21.

13. Francaviglia, *Mapping and Imagination*, 22.

14. Francaviglia, *Mapping and Imagination*, 37.

15. Trimble, *Sagebrush Ocean*, 67.

16. "A flat playa of clay, often salt-encrusted, gleams in the low point of a typical basin," writes Trimble. "Great Basin biogeography starts in the white glare of these centers and goes outward and upward." Trimble, *Sagebrush Ocean*, 64.

17. Mozingo, *Shrubs of the Great Basin*, 5.

18. Rudolf Wittkower, *Architectural Principles in the Age of Humanism* (London: Alec Tiranti, 1952), 91.

19. Fox, *The Void*, 11.

20. Joan Woodward, *Waterstained Landscapes* (Baltimore: Johns Hopkins University Press, 2000).

21. John T. Lyle, "Archetypes in the Arid Landscape," in *Sustainable Landscape Design in Arid Climates*, ed. John T. Lyle, 25–33 (Geneva: Aga Khan Trust for Culture Symposium, 1996).

22. Marc Reisner, *Cadillac Desert: The American West and its Disappearing Water* (New York: Penguin Books, 1986), 469.

23. Kamran T. Diba, "Sustainable Development in Tehran," in *Sustainable Landscape Design in Arid Climates*, ed. John T. Lyle (Geneva: Aga Khan Trust for Culture Symposium, 1996), 36.

24. Ronald Lewcock, *The Old Walled City of San'a* (Paris: UNESCO, 1986).

25. Terry Tempest Williams, *Refuge* (New York: Vintage Books, 1991).

26. See Reisner, *Cadillac Desert*, 3.

27. Data for maps collected from ESRI, http://arcdata.esri.com/data/tiger2000/tiger_download.cfm; U.S. Census Bureau, http://www.census.gov.

28. Robert E. Lang, "Open Spaces, Bounded Places: Does the American West's Arid Landscape Yield Dense Metropolitan Growth?" *Housing Policy Debate* 13, no. 4 (2003).

29. William Fulton, Rolf Pendall, Mai Nguyen, and Alicia Harrison, *Who Sprawls Most? How Growth Patterns Differ Across the U.S.*, Center on Urban and Metropolitan Policy, the Brookings Institution, Washington, DC, 2001.

30. Robbins, "In Search of Western Lands," 8.

31. Urban planning wonks will no doubt notice that many of the places this book visits are at the edges of the Great Basin's metropolitan areas, locations generally frowned upon for growth because of the consumption of unbuilt land and wildlife habitat far from existing neighborhoods, jobs, and infrastructure, and the unwalkable, car-dependent, and boring development that is usually built at the metropolitan edge. There are several reasons this book includes the growing edges of the Wasatch Front and Truckee Meadows in its itinerary, while bypassing many of the built-out parts of these metro areas. (1) The Great Basin edge is where most recent development has happened. As reporters say, this is where the story is. (2) The edge is where the

built environment is interfacing most with the Great Basin landscape, a relationship this book seeks to study. (3) Due to the Great Basin's natural barriers of topography and water, public lands, and lack of water and water rights, development often cannot occur in a neat concentric pattern. These constraints have led development to "hopscotch" over unbuildable areas. However, the degree of this hopscotching is a major political contention. (4) Also in part because of the above constraints, the Great Basin metropolis displays a relatively even medium to low density that has reduced opportunities for major infill projects or concentrated development along established transit-served corridors. This is especially true in Salt Lake Valley. One major infill opportunity is the underutilized land along the Interstate 15 freeway corridor, much of which has become part of the Trax light rail corridor and presents many opportunities for future transit-oriented development. Yet some places discussed in this book, like the Great Salt Lake shorelands, are at the same time at the edge of the Wasatch Front and within a mile or two of its transit-served urban spine—these are quintessentially Intermountain places that really interest me. (5) Planning efforts in both metro areas are addressing where growth should and will be concentrated at a regional scale. (6) There are appropriate approaches to growth in different areas of metro regions. New urbanists address this through the transect model, which posits a spectrum of intensity from the urban core to the rural edge, but the Great Basin, as I argue in later chapters, doesn't fit that model. This book, in part, is about finding what does fit.

32. Dieterle, "Five Minutes to Midnight," 14.

33. John Evanoff, "What Do a Space Ship and Wild Horses Have to Do with Each Other?" *VisitReno* (September 2005), http://visitreno.com/evanoff/september-05.php.

34. Joel Garreau, *Edge City: Life on the New Frontier* (New York: Doubleday, 1991).

35. What is created is what is sometimes called by planners a "fused grid"—what would otherwise be a disconnected suburban street pattern of cul-de-sac stubs resulting in long walk distances between destinations becomes, at least for walking, a connected street network. In general, urban designers usually prefer a completely connected network because it not only allows for easier walking, but also can distribute auto traffic among all streets instead of funneling cars onto a few arterial streets that then become large barriers for walkers. Woodland Village's fused grid is interesting because it creates not only a network for walking and bicycling, but also a framework for recreation and the processes of the watershed. Very Great Basin.

36. Susan Voyles, "Area Growth Takes Top Priority in Upcoming Elections," *Reno Journal-Gazette*, June 12, 2006.

37. Lifestyle Homes, *Woodland Village Landscape Manual*, June 2004.

38. Information gathered from Lahontan Audubon Society, interpretive signage at Swan Lake.

39. John Elder, *Reading the Mountains of Home* (Cambridge, MA: Harvard University Press, 1998).

Chapter 3. Shorelands

1. Dale Morgan, *Great Salt Lake* (Salt Lake City: University of Utah Press, 1947), 19.

2. Writer Barry Lopez called the Black Rock Playa in Nevada "a stage"; see Trimble, *Sagebrush Ocean*, 64.

3. Morgan, *Great Salt Lake*, 20.

4. Trimble, *Sagebrush Ocean*, 64.

5. Tim Westby, "The Great Salt Lake Mystery," *High Country News*, April 29, 2002.

6. Interview with Chris Brown, by author, Nature Conservancy's Great Salt Lake Shorelands Preserve, January 3, 2007.

7. Marlin Stum, *Visions of Antelope Island and Great Salt Lake* (Logan: Utah State University Press, 1999).

8. Wallace Stegner, *Mormon Country* (New York: Deull, Sloan and Pierce, 1942), 21.

9. D. W. Meinig, "The Mormon Culture Region," *Annals of the American Association of Geographers* 55, no. 2 (June 1965): 200.

10. Parera, "Mormon Town Planning."

11. U.S. Census Bureau, "Census of Population and Housing," Summary File 3, 2000, http://www.census.gov.

12. Mark Cannon, "Mormons in the Executive Suite," *Dialogue* 3, no. 3 (Autumn 1968): 100.

13. Bitton, Davis, "Anti-Intellectualism in Mormon History," *Dialogue* 1, no. 3 (Autumn 1966): 124.

14. Daughters of the Utah Pioneers, *East of Antelope Island* (Bountiful, UT: Carr, 1948), 19.

15. Lyle, "Archetypes," 25.

16. See Wallace Stegner, "Living Dry," in *Marking the Sparrow's Fall* (New York: Henry Holt, 1998), 224. Stegner writes, "Now, 140 years after their hegira, [the Mormons] have managed to put only about 3 percent of Utah's land under cultivation; and because they took seriously the Lord's command to be fruitful and multiply, Zion has been overpopulated, and exporting manpower, for at least half a century. One of the bitterest conflicts in modern Utah is that between the environmentalists who want to see much of that superlative wilderness preserved roadless and wild, and the stubborn Mormon determination to make it support more Saints than it possibly can."

17. Daughters of the Utah Pioneers, *East of Antelope Island*, 202.

18. Stum, *Visions*, 93.

19. Great Salt Lake Hydrologic Basin Observatory, Great Salt Lake Description, University of Utah, 2004, http://www.greatsaltlake.utah.edu/description/greatsaltlake.

20. U.S. Census Bureau, "Census," 1990; "Census," 2000; "Population Estimates," 2005; http://www.census.gov.

21. U.S. Census Bureau, "Census of Population and Housing," 2000, http://www.census.gov.

22. Utah Education Network, http://www.uen.org/counties/davis.shtml.

23. Tom Busselberg, "Syracuse Fires City Manager," *Davis County Clipper*, February 8, 2007.

24. Andrew Aragon, "I've Got Your School Name Right Here," *Salt Lake Tribune*, February 3, 2007.

25. Utah Foundation, *Utah Water Use and Quality*.

26. Syracuse City Planning Commission minutes, April 4, 2006.

27. Peter Hall, *Cities of Tommorrow* (Malden, MA: Blackwell, 1988).

28. Most of the history of Ivory Homes was adapted from Ron Clifford, *The Ivory Legacy* (Salt Lake City: Ivory Homes, 2001).

29. Jennifer Nii, "Ivory Homes Reaches 10,000 Milestone," *Deseret News*, July 15, 2006.

30. U.S. Census Bureau, "Census of Population and Housing," Summary Files 3, 2000, http://www.census.gov.

31. Syracuse City Planning Commission minutes, April 4, 2006.

Chapter 4. Urban Realities of Rural Places

1. Robert Moses in Marshall Berman, *All That Is Solid Melts into Air* (New York: Penguin Books, 1982), 294–95.

2. Tooele County Engineering Department, 2002, http://www.co.tooele.ut.us/PDF/Economics%20Tooele%20Valley%20master%20plan.htm.

3. Interview with Drew Hall, by author, Tooele, Utah, October 2, 2006.

4. Tooele Army Depot, "Tooele Army Depot History," 2010, http://www.tooele.army.mil/history.

5. Aaron Hughley, "2000 Census Reveals Interesting Trends," *Echo* (March 2003).

6. Robert E. Lang and Arthur C. Nelson, "The Rise of the Megapolitans," *Planning* (January 2007): 8.

7. Daibhi MacDomhnaill, Dublin City council minutes, October 20, 2005.

8. Abbott, *Metropolitan Frontier*, 169.

9. Susan Voyles, "Street-widening Heralds More Growth in North Valleys," *Reno Gazette-Journal*, March 21, 2006.

10. Associated Press, "Annexation Plan That Could Mean 5,700 New Homes in Reno Opposed," news release, January 30, 2005.

11. "High Desert Forum," KUNR, Reno, February 17, 2007.

12. Associated Press, "Citizens Sue over Annexation That Could Mean 5,700 Homes in Reno," news release, April 3, 2005.

13. Interview with Tony Midmore, by author, Cold Springs, Nevada, October 21, 2006.

14. Richard Walker, "Industry Builds Out the City," in *Manufacturing Suburbs: Building Work and Home on the Metropolitan Fringe*, ed. Robert Lewis (Philadelphia: Temple University Press, 2004), 110.

15. Carol Cizauskas, "Growing Out: Activists Fight Sprawl into Areas Remote from the Truckee Meadows," *Reno News and Review*, May 31, 2007.

16. Letters, *Reno Gazette-Journal*, January 30, 2007.

17. City of Reno, http://www.cityofreno.com/Feb06/pdfs/0622Feb15BB1B2.pdf (accessed February 2007).

18. Interview with Dwight Dortsch, by author, November 2006.

19. Interview with Jeff Hardcastle, by author, February 2007.

20. U.S. Bureau of Labor Statistics, "Location Quotient Calculator," http://data.bls.gov:8080/LOCATION_QUOTIENT/servlet/lqc.ControllerServlet (accessed February 2007).

21. Tahoe-Reno Industrial Center promotional materials, http://www.lancegilman.com.

22. Ken Ritter, "Lyon County Overtakes Clark County as Fastest-growing in Nevada," Associated Press news release, April 14, 2005.

23. U.S. Census Bureau, "Census of Population and Housing," Summary File 3, 1990, 2000, http://www.census.gov.

24. U.S. Bureau of Labor Statistics, "Location Quotient Calculator," http://data.bls .gov:8080/LOCATION_QUOTIENT/servlet/lqc.ControllerServlet (accessed February 2007).

25. Interview with Mick Casey, by author, December 19, 2006.

26. U.S. Bureau of Labor Statistics, "Location Quotient Calculator," http://data.bls .gov:8080/LOCATION_QUOTIENT/servlet/lqc.ControllerServlet (accessed February 2007).

27. Interview with Nicole Cline, by author, October 2, 2006.

28. Tooele County Planning Commission minutes, December 1, 2004.

29. Tooele County Planning Commission minutes, July 27, 2006.

30. Tooele County Planning Commission minutes, April 20, 2005.

31. Interviews with staff of City of Tooele Dept. of Community Development, by author, October 2006.

32. Interview with Mark Simpson, by author, November 2006.

33. Clarence Perry created a diagram called the Neighborhood Unit in the 1920 New York Regional Plan, which used a five-minute walking radius as the basis for a residential neighborhood with commercial areas at its edges and schools and parks in its center.

34. "City of Tooele Finds New Way to Benefit Residents with Progressive Water Treatment in Golf Course," Overlake promotional materials, http://www.trilobyte. net/overlake/press/water.html.

35. Envision Utah, *Urban Planning Tools for Quality Growth*, 2002, http://www .envisionutah.org/Urban%20Planning%20Tools%20for%20QG_ch5_sup.pdf.

36. Overlake promotional materials, http://www.trilobyte.net/overlake/jacks.html.

37. Karen Hunt, "Overlake First Ward Sets Record for Most Mormon Twins," *Tooele Transcript-Bulletin*, April 14, 2006.

38. Michael Bernick and Robert Cervero, *Transit Villages in the 21st Century* (New York: McGraw Hill, 1997), 83.

39. "Where the Jobs Are," CNNMoney.com, July 2007, http://money.cnn.com/ galleries/2007/moneymag/0707/gallery.BPTL_job_growth.moneymag/index.html.

40. Tim Gillie, "Allegheny Technologies to Begin Producing Titanium This Week," *Tooele Transcript-Bulletin*, December 29, 2009.

41. Mark Watson, "Dunlavy: Lawsuits Costing Too Much," *Tooele Transcript-Bulletin*, December 22, 2005.

42. Berman, *All That Is Solid*, 83.

43. I am ambivalent about Tooele's foray into the urbanized Wasatch Front, since the urbanization of this valley is based on the notion of a bedroom suburb for Salt Lake Valley jobs and long, fuel-burning commutes. Even Overlake, at its core, is built for commuters to the valley to the east. Hall's notion of time over distance became true for thousands of Tooele residents and signals a shift to urbanization, but I don't know that this is the most urban way to think of space. A challenge of urbanism is to increase mobility in established urbanized areas without resorting to the highway

out of town. But, as I argue, the incorporation of Tooele into the urbanized region is reality, and this chapter demonstrates markedly different approaches to the realization of this urbanization. One key for Tooele County in the coming decades will be to match job growth to its residential growth.

Chapter 5. Public Land, Private Politics

1. Daybreak promotional materials, Kennecott Land Company, n.d.

2. Five million square feet of office space is what Joel Garreau considers to be "critical mass" for an "Edge City" in his book of the same name. See Garreau, *Edge City,* 470.

3. Interview with Nathan Francis, by author, Daybreak, Utah, September 29, 2006.

4. Michael Sorkin, "Can New Urbanism Learn from Modernism's mistakes?" *Metropolis* (August–September 1998), http://www.metropolismag.com/html/content_0898/aug98wha.htm.

5. Envision Utah, *History,* 19.

6. See Sophie Watson, *City Publics: The (Dis)enchantments of Urban Encounters* (London: Routledge, 2006), 2: "[Writers] mourned the passing of (imagined) rural cohesive communities (Gemeinschaft) for places of loose association (Gesellschaft)."

7. See, among others, Anthony Downs, *New Visions for Metropolitan America* (Washington, DC: Brookings Institution, 1994), 17–26; "Old Regionalism, New Regionalism, and Envision Utah: Making Regionalism Work," *Harvard Law Review* 118, no. 7 (May 2005): 2291-2313.

8. "Old Regionalism, New Regionalism."

9. Myron Orfield, *Metropolitics: A Regional Agenda for Community and Stability* (Washington, DC: Brookings Institution Press, 1997), 11–12.

10. Jared Farmer, *Glen Canyon Dammed: Inventing Lake Powell and the Canyon Country* (Tucson: University of Arizona Press, 1999), 130.

11. Hall, *Cities,* 88.

12. Hall, *Cities,* 95.

13. Sorkin, "Can New Urbanism Learn."

14. John A. Dutton, *New American Urbanism* (Milan: Skira, 2000).

15. Dutton, *Urbanism,* 11.

16. Dimitrios I. Roussopoulos, *Public Place* (Montreal: Black Rose, 2000), 7.

17. S. Watson, *City Publics,* 11. Also see S. Watson, 14: Richard Sennett, noted for his scholarly defense of the public realm, champions the "richer types of relationships that are possible among strangers."

18. Roussopoulos, *Public Place,* 3.

19. Dutton, *Urbanism,* 17.

20. "Public life can support the essential communication system of cities, the linkage that holds them together, helping to orient people, enabling connections both to community and preurban nature," writes Stephen Carr; see Stephen Carr, *Public Space* (New York: Cambridge University Press, 1992), 24.

21. Lewis Mumford believed the fall of the public realm began during the Middle Ages as soon as residential life was uncoupled from the other domestic functions of production and selling, which "weakened the public interest among the middle class citizens." See Carr, *Public Space,* 24.

22. Alan Berger, *Drosscape: Wasting Land in Urban America* (Princeton, NJ: Princeton Architectural Press, 2006).

23. Mike Davis, *City of Quartz: Excavating the Future in Los Angeles* (New York: Vintage, 1992).

24. Kara Platoni, "The Case of the Missing Web Page," *East Bay Express*, November 29, 2006.

25. Rosemary Winters, "Being Green in the Land of the Saints," *High Country News*, December 22, 2003.

26. Thomas G. Alexander and James B. Allen, *Mormons and Gentiles: A History of Salt Lake City* (Boulder, CO: Pruett, 1984), 279.

27. Charles Sellers, "Mormons as City Planners," *Dialogue* 3, no. 3 (Autumn 1968): 80.

28. See the telling of this story in Barber, *Reno's Big Gamble*, 225.

29. American Civil Liberties Union of Utah, "ACLU Returns to Court in Controversy Over Free Speech in Salt Lake City's 'Main Street Plaza,'" 2008, http://www.acluutah.org/mainstreetplaza.htm#returns.

30. U.S. Department of Agriculture, *Agricultural Outlook*, no. AGO-292 (June–July 2002): 18.

31. Salt Lake City, *County Watershed Report*, 2003, http://www.epa.gov/nps/toolbox/surveys/SL_Watershed_Report.pdf.

32. Susan Voyles, "BLM Might Sell Some Land in Smoke Creek Desert," *Reno Gazette-Journal*, March 18, 2005.

33. Interview with Truckee Meadows Regional Planning Authority staff, by author, October 18, 2006.

34. Brian Wargo, "Saving the Master Plan," *Las Vegas Sun*, May 15, 2009.

35. Ronald R. Bateman, "South Jordan," in *Utah History Encyclopedia*, University of Utah online resource, http://www.media.utah.edu/UHE/s/SOUTHJORDAN.html (accessed February 2007).

36. Interview with Ricky Horst, by author, September 29, 2006.

37. City of South Jordan, South Jordan City Demographics, http://www.sjc.utah.gov/demographics.asp.

38. U.S. Census Bureau, "American Community Survey," 2005, http://www.census.gov.

39. U.S. Census Bureau, "Census of Housing and Population," Summary Files 1 and 3, 2000, http://www.census.gov.

40. Bateman, "South Jordan."

41. Wasatch Homes promotional materials, 2008, http://www.wasatchhomes.net/sjhighpointe.html.

42. South Jordan Planning Commission minutes, November 14, 2000.

43. South Jordan Planning Commission minutes, March 27, 2001.

44. "Old Regionalism, New Regionalism," 2292.

45. Envision Utah, *History*.

46. Nicole Warburton, "Trax and Taxes: Would an Expanded System Be Worth the Price?" *Deseret Morning News*, April 30, 2006.

47. See Envision Utah, *History*, but this history is already well told in coalition in-house documentation, state documents and articles from local newspapers and national magazines and journals.

48. Envision Utah, *History*.

49. Envision Utah, *History*.

50. Lois M. Collins, "Churches' Role in Meeting Community Needs to Increase," *Deseret News*, January 29, 1998.

51. Remarks by Alexander Morrison at Utah Botanical Garden award ceremony, August 26, 2006.

52. James E. Faust, *Ensign* (May 1999): 46.

53. U.S. Environmental Protection Agency, "Kennecott Mining Site: Transformation through Collaboration at a Superfund Alternative Site," *Abandoned Mine Lands Case Study* (June 2, 2006): 3, http://www.epa.gov/aml/tech/kennecott.pdf.

54. Glen Warchol, "Daybreak Disclosure Has Yet to Slow Sales," *Salt Lake Tribune*, March 29, 2006.

55. EPA, "Kennecott Mining Site," 11.

56. South Jordan City council minutes, April 20, 1999.

57. Sam Newberg, "Humans/Nature," *Urban Land* (April 2006): 58.

58. James Hardie, "Tailored to the Landscape," http://www.jameshardie.com/pdf/streetscapes_20.pdf (accessed February 2007).

59. Matt Canham, "Avenues Wards Continue to Lose Members," *Salt Lake Tribune*, July 24, 2005.

60. Daybreak promotional materials, Kennecott Land Company, n.d.

61. Explains Brigham Young University's Center for the Study of Elections and Democracy: "Linking Nevada's various subpopulations is a militantly individualist political culture: the state as a whole is, of course, sin-tolerant but also unusually tax averse. . . . Gun control and environmental liberalism are relatively unpopular issues." See Michael Bowers, Tim Fackler, Nathalie Frensley, Erik Herzik, Ted G. Jelen, and Todd Kunioka, " The 1998 Nevada Senate Race," *Outside Money: Soft Money and Issue Ads in Competitive 1998 Congressional Elections*," ed. David B. Magleby, Center for the Study of Elections and Democracy, Brigham Young University, 1998.

62. Plus, as former Albuquerque mayor David Rusk points out, "State legislatures must serve as regional policy bodies because they are the only ones that can. Legislatures must set new ground rules for how local governments must share common responsibilities for common problems." See Orfield, *Metropolitics*, xii.

63. *Enlibra*, meaning "move toward balance" or "collaboration," is meant to symbolize what former Utah governor Mike Leavitt considered his collaborative approach to solving environmental problems.

64. Susan Voyles, "Street widening heralds more growth in the North Valleys," *Reno Journal-Gazette*, March 21, 2006.

65. Interview with Julee Olander, by author, November 2006.

66. Jan Gehl, *Public Spaces, Public Life* (Copenhagen: Danish Architectural Press, Royal Danish Academy of Fine Arts, 1996).

67. Evan McKenzie, *Privatopia* (New Haven, CT: Yale University Press, 1994), 7, 18.

68. Sam Bass Warner, *The Private City: Philadelphia in Three Periods of Its Growth* (Philadelphia: University of Pennsylvania Press, 1968).

69. Harvest Park promotional materials, http://www.harvestpark.net.

70. Wasatch Homes, *South Jordan High Pointe Design Guidelines*, http://www .wasatchhomes.net/sjhpvol2.pdf.

71. Ivory Homes promotional materials, *Utah's No. 1 Homebuilder Launches Flagship Community*, October 2006.

Chapter 6. The Depot

1. From Rio Grande Depot's National Register of Historic Places nomination form, National Park Service, U.S. Department of the Interior, 1972.

2. Alexander and Allen, *Mormons and Gentiles*.

3. This is not to say that the early Mormon Church was not involved in the development of the railroads—they were—but railroads and their connection to the national economy brought a diversity of Gentiles into the heart of the Mormon headquarters; these migrations did not fall in line with the original intent of the settlement.

4. Heather May and Joe Baird, "Depot Area Set to Bloom," *Salt Lake Tribune*, May 31, 2004.

5. May and Baird, "Depot Area."

6. Salt Lake City (SLC), "Gateway District Development and Land Use Master Plan," http://www.slcgov.com/ced/rda/Brownfields/Text%20links/gateway.pdf.

7. May and Baird, "Depot Area."

8. SLC, "Gateway Master Plan," 2.

9. See Timothy Davis, "The Miracle Mile Revisited: Recycling, Renovation and Simulation along the Commercial Strip," in *Exploring Everyday Landscapes: Perspectives in Vernacular Architecture*, vol. 7, ed. Annmarie Adams and Sally McMurry (Knoxville: University of Tennessee Press, 1997).

10. Telephone interview with Katherine Perez, executive director of Los Angeles County–based Transportation and Land Use Collaborative, by author, June 2003.

11. Tim Sullivan, "Restoring Livability: Latinos Bring Back the Concept of Walkable, Vibrant Neighborhoods," *Salt Lake Tribune*, August 2, 2003. Thanks to Katherine Perez, John Taveras, and Michael Mendez for their insights.

12. Tim Sullivan, "Salt Lake Area Has Pluses, Minuses in Integration, Visitors Say," *Salt Lake Tribune*, October 6, 2002.

13. Tim Sullivan, "A Sad Adios," *Salt Lake Tribune*, April 29, 2003.

14. Patty Henetz, "Depot District: High Hopes," *Salt Lake Tribune*, January 5, 2007.

Epilogue

1. Urban Land Institute and PricewaterhouseCoopers, *Emerging Trends in Real Estate 2010*, http://www.pwc.com/us/en/asset-management/real-estate/publications/emerging-trends-in-real-estate-2010.jhtml.

2. Lesley Mitchell, "Development Marches on at Daybreak," *Salt Lake Tribune*, April 24, 2009.

3. Linda Baker, "Overlooking the Mormon Temple, a New Center," *New York Times*, May 12, 2009.

Index

About the Author

Tim Sullivan has reported for several western newspapers and magazines, including *The Salt Lake Tribune* and *The Oregonian,* and now works as an urban planner and designer. A native of Salt Lake City, he currently lives in Oakland, California.